THE FAMILY AND THE SCHOOL

The first edition of *The Family and the School*, published in 1985, drew together for the first time developments in the applications of systems theory to family therapy and consultation to schools. It was widely accepted as a seminal text in the field.

This second edition is fully revised and updated. It now contains more material specifically related to work with schools, and the book has been entirely recast to reflect the major changes in society, in legislation and in the nature of the interaction between families and the education system in general, which have taken place in the last decade. The distinguished contributors all have links with the Child and Family Department of the Tavistock Clinic and include educational and clinical psychologists working with schools and hospitals, family therapists, child and family psychiatrists and teachers.

Emilia Dowling is Consultant Child Psychologist and Head of Child Psychology at the Tavistock Clinic. **Elsie Osborne** is a chartered child psychologist and on retirement was Head of Discipline in the Child and Family Department of the Tavistock Clinic.

THE FAMILY AND THE SCHOOL

A joint systems approach to problems with children

Edited by Emilia Dowling and Elsie Osborne

London and New York

First published 1985
by Routledge & Kegan Paul

Second edition published by Routledge 1994
11 New Fetter Lane, London EC4P 4EE

Simultaneously published in the USA and Canada
by Routledge
29 West 35th Street, New York, NY 10001

Typeset in Times by Florencetype Ltd, Kewstoke, Avon
Printed and bound in Great Britain by
T. J. Press (Padstow) Ltd, Padstow, Cornwall

British Library Cataloguing in Publication Data

A catalogue record for this book is available from the
British Library

Library of Congress Cataloging in Publication Data
The Family and the school: a joint systems approach to
problems with children/edited by Emilia Dowling and Elsie
Osborne. 2nd ed.
p. cm.
Includes bibliographical references and index.
1. Problem children. 2. Psychological consultation.
3. Psychiatric consultation. 4. Problem children –
Education.
5. Home and school. 6. Family psychotherapy. I. Dowling,
Emilia, 1951–. II. Osborne, Elsie L. (Elsie Letitia)
RJ506.P63F35 1995
362.2′083–dc20   93–44329
                                                                          CIP

ISBN 0–415–10127–1 (hbk)
ISBN 0–415–10128–X (pbk)

CONTENTS

Notes on contributors   vii

Foreword to first edition   xi
John Bowlby

Foreword to second edition   xiii
John Byng-Hall

Introduction   xv
Elsie Osborne and Emilia Dowling

1 THEORETICAL FRAMEWORK: A JOINT SYSTEMS
   APPROACH TO EDUCATIONAL PROBLEMS WITH
   CHILDREN   1
   Emilia Dowling

2 SOME IMPLICATIONS OF THE THEORETICAL
   FRAMEWORK: AN EDUCATIONAL
   PSYCHOLOGIST'S PERSPECTIVE   30
   Elsie Osborne

3 THE CHILD, THE FAMILY AND THE SCHOOL: AN
   INTERACTIONAL PERSPECTIVE   45
   Elsie Osborne

4 TAKING THE CLINIC TO SCHOOL: A
   CONSULTATIVE SERVICE FOR PARENTS,
   CHILDREN AND TEACHERS   59
   Emilia Dowling

5 JOINT INTERVENTIONS WITH TEACHERS,
   CHILDREN AND PARENTS IN THE SCHOOL
   SETTING   69
   John Dowling and Andrea Pound

6 PARENTS AND CHILDREN: PARTICIPANTS IN
  CHANGE   88
  Neil Dawson and Brenda McHugh

7 THE TEACHER'S VIEW: WORKING WITH TEACHERS
  OUT OF THE SCHOOL SETTING   102
  Elsie Osborne

8 SOME ASPECTS OF CONSULTATION TO PRIMARY
  SCHOOLS   112
  Caroline Lindsey

9 SCHOOLS AS A TARGET FOR CHANGE:
  INTERVENING IN THE SCHOOL SYSTEM   127
  Denise Taylor

10 CONSULTATION TO SCHOOL SUBSYSTEMS BY A
   TEACHER   148
   Muriel Barrett

11 THE CHILDREN ACT 1989: IMPLICATIONS FOR THE
   FAMILY AND THE SCHOOL   160
   Caroline Lindsey

12 ISSUES FOR TRAINING   168
   Emilia Dowling and Elsie Osborne

Bibliography   176

Name index   185

Subject index   188

CONTRIBUTORS

Emilia Dowling is Consultant Child Psychologist and Head of Child Psychology in the Child and Family Department at the Tavistock Clinic, and a staff member of the Institute of Family Therapy (London). After completing her training as a clinical psychologist in Javeriana University, Bogotá, Colombia, she worked in the Paediatric Hospital in Bogotá where she developed a psychological service for children. Her interest in children and their families brought her to Europe where she undertook post-graduate studies in Madrid and the Tavistock Clinic in London. She is a chartered clinical psychologist.

From 1973 she worked at the Family Institute in Cardiff where she was involved in the practice, teaching and research of family therapy. In 1979 she joined the Tavistock Clinic, where she has developed a special interest in the systems approach to families and schools and in the practice and teaching of consultation. She is involved in the training of family therapists and of educational and clinical psychologists and has recently set up a clinical Ph.D. programme in Child and Family Psychology jointly with Birkbeck College, University of London.

Her interest in training and research in family therapy is reflected in a number of her publications, which include a study of co-therapists' behaviour, involvement of young children in family therapy and follow-up studies of clients and of students' views of their training programme. Currently she is engaged in examining children's perspective of the divorce process. Other publications cover her interest in consultative work in schools.

Elsie Osborne was employed as a clinical child psychologist in the Child and Family Department of the Tavistock Clinic for many years, after primary school teaching, training and subsequent work as an educational psychologist in local authority child guidance and school psychological services. She became head of the psychology discipline in the department at the Tavistock and Senior Tutor to the postgraduate training course for educational psychologists and established the link with Brunel University to convert this to a Master's degree. She chaired the department for some years prior to her retirement from full-time employment in 1988. She is a chartered educational psychologist.

Since then she has continued to be involved in teaching, lecturing and consulting in Britain and overseas, as well as in editing and writing. She has been an active member of the Division of Child and Educational Psychology of the British Psychological Society throughout her career, has chaired its training committee, taken part in its working parties and its Educational Psychology course evaluation teams.

Major interests that are reflected in publications include learning and examination difficulties in children and adolescents, process, practice and training in supervision, educational therapy and group relations. She is currently editing and contributing to a series of books on child development for parents and was co-editor of *The Emotional Experience of Learning and Teaching*.

Muriel Barrett began by teaching in primary schools. After a break to have children she resumed her teaching career as a member of a School Psychological Service, working with older children who had not reached their potential in school. She then became a clinic teacher at the Tavistock Clinic where, amongst other clinical, consultative and teaching duties, she was organizing tutor for postgraduate training in educational therapy for teachers, which she had taken a leading part in establishing. After leaving the Tavistock she continued her teaching and consultation roles and is currently teaching on a Diploma in Educational Therapy course in Plymouth.

Muriel Barrett was co-author of *Attachment Behaviour and the School Child: an Introduction to Educational Therapy*.

John Byng-Hall is a consultant child and family psychiatrist in the Child and Family Department at the Tavistock Clinic. He is a member, and ex-chairman, of the Institute of Family Therapy (London). He trained at Cambridge University, the Maudsley Hospital and the Tavistock Clinic. He has published in the field of family myths, legends and scripts, attachment theory and family therapy, distance regulation in families and couples, and supervision in family therapy.

Neil Dawson is joint teacher in charge of the Education Unit at the Marlborough Family Service in London. He is also a family therapist registered by the United Kingdom Council for Psychotherapy, having trained at the Institute of Family Therapy (London). At present he is a clinical supervisor on the M.Sc. and Advanced Clinical Trainings in Family Therapy at the institute. He is an honorary lecturer at University College, London and Birkbeck College, supervising and teaching on the Diploma in Family Therapy based at the Marlborough.

Together with Brenda McHugh he has published accounts of work with children presenting emotional, behavioural, developmental or learning difficulties at school, using family systems principles, and run many training courses for teachers in Britain and internationally. He is currently developing and co-ordinating multi-disciplinary trainings in child protection work, specifically designed for teachers.

John Dowling is Principal Educational Psychologist for the City of Westminster. He trained as an educational psychologist at the Tavistock Clinic. Whilst working for South Glamorgan Local Education Authority he developed a special interest in the problem of school refusal and carried out research into the transfer from primary to secondary school.

Since moving to London in 1979 he has undertaken advanced training in consultation at the Tavistock Clinic and is now a course tutor. He has pursued his interest in systems work and organizations and completed an M.Sc. in occupational psychology at Birkbeck College, University of London.

He is a chartered educational psychologist.

Caroline Lindsey is a consultant child and adolescent psychiatrist and Chair of the Child and Family Department at the Tavistock Clinic. As a family and group therapist, she is interested in systemic work with professional and family systems and in applying these ideas to consultation in school-based settings. She is involved in the training of child mental health professionals including systems therapists. She has a specialist interest in child care consultation, in particular in fostering and adoption. She is the author of papers on family therapy and consultation work.

Brenda McHugh is joint teacher in charge of the Education Unit at the Marlborough Family Service in London. She is also a family therapist registered by the United Kingdom Council for Psychotherapy, having trained at the Institute of Family Therapy (London). Currently she is a tutor and lecturer on the M.Sc. and Advanced Clinical Trainings in Family Therapy at the institute and is an honorary lecturer at University College, London and Birkbeck College, supervising and teaching on the Diploma in Family Therapy based at the Marlborough Family Service. She has recently qualified as a family mediator.

She has co-authored several articles on the application of family systems principles in relation to joint work with schools and families, and is currently writing and producing, with colleagues, a video and computer distance learning pack, on Family Therapy Basics.

Andrea Pound is Head of the Psychology Service at the Royal London Hospital and has worked in children's mental health services for many years. She has also been involved in research on the effect of maternal depression on young children and on the evaluation of Newpin, a pioneering befriending scheme and therapeutic network for young families. She is a chartered clinical psychologist.

Denise Taylor was a principal psychologist in the Department for Children and Parents, Tavistock Clinic, where she initiated the Advanced Course in Consultation and Community Mental Health, the first course in consultation for experienced professionals working in the community. She formerly worked as an educational psychologist in the Hertfordshire School Psychological Service. Her publications include accounts of family consultation in a school setting and of group work with the counsellors of the bereaved.

As a qualified psychoanalytic psychotherapist she is a full member of the British Association of Psychotherapists of which she served as Chair from 1989 to 1992; she continues to be a member of Council and to conduct her private practice.

FOREWORD
TO THE FIRST EDITION

John Bowlby

When the child guidance movement started in Britain before the war it aimed to provide a service that took into account not only the potentials and limitations of the child himself but also the two principal parts of his environment – his family and his school. To achieve this it set up the clinical team of psychiatrist, psychologist and social worker who, working together, would be able to take all these variables into account and plan effective action. Today we can see how right that aim was, even if it has proved far more difficult to realize than was ever imagined in those optimistic days.

There were formidable difficulties. One amongst many was the depth of our ignorance of the nature of the problems we were grappling with. Another, just as formidable, was the tradition, engrained from the start, that expected each piece of the jigsaw to be the responsibility of a single member of the team based on the assumption that, once information was pooled, the whole picture would emerge and the therapeutic role of each member in his own part of the field could be specified. What this tradition failed to recognize was that when you separate the parts of a dynamic whole you lose the chance to see how the parts of the system are interacting and endlessly influencing each other. You lose the chance, too, of intervening in the system itself with a view to changing the pattern of interaction for the better.

During the past twenty-five years many efforts to adopt a new perspective and a new tradition of working practice have been made. The key principle is, whenever possible, to see two or more members of an interacting social group together in a joint session. In this way vicious or virtuous cycles of interaction become plain and, once sanction is obtained, direct interventions become possible. In these interventions the usual roles of the professional are those of mediator, clarifier and facilitator. The aim is to help each member of the interacting group to see the problem from the point of view of each of the other members, which requires that each is given an opportunity to describe what he thinks and feels. In this process the professional strives to maintain a neutral stance and, on occasion, feeds in any information that seems necessary for a solution to be found. Experience shows that, given these conditions, human beings are far more capable of being both co-operative and constructive than they are often given credit for.

Nevertheless, it must be recognized that for anyone long accustomed to think only in terms of linear chains and to deal only with individuals, the necessary shift in thinking and practice is not easy. Furthermore, there is fear of what may be lost. For example, some are apprehensive that a systems approach may preclude work with individuals. Experience shows the reverse to be true. Invaluable though joint sessions with all those concerned with a problem undoubtedly are, it often becomes clear during such sessions that one or more members can be helped individually. When begun within this framework, it is found, help to individuals is greatly facilitated.

The work described in this book constitutes a substantial step towards establishing the new perspective and the new working principles in a part of the field to which they have hitherto been too little applied. What will impress the reader is the great variety of techniques and practices that can be employed to enable each of those who play a part in a child's educational progress to gain a better understanding of how the others concerned view the problem and, in the light of that knowledge, to revise their own opinion and, ultimately, agree a plan of action. At the start, children, siblings, parents, class teachers, head teachers and others each have a distinctive perspective and favour a solution that commonly takes into account only a part of the problem. Coming afresh to the situation, the outside professional has an opportunity not only to get to know how each participant is tackling the problem presented, but also to enable each of them to understand the viewpoint and expectations of the others.

In all this work there is no outcome more to be hoped for than one in which the corrosion of mutual blame is banished and its place taken by mutual respect and goodwill. For it is only then that durable solutions can be expected.

FOREWORD
TO THE SECOND EDITION

John Byng-Hall

Sadly, since the first edition of this book, John Bowlby died in 1990 aged 83. His ideas, however, live on. He is emerging as one of the greatest figures in the field of child development in the twentieth century. There has been a flood of research findings that support his theories about human attachments. Happily, he lived long enough to see many of his ideas confirmed – and he was absolutely delighted; but the research has continued apace since his death. His theories about attachment and loss have proven to be very useful and have had a profound effect on child care, and will continue to do so.

Children who are securely attached to their parents are able to explore their world, safe in the knowledge that their parents are available when needed, such as when they are anxious or distressed. This helps children to be free to explore ideas and to think. Insecure children are less autonomous and are more likely to have emotional problems by school age, such as having difficulties with peers or in concentrating. So it is important for learning that children have secure and reliable relationships with the adults in their lives. Recent research shows that parents who have a clear and coherent understanding of their children's needs and vulnerabilities are more likely to have secure children, whereas parents who cannot easily empathize with their children, and so find it difficult to respond appropriately when they are in need, are more likely to have insecure children.

The knowledge about parent–child attachments has been extended to understanding how the family as a whole can provide a secure base from which the children can explore and develop (Byng-Hall, 1991). What happens in other family relationships can influence how parents provide security for their children. If parents and other relatives are supportive of each other then this helps enormously. If they undermine each other, however, the children are inevitably affected, especially if one parent involves a child, sometimes in a subtle and hidden way, in a battle with the other parent. In this situation the child has divided loyalties, and loses out on appropriate parental care, becoming a partner rather than a child to one, and distanced from the other. This can affect the security of the child whether or not the parents are separated, so parental battles in the child's presence are not the only thing to create anxiety. When parents get down to sorting out their own conflicts children can relax and get on with their lives, safe in the knowledge that they are not needed for the fray.

Can we apply some of the principles of how family attachments influence security to how relationships between social systems such as the school, the family, and the psychological services affect the child's security? Children feel more secure if they sense that each group is supportive of the other. However, if children, especially those in difficulties, sense that there is mistrust between the various organizations their capacity to feel secure in each may be reduced, and learning can suffer. It is all too easy for each social system to pull in opposite directions – often without really being aware of doing so. Collaboration between all the adults is important for children.

One of this book's most valuable assets is its coherent and lucid account of how the various social systems interact, and how this interaction affects our troubled children. It is to be hoped that both teachers and those in the psychological services will read it. The shared model that it provides will be invaluable, especially for thinking about how to co-ordinate changes that are taking place. Since this book was first published in 1985 the degree of reorganization of the many social systems that surround children who may be having trouble at school has been quite extraordinary. Radical changes are being asked of education, of the health service, of children's law, and of families themselves. To complicate matters further all of these changes are happening simultaneously. The models behind the reforms may also be clashing; for instance the notion that competition is a spur to success – which may make some children feel more insecure – can jostle uncomfortably with the idea that collaboration and a sense of security facilitates learning and creativity.

The first edition of this book has become a classic in its field, and it provides an invaluable model for those struggling to adapt to multiple changes. It is very timely that it should now be brought up to date in view of the organizational changes, and the need to include various advances in the field. All will benefit from the revision of this book – especially children.

INTRODUCTION

Elsie Osborne and Emilia Dowling

The Family and the School in its first edition looked in a new way at the interaction between families and schools. It aimed to provide a bridge between theory and practice, and to draw together separate advances in the application of systems theory to the fields of family therapy and of consultative work in schools, in order to suggest a model for working jointly with both families and schools.

The shift towards an interactionist view of problems presented by children in the two contexts of family or school had developed quite separately in the clinical and the educational fields, with little cross-fertilization. The attempt by the first edition to consider how the two systems of family and school overlap and interact with each other was seen by professional workers and reviewers as its special value, and as something not attempted elsewhere.

Since the publication of the first edition there have been many shifts in both of the contexts which are our main concern, and in the nature of the interaction between them, following legislation as well as general social changes. The second edition therefore provides a welcome opportunity for a major revision and update.

The aim in this revision remains one of bringing together the different strands of development in systems theory and their application to families and schools. In spite of an increasing use of a systems orientation in many areas, and by many professionals, we think there is still a considerable need for this linking work to be done, and we are not aware of any comparable attempt in the years since *The Family and the School* first appeared.

Those who are familiar with the first edition will find that certain key chapters have been retained, but with alterations and updating to allow for more recent work. Other contributions have been substantially rewritten and a number are completely new. Much of the book is derived, as before, from work in the Child and Family Department at the Tavistock Clinic and we are proud to retain the original foreword written by John Bowlby.

As chairman of the Department for many years Dr Bowlby initiated and encouraged the development of family interviewing. His seminal paper 'The study and reduction of group tensions in the family' (1949) was instrumental in much of the subsequent development of family therapy, not only in Britain but also in the United States. A full account of this early influence is given in the book *Family and Marital Psychotherapy*, edited by Sue Walrond-Skinner (1979). With his initiating and active support the Tavistock Neighbourhood Schools Project pioneered an emphasis upon working in a consultative way to school staffs and was reported in a Schools Council working paper by Caspari and Osborne (1967).

In his foreword to this new edition John Byng-Hall places Bowlby's work, in particular attachment theory, into the wider systemic perspective. John Byng-Hall has himself made a considerable contribution to providing cross-theoretical links, with his profound understanding of these two major perspectives, as well as to the development of family therapy practice and training (Whiffen and Byng-Hall, 1982).

The new edition begins with an updated theoretical section which is extended by a second chapter. Chapter 1 presents key concepts in general systems theory and outlines the way in which theoretical thinking about families and schools have evolved in parallel. It examines the interaction between families and schools when problems of an educational nature arise with children, and the development of alternative intervention strategies. The second chapter explores some key concepts which have been found especially relevant for someone working as an educational psychologist in schools, and their relationship to other paradigms in common use as well as to the school as an organization.

The book subsequently moves on to several accounts of application supported by theoretical considerations. Chapter 3 shifts to a focus on the family. It briefly traces theoretical and practical developments in child guidance and school psychological services and gives some examples of the psychologist's use of an interactional approach with various families, including one with a long-term school refuser. This work is clinic based and is followed by two contributions which take the work with families into the school itself.

Chapter 4 describes the innovative development of a school-based service for parents, teachers and children, taking into account the changing context in education and the constantly evolving roles, particularly those of the head teacher and the consultant, and how they have to adapt in order to respond to these contextual changes.

Chapter 5 also describes joint interventions with parents and teachers, this time within a secondary school. It is concerned with the misunderstandings between school and family which can lead to serious problems for the child. Accounts are given of collaborative interventions with the psychologist as facilitator and of a school–family project aimed at improving goodwill between parents and teachers, and to reducing referrals. The approach is systemic and preventive.

Chapter 6 takes us into a base which is neither clinic nor school, although combining aspects of both. It illustrates the functioning of a Health-Service-based Education Unit in which the teacher and family therapists have developed a model of practice based on a joint systems approach to work with children and their families in an educational setting.

At this point we felt it was worth looking at some of the occasions when it can be useful to hold a meeting with teaching staff outside the school setting, and this is the focus of Chapter 7. The meetings described include those concerned with individual children and their families as well as other ways in which groups of teachers might work together by taking themselves outside their own school system. This provides a link with the following three chapters which are all concerned with consultation to schools.

Chapter 8 addresses some general and specific issues for the consultant in a primary school. Whilst working systemically the consultant keeps in mind the developmental characteristics of the life cycle stage of the junior school child and his or her family. Consideration is also given to the influence on the consultancy of this author's profession as a child psychiatrist.

Chapter 9, on schools as a target for change, was a key chapter in the original edition and remains as a major theoretical contribution, especially in taking further the conceptual framework for consultative approaches. It traces the history of consultation and its theoretical underpinning, includes a consideration of schools as socio-technical systems and of action research as a model for use in schools. It draws in particular on work in secondary schools.

The author of Chapter 10 draws on her experience as a teacher consulting to groups of teachers in school and we are again reminded of the need to look at the influence of the consultant's profession. The chapter discusses the issues involved, this time in working with subsystems, such as a special needs department, with particular attention to the importance of the setting up process. The development of the subsystem's role in the wider context of the whole school system is also examined briefly.

The impact of the Children Act 1989 is of considerable interest to all those working with children. Chapter 11 is a new contribution, which looks in an informed way at the influence of the Act on the family and school systems.

In the final chapter the editors join forces in bringing together some of the main themes of the book in order to address the way in which a systemic way of thinking can influence training generally. It also discusses some supervision issues, for instance the importance of being alert to the interaction between supervisor and supervisee and to the systems in which they operate.

We are indebted to many colleagues and trainees as well as families who have worked with us and from whom we have learned so much, within the Tavistock, in the schools and in workshops and conferences elsewhere. We extend our special thanks to Jane Rayner for her patience and skill in preparing the typescript, to Margaret Walker, the Tavistock librarian, for her expert assistance and to John Osborne for his invaluable technical advice and general helpfulness throughout the preparation of the book. We are grateful also to Mari Shullaw, our publisher's editor, for her unfailing support and encouragement.

We hope that this new edition of *The Family and the School* will provide its readers with some new perspectives and encourage reflection on the frameworks and techniques that they use.

1

THEORETICAL FRAMEWORK
A joint systems approach to educational problems with children

Emilia Dowling

Most professionals in the mental health field would recognize that two of the most influential systems in an individual's development are the family and the school. However, not enough has been done to bring these two systems together as part of a therapeutic strategy to deal with problems in children.

Since the first edition of this book there have been interesting developments in the social context in which families and schools function. New legislation affecting these two systems will no doubt have far-reaching effects on children's development in the family and school context in years to come. On the one hand the law has highlighted and recognized the children's needs and rights. On the other hand, the current economic climate has prevented the expansion of children's services and the danger is that these services will be required to focus mainly on 'statutory' work, making the scope for preventive and consultative work increasingly difficult.

In the face of an enormous amount of imposed change, the education system has to continue providing an environment for children to learn. Families in recent years have undergone increasing changes in life patterns and styles. In this changing environment the relationship between families and schools continues to evolve with children as linchpins between these two systems. Continuing efforts to develop work which meaningfully addresses this dual context are described in the second edition of this book.

The aim of this chapter is to examine the concepts of general systems theory as they apply to family and school functioning, with particular reference to the interaction between them when problems of an educational nature arise with children. The relationship between family and school systems, the meaning of organizational culture and beliefs and the implications for therapeutic interventions when problems occur in this dual context, are discussed.

Since the early 1960s clinicians have learned to put the individual in the context of the family, and this has led to the development of family therapy as a therapeutic alternative to individual treatment. Educationists have

GOVERNORS STATE UNIVERSITY
UNIVERSITY PARK
IL 60466

also moved from the belief that all problems reside within the individual to consider how pupils' behaviour is affected by the particular educational establishment of which they are part (Burden, 1981a, 1981b; Gillham, 1978, 1981; Rutter *et al.*, 1979). However, the applications of systems notions to families and to schools have developed quite slowly and separately and the result is two rather divorced schools of thought and practice, with insufficient cross-fertilization between them. On the one hand, there is a wealth of family therapy literature, and on the other, the educational literature, emphasizing school systems interventions.

Since Aponte's seminal paper (1976) advocating the family–school interview, attempts have been made to explore children's problems in the dual context of family and school although not all of them approach the subject from a systems perspective. Tucker and Dyson (1976) described an ongoing project involving families and school staff which, in their view, brought about changes in traditional practices for school psychologists as well as better communication between the two systems. Love and Kaswan (1974) examined the family and school environment of elementary school children from a wide range of socio-economic areas in order to 'identify characteristics of family and school environments that seemed related to children's personal social effectiveness'. Fine and Holt (1983) have examined implications of a family systems approach for school-based consultants. They warn of the problems of identifying the 'client system' and of the complexities of selecting appropriate strategies for both systems. S. Holmes (1982) outlines a series of useful steps in dealing with learning difficulties in a social educational context.

Studies of a more sociological, rather than interventive, nature include those by Craft *et al.* (1980) and Johnson (1982).

In Britain, Taylor (1982) has described a model of family consultation in a school setting. She has also highlighted the dilemmas for the child as the family and school 'go-between', having to negotiate daily the transitions from home to school (Taylor 1986). Recently Cooper and Upton (1990) have described an ecosystemic approach to emotional and behavioural difficulties in schools which seems particularly valuable for teachers. Frederickson (1990) has re-evaluated the systems approaches in educational psychology practice. She advocates the use of soft systems methodology and refers to its application to the school context.

Stoker (1992) looks at the forces militating against change in the role and practice of educational psychologists. He perceptively examines the strongly held belief by many families, schools and education officials 'that children can be "treated" and changed without any undue interference with the social system of which the child is a part'. He suggests that to challenge such a belief is to challenge a very entrenched power structure which will not readily welcome change. He alerts educational psychologists to be aware of these dynamics and proposes three models of service delivery which might help to address the issues and be of interest to educational psychologists wishing to effect systemic change.

Although the literature on the subject is scarce, in recent years an increasing number of practitioners recognize the importance of viewing families and schools as open systems in constant interrelationship with each other. The contributions to this book reflect some of the developments in this field.

A SYSTEMS PERSPECTIVE

A systems way of thinking refers to a view of individual behaviour which takes account of the context in which it occurs. Accordingly, the behaviour of one component of the system is seen as affecting, and being affected by, the behaviour of others. Ackoff (1960) defines a system as 'any entity, conceptual or physical which consists of interdependent parts'. However, it is important to remember that systems theory stems from the physical sciences, which are more exact and predictable than the social sciences. The boundaries around physical systems are more clearly defined than those in social systems, where they are often arbitrarily determined.

General systems theory, which was conceived by von Bertalanffy (1950), provides an alternative theoretical framework to the linear model, which looks for causes in order to explain effects. Most professional trainings are based on a linear model, and in fact the mental health professions have been influenced by the traditional medical model in their search for the aetiology of pathological phenomena in dealing with emotional problems. The traditional scientific method by which variables are isolated in order to test out whether they cause a particular phenomenon is another example of how well-trained minds depend on linear thinking.

Plas, in her book *Systems Psychology in the Schools* (1986), offers a very thorough review of the theoretical and philosophical basis for systemic theory. Her work is particularly important as it refers in detail to some crucial precedents to the development of systems ideas: for example, Gestalt theory (Kofka, 1935), field theory (Lewin, 1952), and transactional theory, in particular the influence of Dewey and Bentley (1949), whose work was concerned with the relationship between the observer and the observed. This notion is, of course, central to the systemic epistemology, which holds that *what* we know depends on *how* we know (Keeney, 1983).

The application of Plas's ideas to work with school systems is explored further in Chapter 2.

3

KEY CONCEPTS OF GENERAL SYSTEMS THEORY

Context

One of the basic tenets of general systems theory is the emphasis on the context in which the phenomenon occurs:

> Living systems, whether biological organisms or social organizations are acutely dependent upon their external environment and so must be conceived of as open systems . . . open systems [which] maintain themselves through constant commerce with their environment, i.e. a continuous inflow and outflow of energy through permeable boundaries.
>
> (Katz and Kahn, 1969, p. 91)

In terms of social processes this means a move from the intrapsychic to the interpersonal level, from an individual to an interactional view of behaviour. This conceptual shift in the social sciences has taken place in parallel with developments in the physical sciences, where the focus has also moved away from a concern with the intrinsic properties of the matter to the way in which the matter is organized and the ways its particles relate to one another.

Circular causality

If we view behaviour in terms of cycles of interaction, instead of asking whether A causes B, the behaviour of A is seen as affecting and being affected by B and C, as shown in Figure 1.1.

When families find themselves locked in dysfunctional interaction patterns, a linear explanation of the 'cause' of the problem is not very helpful as it just swings the blame from one person to the other. In the case of a mother who complains about her husband's lack of involvement in the care

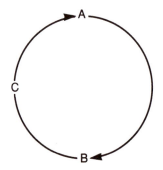

Figure 1.1 Cycle of interaction

4

of their child, it is more useful to identify the sequences of interaction which contribute to the perpetuation of the problem, than to apportion blame for it. The sequence can be translated as follows: the more she tells him that he never helps, the less he will help, since he feels so incompetent next to her, the more she does not let him try, the less he can learn, and so it goes on, only escalating as the recriminations extend to other areas, and consequently further uninvolvement and discontent will be triggered. A similar cycle could be identified in a school where the head teacher, who behaved in an authoritarian and autocratic manner, complained about his staff not supporting or helping him; the more he made his own decisions – without consulting, as he thought he would not be supported – the more his decisions were perceived by the staff as impositions; therefore they felt infantalized, did not take part in the planning of events and, on occasions, even behaved like irresponsible adolescents.

This view of events implies a different epistemology; the question *why* (linear, cause–effect model), is replaced by *how* the phenomenon occurs, and attention is paid to the sequences of interaction and repetitive patterns which surround the event.

Psychological functioning involves a reciprocal interaction between behaviour and its controlling conditions, and as actions are regulated by their consequences, the environment is, in turn, altered by the behaviour (Bandura, 1969).

Plas suggests that the term *recursive*, identified by Bateson (1979), captures the essence of non-linearity. 'A recursive phenomenon is the product of multidirectional feedback, which occurs as functional and arbitrarily identifiable parts of a system engaged in transaction across time and space. A recursion is non-linear; there is mutuality of influence' (Plas, 1986, p. 62).

Punctuation

The notion of circularity is intimately linked with the concept of *punctuation*, that is, the point at which a sequence of events is interrupted to give it a certain meaning. If reality is viewed in terms of interactional cycles, it is easy to see how a certain interpretation of *what* causes *what* depends on the way reality is punctuated. 'Every item of perception or behaviour may be stimulus or response or reinforcement according to how the total sequence of interaction is punctuated' (Bateson, 1973, p. 263).

A secondary school requested that 'something must be done' with a boy who was described as severely disturbed. When teachers were asked for a specific example of how he behaved and what made him appear as severely disturbed, they referred to the fact that he punched a boy who accidentally knocked his lunch tray and spilt milk on his blazer. This was, the head of year said, the proof of how severely disturbed he was – a disproportionate reaction, as he saw it, to a relatively minor incident. The head had chosen to punctuate reality at the point of the boy's behaviour, labelling it as disturbed. Exploration of the context revealed that the mother, a widow living on Social Security, had saved for a year to buy George a new blazer and had threatened to 'beat the hell out of him' if he damaged it. This was the first time George had been allowed to wear his blazer.

No punctuation is right or wrong – it just reflects a view of reality. Our particular view of reality is that behaviour is intimately dependent on the context in which it occurs. When educational problems arise, it is useful to examine the problem in the dual context of the family and the school.

Homeostasis

This term, first used by Walter Cannon (1939), refers to the tendency of living organisms towards a steady state of equilibrium. 'Homeostasis is made possible by the use of information coming from the external environment in the form of feedback. Feedback triggers the system "regulator" which by altering the system's internal condition maintains homeostasis' (Walrond-Skinner, 1976).

However, the application of this essentially biological concept to the understanding of social systems has been challenged by family theorists such as Dell (1982) and Hoffman (1981), who prefer the notion of coherence. Hoffman defines 'coherence' as having to do with how pieces of the system fit together in a balance internal to itself and external to its environment.

Nevertheless, the self-regulating properties of the family system have proved a useful notion to clinicians in understanding the purpose of the present problems and the tendency in families to maintain the status quo and resist change. As Gorell Barnes points out,

> Its value in clinical assessment is that it offers clinicians a way of thinking about key characteristics in the family which are interrelated with the present problem . . . It may also help him consider what the likely effects of improvement in one member of the family may be in other members, since a change in the referred person will require a change in the others. This may either be resisted or resolved by the appearance of a problem in a different family member which allows the overall family balance to remain unchanged.
>
> (Gorell Barnes, 1985, p. 219)

The self-regulating aspects of the dysfunctional individual behaviour in the context of the family system can also be observed in the school setting. The maintenance of disruptive behaviour in certain individuals contributes to maintaining the status quo of an institution which perhaps otherwise might be challenged. So long as 'badness' can be located in a sector of the institution, the rest can be preserved and the equilibrium maintained. Families and schools can collude successfully to maintain this equilibrium at the expense of the 'symptomatic children'. It is useful to ask, in the case of problem behaviour in schools, 'What in the school situation is helping to *maintain* [my italics] the behaviour? In a well-defined institution like a school the (good or bad) behaviour of individuals is, to some extent, kept going by the task and role demands on them, so the antisocial behaviour can be supported by the institution itself' (Gillham, 1981, p. 13).

Information and feedback

The notion of information exchange as a mutually affecting process between the components is particularly useful to our understanding of families and schools. In the feedback model of information exchange each link is modified by its interaction with others and this modification, which takes place in a circular process, is known as a feedback loop.

Families and schools are intimately interlinked over a significant period of time during the family's developmental life cycle. As open systems, i.e. systems that cannot be viewed without reference to their influence on the environment in which they exist, they are closely interrelated in a dynamic two-way relationship. This reciprocal influence determines how these two systems view one another (feedback loop). We are only too familiar with the cycles perpetuated by the way families and schools perceive each other and what they expect of each other (see Figure 1.2).

Galloway *et al.* (1982) comment on head teachers' subjective assessment of problems in their catchment area and quote a head teacher referring to how families' perceptions and attitudes to schools are influenced by the area in which the school is. Turner (1983) found that the comprehensive system has not eliminated the tendency of local schools to draw from particular social backgrounds.

In this cyclical sequence it can easily be seen how a particular point in the circle can be in turn 'cause' or 'effect', depending where reality is punctuated. The definition of a school as good is highly dependent on the perceptions of the parents who in turn are constantly being influenced by the school's attitudes towards them.

A mother-teacher expressed surprise at the fact that, in the middle-class area where she had recently moved, parents were not invited more frequently into the primary school. She compared this attitude with the school she taught in, where mothers were constantly invited to help and become involved in various ways, but rarely responded. It was perhaps the very fact that parents were so ready to 'come in' which made the school staff more wary of asking them. Perhaps at some level they feared the parents might 'take over'. Conversely, in the area where the parents were reluctant to come in, this very fact stimulated the teachers' efforts to get them involved.

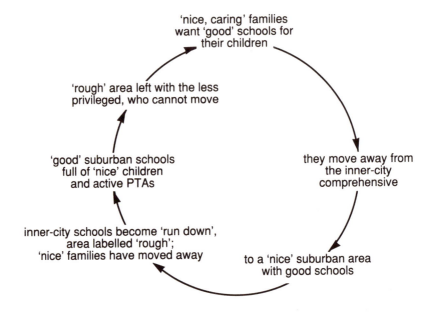

Figure 1.2 A cycle of reciprocal influence

COMMON ELEMENTS TO FAMILY AND SCHOOL SYSTEMS

Hierarchical organization

The structure of these two social systems presupposes a hierarchical organization with different kinds of boundaries: generational boundaries, hierarchical boundaries and boundaries between subsystems. It is important to elicit who in the family and in the school constitutes the executive subsystem: who makes the decisions? Are these carried out through consultation, or imposition, or not carried out? Are there explicit rules related to new decisions? How are these communicated?

It is generally accepted amongst clinicians that for families to function well a hierarchical structure is needed where parents (or other responsible adults) are in charge, and are able to make consistent rules and communicate them clearly to the children. Appropriate limits and rules, enforced consistently, help children feel secure about the fact that someone is in charge and will enable them to learn about limits and begin to understand that breaking rules has consequences.

When children are elevated to a parental position they are not only allowed and expected to make decisions but they also will be burdened with the consequences of such decisions. Blurred generational boundaries with grandparents or other family members can also create difficulty for the children who will not know clearly who is in charge.

8

Minuchin (1974) and his followers have been concerned with the structure of the family in terms of its hierarchical organization, boundaries, alliances and coalitions, and have developed a range of therapeutic techniques under the umbrella of structural family therapy.

In the school systems literature we find the same preoccupation with hierarchical structure boundaries and subsystems. Burden has described a systems approach to problems in school as seeking

> to understand how the explicit and implicit organizational structure of a school affects the perceptions and behaviour of its pupils in a way that leads them to be seen as problematical or disruptive by those faced with the task of maintaining that structure.
>
> (Burden, 1981b, p. 35)

This view is similar to Minuchin's when he describes the techniques of structural family therapy:

> therapy based on this framework is directed towards changing the organization of the family. When the structure of the family group is transformed the positions of members in that group are altered accordingly. As a result each individual's experiences change.
>
> (Minuchin, 1974, p. 2)

It should be noted, however, that the structural approach emphasizes change as opposed to description.

Rules

In any social system there are rules governing the way people should behave towards one another, what should and should not be done, but there are also rules about how rules are made, who makes them and how they are to be negotiated. Ground rules refer to the specifics of the way a system functions, whereas metarules are rules about the meaning of the ground rules (Gorell Barnes, 1982). Conflicts in timetabling which might make it difficult for pupils to do certain subjects may reflect gender-related expectations of society, which have found expression in the school's organization of the timetable. Often certain metarules attributed to a particular school are only reflecting the wider context and may be the vehicle for society's rules to be expressed.

Rigid and inflexible rules in schools have been associated with serious discipline problems (Galloway *et al.*, 1982, and Reynolds, 1976b) and with attendance rates (Reynolds and Murgatroyd, 1977). Dare (1982) refers to a process whereby school-age children absorb family rules, contrast them with rules outside the family system, namely the school, and play back to the family their new, integrated version of intra- and extra-familial rules. It is not difficult to imagine the impossible position in which children can find

9

themselves, torn between different sets of rules and the loyalties demanded of them by each system.

Culture

Morgan (1986) describes *culture* as shared meaning, shared understanding and shared sense. In talking about culture we are talking about a process of reality construction that allows people to see and understand particular events in distinctive ways. Understanding the culture enables us to understand families and schools in relationship to their environment. We come to know and relate to our environment according to the belief system that guides our interpretations and actions.

Morgan suggests that we learn the characteristics of a particular culture through observing the patterns of interaction, the language used, the norms that evolve, the various rituals and the dominant values and attitudes.

Schein (1985), however, argues that these characteristics *reflect* the culture but are not its *essence*. The essence of culture, in his view, lies in the deeper level of shared basic assumptions and beliefs which operate *unconsciously* and define in a basic, taken-for-granted fashion an organization's view of itself and its environment. These basic assumptions are implicit and guide behaviour. For example, if on the basis of experience and education the basic assumption is that people are intrinsically idle then it will be assumed that if they are just sitting doing nothing they can't be thinking, they are wasting time. In a school, if teachers are not teaching the three Rs, the children are not learning.

On the other hand if the basic assumption is that people are essentially good and able, when children are not learning or adults are not being productive the attention will turn to those elements in the environment which may be turning them off. Emphasis will be on creativity and individual ways of doing things because the underlying assumption is that individuals are 'good' and *can be trusted*.

A particular aspect of the culture of an organization is its *ethos*, which refers to its characteristic spirit or tone.

Rutter *et al.* (1979) have pointed out how schools develop an ethos which is intimately related to their characteristic as social organizations. We know how parents with academic expectations for their children seek a school with a good academic reputation. This often means, in the parents' views, good 'old-fashioned' traditional values, and emphasis on discipline and hard work. The schools in turn will develop attitudes and rules that confirm the parents' perceptions of their ethos.

Many secondary schools have preserved their reputation by relying on their pre-comprehensive, grammar-school ethos. Families will seek the values of what constituted for them a good school and, to a certain extent, expect to find those qualities unchanged or at least only slightly diminished by the comprehensive ethos. The school will be defined by what it *used* to be and the school staff might collude with such an identity as they themselves are uncertain of the advantages of the current system.

An important part of the organizational culture are the gender-related beliefs which govern attitudes and behaviour in school. Imber-Black (1989) documents specific problems relating to how schools may view single parents and the commonly held belief that their families are 'incomplete'. He points out how this belief can find expression in the interaction between single mothers and school professionals which involves an implication that the school can make the child behave while the mother cannot. Imber-Black encourages professionals to be critical of unfavourable beliefs about single mothers that undermine their confidence.

When consulting to schools it is important to bear in mind how difficult it is for women in positions of power and authority to develop their own style of leadership.

> As female leadership emerges in previously male-led systems, the women may discover that they are in the untenable position of being criticized for 'acting like men' (e.g. authoritatively and hierarchically) while also being expected to do so. Conversely, they may find that they are expected by others to be 'feminine' and criticized for being so. Women leaders who behave in collaborative ways with an emphasis on relationships may find that they are not taken seriously by the male hierarchy.
>
> (Imber-Black, 1989, p. 350)

Belief systems

In order to make sense of individual behaviour in the context of a family or a school, it is important to understand the belief system or the system of meaning which governs a particular behaviour. 'Meaning and behaviour have a *recursive or circular relationship*. We voluntarily behave as we do because we have certain beliefs about the context we are in, and our beliefs are supported or challenged by the feedback from our behaviour' (Campbell *et al.*, 1988, p. 16). Beliefs held by families and schools have been usually supported over time by events and they come to form the family or the organization's culture, that is, the way the world is seen and understood.

When parents in the face of a complaint from school about the child's behaviour react angrily by attributing it solely to 'bad' influences from other children, they may be reflecting a belief that all influences outside the family are likely to be negative. Perhaps over time certain difficult situ-

11

ations have been explained through finding the source of the problem outside the family boundary.

Likewise, schools have a particular culture which is partly determined by the belief system. For example there may be a strong belief that accepting or acknowledging difficulties which might require outside help would be a reflection that they are a bad or non-coping school. The belief that strength and goodness are based on self-reliance would govern and influence their attitude to any outside professional intervention. A systemic intervention could contribute to creating a new context in which the problem behaviour is perceived differently, and this different perception may lead to a different belief about the situation.

A common concern

It is evident that the shift from the individual to the family as the focus of concern has been a tremendous impetus to the development of clinical strategies, and family therapy as a treatment modality has flourished since the early 1960s. Likewise, in the world of education the labelling of individuals has come under criticism and an interactional approach to deviant behaviour has been put forward (Hargreaves, 1978), which links with the concept of the feedback loop. This seems to have had less of an impact in practice for educational psychologists and others involved in schools. *It has alerted them to the dangers of labelling behaviour but it has fallen short of equipping them with specific interventive strategies to deal with the problems they encounter.* On the other hand, the education reforms (Education Act 1981, Education Reform Act 1988) have had considerable impact on the work of the educational psychologist, particularly in relation to statutory work and it has become increasingly difficult for practitioners to take a systemic approach which takes account of the context in which problems occur.

The rest of this chapter is concerned with bringing together some of the techniques which can most appropriately be used with families and schools.

STRATEGIES OF INTERVENTION

The notion of problem-determined systems is particularly relevant to working with families and schools, Anderson *et al.* define a problem-determined system as 'an individual, a couple, a family, a work group, an organization, any combination of individuals that is communicatively interactive and organised around a shared language problem'. They go on to say that 'the definition of a problem marks the context and therefore the boundaries of the system to be treated . . . the problem to be diagnosed and treated and the membership of the problem system is determined by those in active communication regarding the problem' (Anderson *et al.*,

1986, p. 7). The view is particularly helpful as it takes away the right–wrong paradigm and replaces it with one of a disagreement in communication. This way different views of reality are legitimized and it is possible to explore them with the relevant members of the system. All those who have a view of the problem are then included as part of the process towards resolution.

It is our experience in the Child and Family Department at the Tavistock Clinic that when problems of an educational nature arise with children, families and schools perceive the problems in a variety of ways:

(1)   The parents see the problem as having originated in the school, and implicitly or explicitly place responsibility with the school for the existence of the problem, its origin, and its resolution; in most of these cases the families, at least initially, deny any problems at home. The school may refer the child to the school psychological service, or directly to a clinic, or they may encourage the parents to refer themselves. The intensity of the problem may vary from concern on the part of the school about the child's low attainment, lack of concentration and possibly behaviour problems, to the more extreme and uncompromising position where the school is saying it has 'done all it can' and the expectation of the intervention is the removal of the child from the school.

Campion (1984), in her study of 72 children who received family therapy through a school psychological service, points out how the parents usually see the child's problem as the school's responsibility. She refers to the difficulties of engaging the family when the parents do not see a connection between the child's behaviour at school and his behaviour at home.

However, when parents blame the school for a learning problem they may be questioning the context in which the child is learning and asking for help in changing schools. Exploring their views about how their child's needs can best be met can contribute to an understanding of what the best way forward should be.

(2)   The child's problem is manifested in the school but the school staff attribute its origin and cause to the family situation at home. This often coincides with some developmental crisis having occurred at home – separation, divorce, arrival of a new baby, moving home, etc. – and responsibility is placed on the family for not having resolved the home situation appropriately. Remarks like, 'It's to do with the family background, nothing we can do about it', 'What can you expect, Father is never there', or 'Mother is always out with different men', are attempts to provide an explanation of the problem as residing outside the school. Whatever the reasons, the assumption is often that the school can do very little unless family circumstances change. Even if temporary improvements occur they are regarded with scepticism, and school staff often predict relapse.

Whatever the 'cause' of the problem may be, in these situations there often appears to be a gulf between the family and the school; their views are polarized and more often than not they have stopped talking and certainly no longer find it possible to agree on a solution.

Often the parents' own experience of schooling will influence their perception of teachers as figures of authority and will determine their relationship and attitudes to them.

Osborne describes some of the underlying feelings that contribute to maintaining this polarized position:

> At times the nature of the rivalry between parents and teachers, arising from the desire of both to gain positive attitudes from the child, can be such that both sides avoid each other altogether. The parents' unresolved feelings from their own school days, for instance, feelings of fear or rebelliousness which relate back to their childhood, may hold back or distort their contacts with the school staff. Parents may also be anxious about being criticized over shortcomings in the upbringing of their child on the one hand whilst on the other hand teachers may anticipate being blamed for learning and discipline failures, which may either lead to angry exchanges or inhibit communication altogether. In such circumstances of mistrust the teacher may unwittingly enter into an alliance with the child's wish to demonstrate superior knowledge and skills in contrast to what are seen as the parents' old-fashioned ideas.
>
> (Osborne, 1983, p. 116)

(3) The school and the family recognize the problem in the child and are united in demanding that something must be done. Whether they agree on what causes the problem or not they are united in seeing the locus of the problem in the child himself and notions such as 'personality', 'temperament' or 'lack of ability' are suggested as reasons, permanent and irrevocable, for the presenting problem. More often than not they find an 'expert' who will collude with, and confirm their view of, the problem with a diagnostic label and with the decision that the child needs individual 'help'. The context of the problem is played down and the emphasis is placed on diagnosis and finding a remedy for the 'problem child'.

Differences between the school and the family are usually minimized or not investigated, and the emphasis is placed on what the child *is* rather than what the child *does*. Vague definitions like 'depressed', 'unhappy' or 'withdrawn' can be a useful device to avoid exploration of the problem behaviour in an interactional context.

A JOINT SYSTEMS APPROACH

A joint systems approach which addresses the problem in the dual context of family and school and focuses on the relationship between these two systems has the following aims:

1 To facilitate communication between school, staff and family members. In a study of 58 pupils suspended from Sheffield schools (Galloway *et al.*, 1982), relationships between parents and teachers were found to be remarkably limited. The authors report 'a quarter of the parents said they had never met their child's teacher though some admitted there had been indirect contact via the educational welfare officer' (1982, p. 44).

  In over half of the cases the suspension was notified via the child. As the authors comment, 'The schools were therefore relying on pupils who in most cases they regard as unreliable, to give their parents news of their suspension.'
2 To clarify differences in perception of the problem by focusing on *how* it occurs rather than *why*.
3 To negotiate commonly agreed goals.
4 To begin to explore specific steps towards change.

Aponte (1976), in describing what he called an *ecostructural* approach, defined the family school interview as an 'instrument to learn about the presenting problem, the relationships among the people that contributed to the problem and the ways in which these people can help bring about change' (1976, p. 304).

It must be made clear, however, that a joint systems approach must be regarded as a general framework for conceptualizing problems in this dual context. The decision as to how to intervene depends on many factors and may take several forms:

1 A joint family–school intervention in connection with an individual referral. (This may on occasions be contra-indicated; see Dowling and Pound, Chapter 5).
2 An initial contact with the family and with the school but the focus of treatment will be the family, alongside consultation with the relevant school staff (Osborne, Chapter 3).
3 An ongoing school-based intervention for parents and teachers in a particular school, geared to deal with the problems in the school context and to help the school staff develop skills to contain the problems within the school (Dowling, Chapter 4).
4 A family-systems-based model in an educational context (Dawson and McHugh, Chapter 6).
5 A family consultation in the school setting as described by Taylor (1982).
6 An intensive consultative service to a school or a subsystem of the school which may or may not include interviewing families when appropriate

(Barrett, Chapter 10; Dowling and Pound, Chapter 5; Lindsey, Chapter 8).

Relevant questions

The decisions made partly depend on external factors such as time, resources, etc., but the following questions can be helpful in determining the focus of an intervention:

1 *Who* is concerned?
2 *What* is the concern about?
3 What are the *expectations* of those concerned about our intervention?

Let us take a familiar example: when a pupil is presenting a problem the school may contact the school psychologist or education social worker or it may advise the parents to approach a child guidance clinic. The child may be defined as disturbed, deviant or disruptive, or failing to achieve. This familiar type of referral may elicit different responses from different workers in different settings. To take some examples, an educational psychologist may choose to interview the teacher in order to find out exactly what the problem is, then perhaps assess the child and interview the parents, and make recommendations based on the findings. A social worker may interview the parents first. A psychiatrist may see the child. A family therapist may decide at the referral stage to see the whole family for treatment. If we take the joint systems viewpoint we will approach the problem with an open mind.

Who is concerned?

The answer to this question will help us determine who should be involved in an interview: is it one teacher, is it the head, is it all the teachers in a comprehensive school? Sometimes not all this information is available at the time of referral so that a decision may have to be made on the evidence available for each case. Maybe the first stage of the intervention will have to be an information-gathering process in order to establish who is concerned.

At this point we can see that decisions begin to get complex, and even before we tackle the actual problem we are grappling with issues of context: different perceptions of an individual by different people, in different settings – home and classroom, different behaviour in different activities (good at games, poor at English). Most professionals working in the school context have experience of parents being directed to school to discuss a problem in their child that perhaps they do not see or do not accept. Likewise, family therapists know very well how difficult it is at times to get co-operation or even information about a child's behaviour in

16

school, as teachers might say, 'It is all to do with the family background – nothing we can do', and this type of attitude contributes to the labelling process we are all familiar with.

However, it may be that quite appropriately the school wishes to manage the difficulty with its own resources, at least to begin with, and the presence of an 'expert' outsider might be a threat to its belief that it should be able to seek a solution to the difficulties without outside help.

What is the concern about?

Jay Haley (1976) defined a statement about someone's problem as a statement about someone else's inability to handle it. When parents say Johnny is difficult to control, they are also saying they find it difficult to control Johnny. When a teacher says, 'Peter is withdrawn', she may also be saying she cannot get through to Peter. The problem from a teacher's point of view may be that a child is not learning properly. In the parents' view, the child is not being taught properly. The child usually does not know *what* the problem is, and if he or she does, is rarely given a chance to say so.

What are the expectations of the intervention?

From the teacher's point of view these may range from expecting some miraculous cure by an outside agent which is usually conveyed in vague words like 'this child needs help', to expectations of removal to a different school altogether. The parents usually expect change within the school, in the teacher or in the teaching methods, and there is often a tendency to blame the school, or at least place the responsibility with them.

INITIAL STAGES OF A JOINT SYSTEMS APPROACH

Setting the scene

(1) *Who is to attend the initial interview*: Having established who is to be involved in an initial interview, using information gathered about who is concerned, we may encounter practical problems. As systems therapists we will be taking note of how these problems are presented, since they will provide useful information about relationships, power, alliances and coalitions within these systems. Not everybody who *should* be involved will be found willing or able to attend.

More often than not we will be notified of their inability or unwillingness by someone else. For example, a head teacher may warn us about the difficulties the class teacher will have at a particular time. A mother will give us very powerful reasons as to why it is impossible for the father to attend; a parent may anticipate that not all the teachers will be there. We should note this information, take it seriously, but not share our inferences about its meaning at this stage. They will only be inferences in any case, and we will need to gather more data to prove or disprove our hypothesis.

The relationship between the family and school will also become apparent if we suggest the possibility of meeting together. A comment by a head teacher may suggest to us how she views the mother and likewise, parents' reactions to meeting with school staff will indicate how far apart they see their own views and those of the school. Sometimes these perceptions are based on inference or hearsay, rather than on direct firsthand experience. Reluctance about involving 'well siblings', i.e. brothers and sisters who have not been referred as a problem, can provide valuable clues as to how firmly the problem is located in one child. It can also reveal fears about 'contaminating' the other children. 'My daughter is doing her GCSEs, I don't want her to worry; the little ones know nothing about it', was a parent's anxious reply to the suggestion of an initial interview with the whole family.

Do not try to convince either school staff or family members that you are right and they are wrong. Go along with their convictions but suggest firmly that their presence in the interview is crucial for *you* to get a clear picture of the problem. In other words, the emphasis shifts from *you* as an *expert* offering help to them, as *them as experts* in their knowledge of a given situation helping *you* to understand it better.

(2)   *Where to meet*: The decisions about where to meet depend on a variety of factors, some of them very practical, and there are advantages and disadvantages about each setting. Gorell Barnes comments on the problems of territorial rights for social workers working in schools:

> The problem of working in someone else's territory is a delicate one. As an outsider the social worker entering schools finds himself drawn into a network of details about school management and school relations which can leave him quite bewildered.
>
> (1975, p. 690)

Meeting at school is obviously the most convenient place for teachers and there are also specific advantages for interviewing families, as mentioned by Taylor (1982). On the other hand, it may be useful to meet in neutral territory; for example, for a family to organize itself to go to the worker's office may, in itself, be therapeutic. The benefits of inviting teachers to meet outside the school environment are described by Osborne in Chapter 7.

Home visits provide an opportunity to see the family in its natural environment but, on the other hand, most practitioners will agree on how difficult it can be to set a firm boundary around time and space in the family home. Osborne comments on the opinions of teachers on the value of home visiting:

> In some cases it was clear that there were great advantages of informality, of greater awareness of the child's background and of meeting the family on its own ground. However, care was needed where child or parents, or both, felt the visit to be an intrusion into privacy.
>
> (Osborne, 1983, p. 114)

RESPECTING THE EXISTING HIERARCHIES

Both educationists advocating the systems approach and family therapists have emphasized the need to make an alliance with those in power in either system. Burden (1981a) suggests that an alliance with the head teacher is essential if change is to be brought about in schools. Likewise, structural therapists believe in reinforcing the hierarchical structure within the family by putting the parents in charge, and supporting them in that role.

If an interview is to be held at the school, it is most likely to take place in the head teacher's office. This reinforces the school's position of power and control, since the meeting is taking place in its territory. The worker can make therapeutic capital on this, for example, by putting the head in charge of deciding the time boundary and communicating it to all participants. This will provide an opportunity to see whether the style of communication is clear or ambiguous whilst at the same time supporting the position of the head as in charge in the school setting. The teachers themselves often welcome the head acting as an intermediary between them and parents, particularly where parents demand to see them unexpectedly. As Osborne points out when describing relationships between teachers and parents:

> It was often the case that individual teachers were not readily available to see parents making an unexpected visit, and the head acted as a first contact. Instead of feeling resentful many teachers appreciated this protection and felt this left them free to get on with their primary task of teaching. There were also gains in having one person in the school with a detailed and ongoing knowledge of the family, the history of previous contacts and, therefore, more chance of dealing with requests, complaints or worries in an informed way.
>
> (Osborne, 1983, p. 114)

AVOIDING TRIANGULATION

'Triangulation describes a relational triad in which two members form an alliance against the third' (Cooper and Upton, 1990, p. 307). Whilst it is important to side with those in power in order to get the interview off the ground, it is crucial for workers to remain 'meta' to the system in order to be free to intervene effectively. A permanent alliance with the head teacher can trigger off resistance and apprehension on the part of the family who will see the worker as 'one of them' (the school). Likewise, a strong identification with the family's viewpoint will make it difficult for school staff to trust workers, and there is a risk of seeing them as not really understanding the situation and therefore disqualifying their interventions and rendering them impotent. The same applies to taking sides permanently with children or adults. It is important that both have the opportunity to experience the worker as sensitive to their viewpoint.

KEEPING BOUNDARIES

This is particularly relevant when intervention with the two systems is conducted simultaneously and meetings with the families and schools take place in parallel but separately. The sharing of information can be useful provided there is a clear purpose to it and explicit consent from either side to make it available to the other. Example: a teacher expressed anxiety to a therapist about a mother's repeated threats to leave home. Her anxieties were based on information one of the daughters shared with her, including the fact that the mother had actually left home on one occasion.

The therapist, who was having regular meetings with the family, could then tactfully elicit what happened when the theme of Mrs B's exasperation with the children came up in the session. Mrs B was able to share with the therapist and with her family her attempts to flee the frustrating situation, her guilt feelings after she had left and her need to return home. The therapist was then able to encourage more appropriate ways of controlling the children's behaviour and to enlist the husband's support for the wife. If the therapist had disclosed the contents of the teacher's anxiety, she would have betrayed the confidential quality of the conversation between child and teacher and probably would have created misgivings in the mother about how she was seen by the teacher, not to speak of the teacher feeling betrayed by the therapist.

INTERVENTIVE TECHNIQUES

Joining manoeuvres

The initial phase of the intervention is a very delicate stage in which an information-gathering process characterized by a nonjudgemental attitude takes place.

The worker has to utilize joining manoeuvres and accept definitions of the problem as it is presented initially. Early attempts overtly to challenge or disagree with the perceptions of those who are experiencing the problem are often fruitless and will only exacerbate their need to prove how legitimate their worries are by stressing how bad or serious the problem is.

The joining process has been described both in relation to the family and the school systems (Burden, 1981a; Minuchin, 1974) but with no cross-reference between them. For Minuchin,

> to join a family system the therapist must accept the family's organization and style and blend with them. He must experience the family's transactional patterns and the strength of those patterns; that is, he should feel a family member's pain at being excluded or scapegoated and his pleasure at being loved, depended on, or otherwise confirmed within the family . . . He [the therapist] has to follow their [the family's] path of communication, discovering which ones are open, which are partly closed and which are entirely blocked . . . Like the anthropologist, the family therapist joins the culture with which he is dealing.
>
> (Minuchin, 1974, pp. 123–4)

Burden refers to the initial but crucial stage of 'cultivating the host culture' in schools and outlines the purpose of this process as follows:

> To get the feel of the school and its approach to education, to find out who are the high formal and informal status members of the staff room and to establish these as allies; to work out where the power structure lies; to gain a grasp of staff satisfactions and dissatisfactions, to sort out where the school's educational priorities lie; to obtain some idea of the 'tone' of the school both from its appearance and from observation of teacher–teacher, teacher–pupil and pupil–pupil interactions.
>
> (Burden, 1981a, p. 44)

Defining the problem

An important step in the early stages of an intervention is to obtain a definition of the problem by those concerned. It is particularly useful to get a description of the problem in behavioural terms. In other words, in response to labels suggesting what individuals causing concern *are*, we may ask what is it that they *do* to make them appear disturbed, violent, depressed, etc. It is surprising to find how difficult it is for people to shift their thinking from general labels to specific behavioural examples. It is often useful to encourage those concerned to gather baseline data about the disturbing behaviour before attempts to change it are made. Baseline data should include frequency, intensity and as much detail as possible of the context in which the behaviour occurs. It is useful to ask those involved to note what preceded and what followed an incident, in order to identify the patterns of interaction that surround the disturbing behaviour. The exploration of the context helps to establish what responses the disturbing behaviour elicits and what seems to 'trigger it off'. Often the task, on its own, of gathering baseline data puts the problem for those concerned in a different perspective. It is not uncommon to hear teachers and parents say, 'Actually, since you asked me to keep a record he seems to have been much better.'

Formulating the problem in interactional terms

Using the information gathered in the initial stages, it is possible to make a formulation which will go beyond the individually expressed symptomatic behaviour and will include the interactional elements perceived in the analysis of the context of the problem.

The formulation of the problem in interactional terms is crucial to the decision of a particular strategy and it facilitates the next step in the intervention, i.e. the formulation of goals. The formulation need not be final, but just a starting-point which will help identify the repetitive and dysfunctional interactional sequences that contribute to perpetuate the disturbing behaviour.

Using circular questioning

Circular questions are widely used in the field of systemic therapy. These questions are designed to explore the connectedness between people but also the links between their beliefs and their behaviour. The questions will elicit information about these possible connections but also have an inter-ventive power, a power which led Carl Tomm to describe their use as 'interventive interviewing' (Tomm, 1988). Campbell *et al.*, in their book *A Systemic Approach to Consultation* (1991), have categorized circular questions as follows:

First, questions which explore the *belief system* amongst those in-volved in the interview, such as what would happen if the problem is resolved. Who would benefit most and least if things change?

Second, questions relating to the *behaviour* of those involved and its connection to their belief system. What happens when Johnny doesn't go to school? How does the school let you know when they feel they can't cope with Mary any longer?

Third, questions about *relationships*. These explore the relationships between people in connection with their beliefs and their behaviour. For example, do you find your husband always disagreeing with the head teacher? Is the art teacher always supportive of your daughter's behaviour?

These questions are intended to explore connections and effects rather than look for causes of behaviour. Therefore they make it possible for the participants in the interview to develop a different view of the situation, which they have probably seen and experienced as difficult for quite a long time.

Future questions

Questions about the future or 'feed forward', 'encourage families to imagine the pattern of the relationship at some future point in time. Questions about the future in conjunction with positive connotation put families in a meta position to their own dilemmas and thus facilitate change by opening up a new solution for old problems' (Penn, 1985, p. 299).

When questions about the future are put to parents and teachers they are encouraged to examine new possibilities and create a new scenario which they are not familiar with. If one asks them questions about the past, it often becomes clear that their view of it is well known. When asking about the future, people have to think of a new script and it is not possible to imagine a different reality. When asked how they saw their 14-year-old in five years' time, parents of a very difficult boy had to try hard to leave the existing script,which was well known and well rehearsed for them. They felt free to imagine that maybe he would have left full-time education but might have found a useful job. They also thought that his talent for music, which at present was just irritating them, might have been put to good use. The scenario of five years hence looked quite different and a lot more hopeful than the present and the past.

More examples of this type of questioning can be found in Chapter 4, 'The clinic goes to school'.

Reframing

To reframe means to change the conceptual, and, or emotional setting or viewpoint in relation to which a situation is experienced and to place it in another frame which fits the 'facts' of the same concrete situation equally, or even better and thereby changes its entire meaning. Meaning . . . is not just a matter of intellectual objective understanding but the *entire personal significance* of the situation in question.

(Watzlawick *et al.*, 1974, pp. 95–6)

In a family where the needs of the older child seemed to be neglected and the younger one had been persistently provoking him throughout the session without the parents doing anything about it, the consultation message was:

We admire Mother's, Father's and John's generosity in agreeing to sacrifice their own needs to those of the youngest member of the family. Mother and Father have succeeded in training John to put the needs of others before his own. But Hugh, as he is always at the receiving end, has not yet had a chance to learn. You, as parents, with your experience, will have to judge when the right time has come as it is quite a burden for a young child to be always in that position.

Reframing is a crucial strategy in Minuchin's structural family therapy and the Milan school has developed the notion of 'positive connotation' (positive reframing) as part of its systemic approach to problems (Palazzoli *et al.*, 1978).

Reframing, or giving a new frame or meaning to a situation can have surprisingly positive effects. A child, whose role as another adult was overtly criticized but covertly reinforced by the parents, constantly interrupted them in the early stages of an interview. The therapist reframed his behaviour as very sensitive and caring in helping his parents with answering difficult questions in an unfamiliar situation. The covert message to the parents, 'You need your child to protect you, he is stronger than you', was aimed at changing the relational pattern in the family without overtly challenging the parents' inability to stop their child interrupting at such an early stage in the intervention.

A mother defined the school her child attended in particular, and the educational system in general, as conspiring to prevent her very bright daughter from developing her full potential. The school staff in turn regarded this mother as difficult and obstructive and their attempts to change her behaviour achieved very little. The situation escalated to such a pitch that the mother was banned from the school. From an interventive point of view, to put pressure on this mother to see the good points of the school or to try to put the school's case to her would have only exacerbated her need to prove that she was right and 'they' were wrong.

A reframing statement about her being a caring parent who knew her daughter well and was aware of her needs lowered her defences and enabled her to accept that perhaps there was an alternative way of putting her feelings across. The situation ceased to be defined as 'her being wrong, the school being right and the expert forcing that view on her'. Instead she was defined as a good, caring parent who might not have found a way of conveying her views to the school successfully.

The situation had up until then escalated into a spiral producing more of the same. The more the mother demanded that the school accept that she was right and they were wrong, the more she was defined as a 'difficult mother'. The more she was defined as 'difficult' the less inclined the school staff were to listen to her views, and as they became more inaccessible the mother's demands increased, and so it went on. The situation reached a stage where attempts to solve the problem had become the problem. Once the mother discovered that the worker did not see her as difficult but as caring she did not need to intensify her 'difficult' behaviour. Instead it became possible to examine alternative ways of approaching the school, including the suggestion that the father conveyed their views to the school. As she felt supported she appeared to be more prepared to 'delegate'.

The teachers in the meantime had grown defensive and persecuted by what they saw as intruding and obtrusive parental behaviour and unreasonable demands. To try to convince them otherwise might have triggered off stronger arguments to prove they were right, with statements such as, 'Don't talk to me about Mrs X, she is the most unreasonable woman I have come across in my experience of n years.' Reframing their behaviour as concerned to do the best they could for the child reassured them that the worker was not there as an envoy of the parents to criticize them.

These first steps in breaking the cycle would have facilitated a gradual exploration of how the school could help the parents share their knowledge of the child in a way that was not felt to be intrusive or undermining by the teachers. Likewise, the parents, having been reassured that they were seen as good, caring parents, would have accepted that the school was not all bad and that the situation was amenable to change.

The reframing of behaviour in a positive way (positive connotation) can be built into a no-change prescription as part of a paradoxical intervention. What happens in the paradox is that more than one message is conveyed at the same time (therapeutic double bind): at one level the therapist is instructing the family members to continue doing as they are doing, but implicit in his message is the fact that what they do is not inevitable but is their choice. On the other hand, if they stop doing it they will show their capacity for change and prove the therapist wrong.

A paradoxical instruction was given to a family where the parents repeatedly complained they had tried every possible way of controlling their children, but without success. In the process of convincing their therapist, they disqualified every attempt he made to suggest a new way of dealing with the problem. The therapist positively connoted the parents as very sensitive parents who should not attempt to control their children until they felt ready to do so. At the next session the parents reported marked improvement in the children's behaviour.

The family was put in a 'therapeutic double bind'. If they did as the therapist said they would prove him right: they were 'not ready' (or able) to control their children. Strategic manoeuvres of this kind have been used successfully with families although criticism has always been levelled against more adventurous clinicians, defining these techniques as manipulative, uncaring, playing games, etc. These techniques, like all other interventive techniques, require skill and sensitivity. It is beyond the scope of this chapter to expand on these therapeutic approaches, but interested readers are referred to Cade (1979); Haley (1976); Madanes (1981); Palazzoli *et al.* (1980); and Watzlawick (1974).

Paradoxical prescription of the symptomatic behaviour in schools has not been documented except for Palazzoli *et al.* (1976), who point out the complexities of using these techniques with larger systems. Our own experience suggests that even without prescribing the symptomatic behaviour to continue, positive connotation of behaviour is always useful in shifting rigid defensive behaviour on the part of school staff. Removing the pressure for change and even expressing a pessimistic view of the scope for change (going along with the resistance) are useful devices in so far as they free the worker from trying to convince anyone that things can be different. We have seen teachers arguing strongly to prove that there is hope in a situation which the worker has described cautiously, as difficult and having no immediate answer.

Task setting

The setting of tasks allows people to experiment with a different way of relating to one another within the framework of a structured specific situation.[1] This technique has been found useful both with family and school systems. The first step in the setting of a task is to gather information regarding the problem situation as it is at present. This must include a clear description of the context in which the problem occurs. Second, the following questions will have to be asked:

Who is to be involved?

It may be appropriate not to ask help of some people who have regarded themselves as key participants. But the reason for leaving out someone from the problem-solving process must always be positively framed.

An intrusive grandmother must never be made redundant as a result of the therapist's attempts to get the parents together. A successful intervention will define her as being free, at long last, of chores that really belong to her daughter, and a substitute role in the system must be found.

In schools, over-involved teachers who, in their attempts to help children, reinforce their disabling labels, must be positively connoted as needing to spread their valuable skills to more children.

What needs to be different?
The task must be carefully planned, it must be possible and be clearly spelt out.

How does it need to be different?
Careful thought is to be given to the way relationships have to be different in order to become functional and render the symptom redundant. An opportunity to experiment with relating in a different and more functional way is ritualized through the task.

A family where only those who shouted loudly could be heard and where the parents found it difficult to set limits on their children, was given the following task: the children were to use a whistle at a special time, decided by the parents. During that special time, anybody who wished to say something, but could not be heard, should blow the whistle. The parents were to ensure then that space would be available for that person to be heard.

The task was geared in the following ways: (a) to restructure the hierarchical boundaries in the family by putting the parents in charge (the discussion about time was initiated in the session and the therapist ensured that the rules regarding the whistle were clearly communicated to the children); (b) to facilitate space and functional communication within the family through a ritualized exercise; the whistle had to be in a special place and was only to be used at the special time decided by the parents; (c) to ensure the children's co-operation by being sufficiently simple and enjoyable; (d) to enable the family to continue creating space for each other after experimenting with a different way of relating in a highly structured and ritualized situation.

The content of the task in itself may be irrelevant but its meaning lies in the restructuring of the relationships. In another instance a headmistress presented a psychologist with a difficult situation where her staff could agree there was a problem but could not agree on the way to solve it. This and similar reported problems showed a pattern of unclear hierarchical structure, mixed messages about authority and general lack of clarity amongst teachers as to how much their views would be heard and implemented.

This particular problem sprung from a new system of referrals suggested by the educational psychologist who, because of the lack of communication amongst the staff, had come to feel that the referrals did not reflect the concerns of the teachers but rather those of the head teacher. The psychologist chose to hold a meeting with the teachers and, because of views expressed at that meeting, suggested a new referral system to the head teacher.

Clearly the head felt her authority and position in the hierarchy was under threat. A rule she had made had been challenged but, even worse, it might be changed without her being a party to it. The only way to recover her position of being in charge of the rules was to block the new system that was being proposed.

She reported back to the psychologist that her staff could not agree on what would be the best referral system. During discussion with colleagues it was suggested to the psychologist that a possible way out of that impasse might be the setting of a task which would reinstate the head in her position of 'in charge' whilst enforcing functional communication between her staff. For example, the head could be asked to convene a meeting with the staff and ask everyone to make a specific suggestion regarding the referral system. The suggestions could then be discussed and an agreement could be negotiated; if a negotiated agreement was not reached, the head teacher could then decide for herself which suggestion would be the best. Although this may not have been the perfectly democratic answer desired by the teachers, changes in the relational pattern could be achieved: the teachers would have been asked by the head about their views in a formal structured context, and the group would have had the option of a negotiated agreement of a most suitable referral procedure. If an agreement was not reached, the head could still take account of her teachers' views, but her position of being in charge would be reinforced as it would be up to her to use her judgement in choosing the 'best' suggestion.

Tasks can be usefully devised to be carried out in parallel by the family and the school, for example, over monitoring progress in a particular situation; occasional joint meetings can be arranged for family and school staff to exchange progress reports and suggestions when things have not worked out. Through a structured situation the experience of a prolonged contest about who is right and who is wrong, with the child usually caught in the middle, is replaced by a co-ordinated effort to effect the desired changes.

Recent developments in family therapy stemming from the social constructivist position (Hoffman, 1988; McNab, 1993; Von Foerster, 1984) have moved on to see the process of therapy as facilitating a co-evolutionary view of the problem, where both the family and the therapist move on to a new construction of the situation. This co-evolutionary process is particularly necessary when the family and school's perspectives on a problem are different and the role of the systems therapist may be to do with bringing forward change in mutual perceptions. Members of the two systems can influence each other towards a different view of the situation where the notion of blame can be replaced by one of understanding and co-operation towards the solution of the difficulties.

CONCLUSION

In this chapter I have outlined the theoretical thinking that has evolved in parallel about families and schools from a systems viewpoint. I have also examined the implications of this conceptual shift in terms of understanding the meaning of disturbing behaviour and developing alternative interventive strategies.

It is clear that, if problems experienced with children are to be dealt with more effectively, a great deal of bridge building is needed between clinicians, educators and policy-makers in an attempt to view the difficulties in the context of these two crucial and constantly evolving subsystems of society: the family and the school.

NOTE

1 For specific references to task setting see Haley (1976) *Problem Solving Therapy*, ch. 2, 'Giving directives'; Minuchin (1974) *Families and Family Therapy*, 'Assigning tasks'; Walrond-Skinner (1976) *Family Therapy: the Treatment of Natural Systems*, ch. 6, 'Task centred therapy'; Watzlawick (1974) *Change*, ch. 9, 'The practice of change'.

2

SOME IMPLICATIONS OF THE THEORETICAL FRAMEWORK

An educational psychologist's perspective

Elsie Osborne

The aim of this chapter is to take as a starting point some of the concepts considered in the first chapter, which outlined the theoretical framework for a joint systems approach and, by reflecting on these and sometimes extending them, to focus on the impact of systems theory on my thinking as an educational psychologist in relation to schools and families.

The intention is to convey some of the changes in attitude and approach that follow from the theoretical considerations, without being prescriptive about the specific action to be taken in particular cases. There will inevitably be some overlap with Emilia Dowling's opening chapter but, true to a systemic way of working, the perspective will be different.

Relevant to the separate development of systems approaches with families and schools is the fact that the development of family therapy was happening at a time when educational psychologists (EPs) were rapidly moving out of the child guidance clinics, where most of them had previously been employed. Many more EPs were being trained and most of them were going directly into school psychological services. This development had many positive aspects: it strengthened their links with education, gave them greater independence and began a process in which many new ways were developed of looking at the problems presented by and to school children and their teachers.

There was some loss, however, in the rejection of the clinical approach which this entailed. In shaking off the perceived medical influence in the clinics, which was increasingly resented, or at least seen as inappropriate, the educational psychologists lost touch with the new methods which were being developed in the clinics, one of which was, of course, family therapy, alongside a growing interest in systems theory.

Certainly ideas about working with schools as institutions, rather than as a base for visits to discuss individual children, were being developed in the school psychological services, but where educational psychologists have become interested in family therapy and sought training or supervision, as they often have in recent years, this has tended to be seen as something quite separate from their thinking about the school system. This has probably reduced the influence of an important aspect of a systemic approach.

In her survey of systems approaches in EP practice Frederickson says,

> In recent years *systems work* has been confusingly used to describe anything and everything which an educational psychologist might do in the course of their work – other than interacting directly with children. It has been used to describe any kind of work (consultation, inservice training, action research) with the school as an organization . . . It has been used to describe projects in which some attempts have been made to introduce some systematic procedures . . . for allocating psychological service time between schools on the basis of need.
>
> (1990, p. 131)

We would agree with Frederickson's conclusion 'in none of these cases is the work described necessarily systems work'. Whilst on the one hand all work done with the school as an institution is not necessarily systemically based, it is equally true, on the other hand, that work based on the individual child can still be influenced by a systemic approach.

Working from a single base as an educational psychologist with family therapy experience has been a helpful reminder that systems theory is not only applicable at the level of the institution as a whole or to working with the entire school system. Systems theory is equally meaningful in relation to any group formed around a task, or where interaction is taking place, for instance in the classroom or staff room. The experience of family therapy, and an understanding of the family as a system, also helps in considering the position of the individual child who has to accommodate to two separate systems, those of the family and the school. Dowling (Chapter 1) has already made reference to the paper by Taylor (1986) in which there is a useful development of this theme. Where there is clear evidence of hostility between the two systems the difficulties for a child caught between them may be obvious, but more subtle shifts of perception may be required and then a broad understanding of family and school systems can help the professional worker appreciate the extent of the stresses involved.

CAUSE AND EFFECT AND BLAMING

A key definition of a system is that it consists of interdependent parts, in which one component affects, and is affected by, the others. This crucially alters the way we look at cause and effect. The importance of this theme has already been well stressed in Chapter 1. If we relate this to the problem of a child who is unable to read the problem may be redefined in a number of ways. For example, if there is a complaint about Tom's reading it does

31

not only imply that Tom cannot learn to read, perhaps because he is dull or has some other deficiency, it also implies that the teacher is unable to teach him to read. Alternatively we may think in terms of Kelly's notion of 'bad fit', which shifts responsibility from a single component to the relations within the system (Kelly, 1968). That is to say, the emphasis is on the relationship rather than a 'bad individual' or a 'bad school'.

We may now be more open to including other important people in the circle of cause and effect, important in terms of this particular issue. Maybe the complaint about Tom's reading reflects the anxiety of a teacher who is feeling unsupported by the head, is concerned that resources are inadequate or that the class has an unreasonable share of children with problems. There are also many possibilities for disagreements within a school over very basic beliefs about the nature of learning and techniques for teaching. Over the years there have been many disputes over the best way to teach reading, provoking intense clashes from time to time.

Alternatively the worry about reading may be related to a disagreement between the teacher and the child's parents about what is needed, over what constitutes acceptable standards or the help required to meet them. Factors at home contributing to the failure to learn may relate to a child's attempt to remain the baby, to resist growing up, which may be related in turn to changes in the family and the relationships between its members.

In any of these cases an attempt only to focus on the problem in the child could lead to failure. The lesson of a systemic approach is that the psychologist might instead target an intervention where it could have the best chance of success.

This is not to say the psychologist does not take seriously the problem as presented. It is almost certainly the case that it is the child who will be seen as the problem, but the aim is not to go through a chain of possibilities in order to find whoever, or whatever, is the *real* cause of blame for Tom's failure to read. The focus on interaction between the various people concerned means that none of them can be seen as carrying the total responsibility for what happens between them; each makes their own contribution. An important consideration here is, of course, the fact that not all members of the system or systems involved are equally influential. The distribution of power and its imbalances are part of the system which must be taken into account in considering how to intervene. However it is still the case that one of the most crucial effects of an interactional way of thinking is that it becomes much more difficult to apportion blame when something goes wrong.

At this point maybe a systemic approach can begin to seem an unduly complex way of working and it is worth pausing to consider why it should be considered worthwhile. We might, for instance, suppose that it is possible to give up a blaming attitude without taking on board the whole of systems theory. For an educational psychologist the systemic approach is a way of thinking which is in tune with the wish to avoid putting people, and children in particular, into categories and labelling them. There is some further discussion of the relationship between this kind of thinking and the rejection of testing, especially intelligence testing, by much of the EP profession, in Chapter 3.

A further important result of shifting the focus from the individual to the interactions they have is that the possibilities for intervention are immediately widened. Instead of putting all our energies into changing the individual (whether child or teacher or parent) the emphasis is upon attempting to change the *situation*. Moreover it becomes possible to choose to intervene in the interaction that looks most amenable to change, or most productive in the longer term.

To return to the rather crude example of Tom's failure to read, it may be possible to bring the class teacher and the head together to discuss the teacher's concerns. It could be that improved communication between home and school looks like being more effective. If family therapy or individual help is offered elsewhere the implications for the school will be considered an important aspect, rather than simply an exercise in co-operation.

OPEN AND CLOSED SYSTEMS

The concept of open and closed systems has also proved to be an extremely useful one in thinking about schools. The closed system is one that resists change and has no exchange with its external environment. It is unlikely that systems involving human beings can maintain themselves indefinitely in this way, but the attempt may certainly be made. Within a system which attempts to close its boundaries there is little opportunity either for change from without or for self-generated change. On the other hand, open systems are maintained through constant exchange with the environment. They may still have clear boundaries, but these boundaries can be breached. They are, therefore, more available to influences for change from outside, even though self-generated change remains difficult.

People are, in themselves, open systems, influencing and being influenced by their environment, despite suppositions that certain troubled people, for example delinquents, are in some way separated off and are therefore frequently seen as outside our recognized system. Where clinics have sought primarily to work with individuals they have taken account of the context in which they live. This has always been true of child guidance clinics, where it was traditionally part of the role of the psychologist to deal with the school, while the social worker took account of the family background. Systems theory extends our understanding of 'the child in context' (Campion, 1985) as the focus of a constantly developing and shifting web of relationships and interactions, influencing as well as being influenced by them all.

EQUILIBRIUM AND RESISTANCE TO CHANGE

Although an open system is, by definition, more readily open to change there is another key concept from systems theory which contributes to understanding the forces which work against change. This concept was discussed in Chapter 1 under the heading of homoeostasis. This notion of homoeostasis, although controversial, has been used by family therapists to help explain how some families will 'sacrifice' one of their members in order to sustain homoeostasis. It can also be helpful in understanding institutions, and therefore schools.

Translated into the attempt which an organization makes to maintain equilibrium, this concept, together with that of open and closed systems, allows us to foresee some of the difficulties we might meet in trying to introduce change into a school system. There is further discussion of this topic in Denise Taylor's Chapter 9, on schools as a target for change. Here I would like to emphasize aspects which are of particular relevance to the educational psychologist.

One aspect of a systemic approach is that it leads us to consider how change in one part of a school will affect other parts, and therefore to reassess the nature of the resistance that we meet. If a different approach to the class is encouraged with one of the class teachers will other teachers resent this because the ethos of the school is then altered in some way? Will a new style of working be seen as attacking a long-established tradition? Efforts to maintain equilibrium are important to the school's stability over time and one way of effecting this could be for other staff to ignore or treat with scorn the attempts at change of the teacher concerned.

Schools are like many other institutional systems in their attempts to preserve equilibrium by encouraging conformity. Those who do not fit in, or who present too great a challenge, may be removed, if not literally then by isolation or denigration. If it is a pupil who is involved then there may be pressure to transfer or exclude the child. If it is a teacher, or any other member of staff, who wishes to introduce an unwelcome change, there are likely to be attempts to exclude him or her from the school's decision-making procedures. The aim and the likely result will be to render the person concerned ineffective.

This is not to say that all teachers in a particular school will work in exactly the same way. Indeed it may be useful to draw on their different perspectives, for instance in discussing a particular child or classroom problem, and to show how these may be valid from different points of view.

The aim here is not to condemn the schools for their resistance to change. Stability is also a factor in maintaining a healthy system. The point is however an important one. Self-generated change is very difficult, even within a comparatively open system.

THE INDEPENDENT PSYCHOLOGIST

This difficulty in self-generated change is also an argument in favour of the educational psychologist retaining an independent role, rather than becoming a member of the school staff. Although it is possible to see staff membership as useful in terms of acceptance by the school, and in the understanding of its particular rules and circumstances, the psychologist who becomes part of the school's hierarchy is then as liable as the others within it to be caught up in the institution's primary task of maintaining its own system.

If the psychologist makes too strong an alliance with the school then it will be more difficult to obtain the trust of some of its families, or to mediate between the family and the school when they are in disagreement, or generally on bad terms with one another.

Psychologists cannot, of course, go in and demand the changes that they think are needed. Attempts to do this would be deservedly rebuffed. Head teachers have a great deal of autonomy and it is essential that the EP has their goodwill. Indeed it is the head teacher who is usually best placed to initiate and support change and who knows what pace best suits the particular school. It is not, of course, the EP's primary task to support and maintain the status quo but the authority of the head has to be acknowledged and care taken not to undermine it. In addition the liaison between head teacher and EP should not be too close where this could mean loss of trust and confidence by the rest of the staff.

Appropriate action is influenced by the EP's understanding of the rules and organization of the school, including its formal and informal systems of communication, its hierarchies and priorities. The informal organization may be especially important, for example where there is a very powerful deputy whose influence alters the formal hierarchy. Such informal features may be vague or include deliberate ambiguities. It is well worth while to try to understand these as well as to know as fully as possible about the satisfactions and the dissatisfactions of the staff and pupils, and also those of its parents.

The psychologist who avoids becoming a part of the school system, who remains 'meta' to the system is also likely to be in a stronger position to resist demands from the school to act in a particular way, for instance to remove a child, to change somebody's behaviour, or to respond to pressure to offer advice and solutions which seem inappropriate or impossible to achieve.

A SUMMARY

The following is an attempt to summarize the issues that have been raised so far.

1 It is useful to think about *whatever* group you are working with as a system, whether you are responding to the referral of an individual child, or a request to help the school implement a major change in how it organizes, say, its special needs department.
2 All children are part of the two overlapping systems of family and school and they usually take the strain of mediating between them and of adjusting to them both.
3 The focus on interactions gives a wider range of possibilities for intervening.
4 We are helped to discover where best to intervene by looking for those interactions which are not functioning well, and by looking for sequences or patterns of behaviour between people rather than by concentrating on acquiring ever more facts and history.
5 This way of working helps the EP avoid the search for who is to blame or who must be compelled to change.
6 It is appropriate for the EP to remain 'meta' to the school system.
7 A systemic approach supports the view that there are many different perspectives and views, all of which may be accepted as valid. It is therefore possible to avoid getting caught up in arguments as to who is right or who is wrong.
8 In resisting demands that he or she should change somebody's behaviour the EP may instead contribute to the shifting of the perceptions that people have of one another.
9 Schools are open systems, but like all institutions they have a major interest in maintaining the status quo in the face of demands to change.

A RANGE OF THEORETICAL FRAMEWORKS

To advocate a wider use of systems theory is not necessarily to consign all previous orientations to the dustbin of history. It certainly challenges what has been seen as the intrapsychic emphasis of psychodynamic approaches, although it was never the case, as noted before, that clinic workers could focus exclusively on the child without paying a great deal of attention to the context of home and school. Whilst it is difficult for me now to imagine working without the structure that systems theory provides, in terms of circular causality, punctuation, feedback and so on, I want to suggest that other theoretical frameworks can and do supplement this structure, with an understanding of some of the forces at work. These are often of additional help in making hypotheses and in the decisions about where and how to intervene. They have the capacity to deepen our ideas about interaction, to help us to look at its irrational dimensions and to understand better the resistance to change that we meet. Our systemic approach means that we do not see resistance as invariably unhealthy, and enables us to avoid the tendency to pathologize the individual.

Attachment theory

The Child and Family Department at the Tavistock Clinic was much influenced by John Bowlby and by attachment theory. In three volumes (1969, 1973, 1980) Bowlby built on his early studies of maternal deprivation to present, lucidly and thoroughly, a reformulation of psychodynamic theory in relation to childhood. Both in theory and in practice he placed the main force of explanation and intervention on the interactions in which a child was engaged. Most famously, he described how the initial bond between mother and baby provided the basis for the establishment of an attachment, the nature of which would influence future relationships. An attachment which was secure enough to allow the baby to be free to explore, created a foundation for future learning.

The implications of attachment theory have been analysed and subjected to experiment by a number of authors. The paper by Ainsworth *et al.* (1978) is something of a classic study of the patterns of attachment as demonstrated by young children presented with a strange situation. Parkes and Stevenson-Hinde (1982) look at many aspects of attachment in everyday behaviour, with an especially important contribution on the nature of grief. More recently Murray *et al.* (1992) have studied the effect of depressed mothers on the cognitive development of their infants, linking the results to attachment theory.

The links between attachment theory and the family system have been explored by John Byng-Hall (1991) and Joan Stevenson-Hinde (1990). The importance of these studies in the context of this chapter lies in their contribution to the deeper understanding of the relationships which are at the basis of the human systems we are concerned with, including the nature of those which facilitate learning. All of these are of considerable significance to the family, the school and the educational psychologist who aims to work with both systems. In Chapter 10 Muriel Barrett discusses attachment theory further, especially in relation to consultation.

Another aspect of a psychodynamic approach which remains an important contribution is the importance attached to the feelings which underlie the interactions we observe. I do not find this incompatible with a systemic view. As psychologists we are still dealing with real people, with feelings, hopes and ambitions, rational and irrational fears, the individual's need to defend against painful feelings and to cope with past experiences and relationships. Individuals are not, in fact, parts of a machine. We need all the help we can find to strengthen our understanding of the (apparently) irrational.

Theories about consultation

The contribution of theories of consultation to our thinking about systems is well explored by Taylor (Chapter 9). She refers to the early and major contribution of Caplan (1970) to the practice of consultation. Of additional interest here is Caplan's approach to the role of the consultant. He specified the most essential aspects as including the issue of respect for appropriate professional boundaries and he offers techniques for preserving these in the interests of the main, work-centred task of consultation. He discusses the consultant's acceptance and management of feelings and personal problems whilst avoiding the temptation to drift into counselling or therapy.

It is a view which shares with systemic approaches the need to be very careful about advice-giving as a prevailing technique, since a major consideration is the respect for the other person's professional integrity and an understanding of the nature of responsibility. This is seen as needing to continue to lie with the appropriate person, and in the light of this view, advice-giving can more clearly be seen as potentially undermining in its encouragement of dependence, and its possible damage to the recipient's self-esteem.

As in systemic approaches, the aim in consultation is to look at different perspectives, to shift perceptions and encourage the setting up of alternative hypotheses and possibilities for intervention, rather than in submitting to the pressure to give an expert opinion, which might then be discredited, and may well not be followed. Choice becomes more central in such a scheme of things rather than a search for the perfect and ultimate cure.

Systems thinking and practice has inevitably developed a great deal since Caplan's early work, without invalidating his central ideas. Campbell *et al.* (1991), for instance, offer a detailed account of a systemic approach to consultation, covering concepts and practice with some illustrative case material. They make a specific link between some of the basic concepts of systems theory, including feedback and negotiating change, with a particular technique focusing on consultation to organizations. In discussing the observer's perspective they say:

> In summary, we are saying that consultation does not change organizations in the way that a gardener might move shrubs and plant trees to change the landscape. It is more akin to moving the observer to a different position, so that the landscape is seen from a different perspective.

(1991 p. 14)

This is in harmony with a view of consultation which is a useful corrective to some of our more extravagant notions about the fashion of 'giving away psychology' or manipulating behaviour. Campbell *et al.* also add the following, which underlines the importance of looking at the influence of change in one place on its influence elsewhere:

> We do not think that talking about problems makes a difference in itself, unless it is connected to a view of the gains and losses of changing the relationships and the culture of the organization. Schein [a reference to Schein's book on Process Consultation, 1987] does not talk about change, but he approaches change via the route of the consultant who has specific solutions for specific problems . . . Thus his questions are problem based rather than systems based . . . limited to solving problems rather than . . . also having an effect on the belief system which governs the way other problems will be solved in the future.
>
> (1991, p. 31)

This long and wide view seems especially relevant to the way we approach schools, where the solution of a single child's problematic behaviour or learning difficulty, for instance, by their removal or cure, leaves the school no better equipped to deal with the next problem, except by calling for the same solution.

Conoley and Conoley (1990) address staff consultation in schools in relation to the work of the educational psychologist. They usefully summarize the strengths and weaknesses of three types of consultation: mental health consultation as proposed by Caplan, which is discussed above, behavioural consultation and process consultation. They conclude that 'few hard and fast generalisations about best practices can be made'. They do not directly refer to systems theory, although many of the points they make, especially in discussing process consultation, are sympathetic to a systemic approach. In their general conclusions they say that 'interpersonal skill (of the consultant) is at least as critical to success as content expertise'.

Conoley and Conoley also warn about the hazards of advice-giving, which may make a consultee dependent and interfere with the empowerment goal of consultation. Their emphasis upon the interactive aspect of consultation is reflected in their final conclusion:

> The key to consultation success is an awareness by all the adults in children's environments that children's problems are at least partially maintained by the actions of the adults. If children's difficulties are seen as signs of individual pathology, then consultation is only of limited usefulness. In contrast, if adults believe that *settings are always part of the problem*, then consultative work is the most-valued service.
>
> (1990, p. 100)

Other systems-oriented approaches

Although her contribution does not specifically relate to consultation, but to a more general methodology, it might be useful here also to consider the approach endorsed by Frederickson (1990) in the chapter previously referred to. She describes soft systems methodology (SSM), as a method derived from systems theory, which is particularly useful for dealing with 'soft systems' such as schools, where 'real world' problem situations are ill structured. SSM is seen as describing problems in terms of 'real world messes or systems of interlinked problems, perceived and defined in different ways by different protagonists'. The similarity with much that has been said before will be clear. Frederickson reports that it is a method now being widely used by EPs, and although it is too soon to draw clear conclusions it is seen as complementing the problem-centred approach, which is the current *modus operandi* for most psychologists.

This seems to be a welcome advance in a systemic approach for educational psychologists for, as Frederickson says: 'teachers are reluctant to reduce [their] fuzzy statements, an approach is needed that can handle the fuzziness and complexity of real world problems'. The methodology, as described by her, emphasizes the importance of different perspectives, without implying that any is right or more accurate. It also accepts that there is subjective judgement, e.g. in selecting which 'relevant system' to develop. (Relevant systems are abstract constructs based on the real world situation and leading to implementation in the final stage of the methodology.) SSM does not focus on the problem but on the situation in which there is perceived to be a problem, or an opportunity for improvement. This is a definition of a systems-based approach which may be compared with Campbell *et al.* above. They move even further away from the presenting problem, to the belief system 'which governs the way other problems will be solved in the future'. Certainly there seems to be agreement that solving problems is more complex than at first appears.

Plas (1986) describes a systemic approach in which she translates familiar family therapy strategies to work with groups in schools. These strategies include positive connotation and prescription carried out by a team of four which is divided into two pairs, one within the room with the school group and another acting as a consultant pair outside the room, acknowledged to the group. The arrangement is as close as possible to that of systemic family therapy, specifically that of the Milan group, but Plas notes the importance of bearing in mind the distinction between the school and the family as one in which the school group (usually a class or special unit of some kind in her own elaboration) is always part of a larger system. It is, therefore, considered crucial to consider the ripples through the wider system. In order to minimize this Plas suggests that strategies should, as far as possible, be modest and simple and confine action to the group directly involved (the target group).

Plas makes it clear that the approach is not designed to work at the interface of home and school. Instead emphasis is placed upon referrals which avoid too direct a connection with family dynamics, and on work with those referrals where the child concerned is seen as a source of discomfort within, or by, the group (e.g. the class). The aim is then to effect improvement through work with the target group within the school and with minimum attention to the family system, other than to obtain parental goodwill and support *as far as possible*. The two systems of family and school are therefore presented as separate and interaction between them is not dealt with. The approach is well argued but it will be clear that it makes a very different application of systems theory from the one which provides the basis for this volume, which attempts to address overlap and interaction between these two systems, and, indeed, to work at their interface.

Plas goes on to make a distinction between her 'systemic' and other systems-based approaches. Within this group she places the ecosystemic approaches, for instance of Aponte (to which there is reference in Chapter 1). All of her examples are derived from work in the USA but we could note that interventions by school psychologists at the level of the school system have their equivalents here, e.g. Burden (1978). Other work of related interest, for instance that of Fine and Holt, has already been referred to in Chapter 1. In summary it seems that there is still a considerable need to address the issues rising from work at the interface between the two systems of family and school.

Schools as organizations

There is a further area of theoretical speculation which is of special importance to the educational psychologist. Again I would refer the reader to Chapter 9 where Denise Taylor discusses schools as socio-technical systems, illuminating the concept of the school as an organization in a number of ways. She draws attention to its special nature because of the immaturity of pupils and their gradual growth, calling for constant readjustment by the adults, and to the overlap therefore between the tasks of the school and the family. She also discusses issues relating to its subsystems. These subsystems comprise groups which are subject to group processes and dynamics, with their implications for power struggles and politics within a hierarchical structure.

Campbell *et al.* (1991) also discuss the nature of organizations, although not with specific reference to schools. Still, there are some elements I would like to draw out of their conceptualization which do seem very relevant. In looking at the relationship between the individual and the organization they stress that it is not necessarily change itself but its perceived meaning that is the problem for the individual. Moreover the process of change is determined by the interactive process between individuals and by mutual feedback. Schools are, of course, crucially involved in interactions; those within the teacher–pupil relationship are essential for without them learning will not take place. The importance of staff interactions may not, however, receive the same attention, and subjective impressions of change may well be left unchallenged.

In their book on understanding schools as organizations, Handy and Aitken (1990) attempt to pin down some of the essential characteristics of the school as distinct from other organizations, as well as those which are shared. In looking at the schools they distinguish the two major tasks of differentiation, with the individual teachers as specialists working independently, and the school organization as a whole needing to provide structures to keep them all pointing in the same direction. They say 'there must be enough integrating devices to match the necessary differentiation'. The difficult task of achieving a collective purpose and setting the boundaries of the system requires time and appropriate structures. Yet elsewhere they point out that a characteristic of schools is that space is not provided for management, which is seen as a chore that should be kept to a minimum. Management is achieved either by giving total autonomy to self-contained units, or by autocracy in which the head teacher takes all the decisions. Neither meets the need of the school for integration, and Handy and Aitken conclude 'schools cannot be run in spare time'.

It can also be the case that in splitting off the management from the teaching task in the way described a situation is created in which it becomes possible to preserve an idealized image of teaching whilst loading 'management' with all the negative feelings.

I find it very useful to understand the central dilemma of schools, which is a source of constant tension, as one about differentiation as against integration. Within the classroom itself I see this dilemma, from the teacher's point of view, as a conflict between treating children as individuals, each with unique needs, and ensuring that they work towards a common aim and within the policy of the school. Neither aim can be denied and, therefore, they must be kept in balance. This is a hard enough task, but without the support of appropriate structures the pressure of the task becomes a source of immense strain.

In looking at the needs of the schools I have a picture of an environment subjected to many pressures. There are external demands for better results, with a wider range of children, for greater parental influence, for more vigorous appraisal, more competition between schools and greater public accountability. Within education there are further pressures on individual teachers to change methods, and to increase their understanding of individual learning difficulties and the effects of handicap.

Schools will, of course, not be exempt from change within a society which is itself undergoing so much change. On the contrary, the education service has been placed at the centre of change, with demands which illustrate the ambivalence with which it is regarded, since it represents, through the children, society's hopes and fears for the future. Therefore attempts to harness the enormous power schools are seen to hold is accompanied by other attempts to lessen their authority, for example by legislation to increase parental power and by controlling the curriculum, both directly and through centrally imposed tests.

In addition the pace of the changes demanded has created further stress and loss of confidence amongst teachers. The previous self-assurance of schools has been considerably shaken. Addressing this is in the interests of their children, but the means have to be found through their staffs, and through the open system which is the school.

The educational psychologist has to be interested in ways of creating the best conditions for the primary task of the school, the learning that takes place. In my view, such conditions would require an open system, amenable to change, with recognizable boundaries which are not too rigid, an organization which allows for external influences without its staff perceiving them as a threat to their integrity. In this climate risks and uncertainty are acceptable and failure an inevitable part of learning. The search for certainty and clear answers is replaced by a willingness to look at alternatives. Respect for individual differences reduces the need for conformity. The task for its management is to exercise an integrating function whereby the staff as a whole can keep in mind a picture of the school's main function, and to create an atmosphere in which all situations, including problem ones, become opportunities for learning.

The account of a school-based consultation service, described by Emilia Dowling in Chapter 4, seems to me to accord with many of the views expressed in this chapter, in the way in which the team involved resisted efforts to define either school or parents as right or wrong, introduced alternative views rather than challenging the view of either teacher or parent, and resisted the temptation to be seen as experts who would produce a short-term resource or as one that would just remove problems. This acceptance of different perceptions as valid, the encouragement to look at alternatives from the child's point of view, and the acknowledgement that conflict between home and school may arise from different priorities which are equally valid is very much in the interests of good home–school relationships. It is an open attitude which is also in the interests of the kind of organizational culture I have been describing. It also brings us full circle, back to systems theory.

CONCLUDING REMARKS

The description of the theories given here, including systems theory itself, is not intended to be exhaustive, indeed it has been very selective of the propositions discussed. There are other paradigms which are of considerable importance in educational psychology. Cognitive psychology is central to much academic educational psychology and to many practitioners. There have undoubtedly been important developments here, including efforts to encompass emotional and social factors (see, for example, Entwistle, 1990). We might also note in passing the importance attached to feedback in cognitive theory, a notion very sympathetic to systemic thinking, where it is, of course, a key concept.

The chapter has also paid comparatively little attention to developments in the understanding of the learning process as such, which is clearly of considerable relevance to educational psychologists. There is also the ongoing debate about Piaget's work, including the major contribution from Donaldson (1979).

The intention of the chapter as a whole has been to translate aspects of theory into an educational psychologist's context. The aim has been to illustrate some of the theoretical possibilities, to make a case for retaining an open mind, and to seek to make meaningful links between the various paradigms presented. This is not to suggest that the EP may pick and choose from a medley of ideas, according to mood.

Later chapters in this book amplify and illustrate some of the ideas presented. The focus here has tended to be on the school, although bearing in mind the dual context of family and school as well as the central importance of the children themselves. The following chapter still has the school in mind, but the family will take centre stage.

3

THE CHILD, THE FAMILY AND THE SCHOOL

An interactional perspective

Elsie Osborne

The work described in this chapter is based on experience of work with families when children are referred with a school-related problem. Referrals to an agency outside the school will almost certainly continue to be made for some time, despite a shared aim to work towards supporting teachers in containing most children with educational difficulties within school. The focus of the work is on the family system and on its perspectives and interactions. A brief account is given of some aspects of developments in clinics and psychological services over the last thirty years or so, including the educational psychologist's role. Whilst the illustrations derive from experience as a psychologist in the Child and Family Department of the Tavistock Clinic, we consider that the principles could prove relevant in other settings.

The educational nature of the referrals raises issues related to success and failure, expectations about achievement, and the coping mechanisms of the family. Two accounts are given of families concerned about school refusal and an example is given in one of these of the use of a family task to explore interactions between family members.

At the moment of referral any agency has to make choices about the nature of its intervention. In the original child guidance model the starting point was usually the child and the intervention to be followed was determined by an accepted routine. Within a systemic approach the child is no longer automatically regarded as the primary focus for investigation or treatment, but the referral is more likely to be regarded as providing a point of entry into a number of relevant systems. Generally the most important of these will be the family and the school.

In addition to its theoretical orientation the agency's response will, of course, also be related to other aspects of its structure, its flexibility, its staff resources, its distribution of authority and responsibility and how it deals with pressures. In other words, its own system. There may be other systems already involved also, as in the case of Linda's family, described later in the chapter.

A BRIEF HISTORICAL REVIEW

Some comments on the history of child guidance have been made else-where in this book (see Dowling, Chapter 1). The methods of the old child guidance team are now largely discarded but perhaps it is worth being reminded briefly of the influence which it has had on thinking about children's welfare before completely dismissing the entire movement. This has probably been put most sympathetically by Sampson, as follows:

> The modern stress on understanding the causes of difficult behaviour, the spread of a therapeutic outlook in dealing with it, and a greater awareness of, and more sympathetic attitude to, individual differences of all kinds are some of the fruits of Child Guidance . . . They have indeed shaped and promoted much of the special educational treatment given in schools, classes and special units . . . There are also many weaknesses to be faced and remedied.
>
> (1980, p. 75)

However the clinics were under a great strain to meet their commitments and the pressures of the waiting lists were virtually unmanageable with the old system of response. Crisis theory suggested one way of defining priorities and prompted a type of response which was more family directed and focused on the current problem, with an emphasis on brief inter-ventions. (See Chapter 9 for a fuller account of crisis theory.) This was followed by the major influence of family therapy on clinics and many social work agencies.

Family therapy has generally been regarded as offering briefer and more effective opportunities for intervention, sometimes to the exclusion of any other type of intervention. The insistence on the involvement of the whole family has often provided a turning-point for the family members, the clinician's certainty of its usefulness being conveyed to the family as reassuring and confidence-building. The fact that, nevertheless, not all families are willing to be involved is a test of flexibility and skill. Attempts to define suitability for family therapy were made quite early in the history of family therapy in Britain. Walrond-Skinner (1978) attempted to produce some guidelines at a time when techniques were developing fast. In particular she provided some contra-indications: these included major practical difficulties, when emotional equilibrium in the family is too precarious and the risks of attempting to change it are too high.

Subsequent techniques will no doubt have modified these reservations, but the point to be made here is that we still need to pay attention to the starting-point offered by the family, that is to say the problem that they choose to bring, their motivation and expectations of intervention. This work may need to be carried out with particular care in relation to problems presented as educational in nature, where the family, and the school, are especially likely to locate the problem firmly in the child.

The movement out of the clinics by the educational psychologists has already been remarked upon in Chapter 2. Within the clinic, the team's contribution was usually seen as assessing the children referred. The case against this aspect of the traditional approach was strongly made some years ago in a volume edited by Gillham (1978). The general view of its authors was that there was little place left for the traditional assessment role and the use of psychological tests. Gillham himself put it most strongly in his chapter on 'the failure of psychometrics' in which he argues that these tests have ceased to serve any useful function at all, and, on the contrary, they fail to deal with the real complexities of a child's cognitive ability.

Some of the authors in Gillham's book advocated more school-based approaches, for example Burden (1978) and Hargreaves (1978) suggested realistic ways in which a shift in traditional assumptions could be made, away from individual assessment and the labelling which is seen as its consequence. They suggested that the most fundamental changes required were in attitude. About the same time, however, a survey by Wedell and Lambourne (1980), carried out for the Division of Educational and Child Psychology of the British Psychological Society, showed that assessment and related activities still took up the highest proportion of an EP's time, up to 41 per cent for field workers.

Subsequently Jones and Frederickson (1990) provided a further review of the work of the educational psychologist, taking into account later developments in practice. Their survey reaffirms the shift in focus from work with individual children to work with children and schools. Ironically, the influence of the Education Reform Act 1988 has been to assert the importance of the EP's assessment role, especially in relation to statementing. Also, the withdrawal of psychologists from the routine use of tests is paralleled by an increase in the reliance of state education upon a greater use of tests at regular stages. There is currently a great deal of debate about these standard assessment tests (SATs) and the extent to which they are too much based upon factual knowledge, so that their final form is still in doubt; but that they are likely to stay in principle seems generally to be accepted.

Where psychologists have continued to work in clinical bases confidence in their assessment techniques has also been undermined. The development of family therapy and the need to work with the family as a whole has been inimical to any idea of individual assessment. Here too, external pressures from educational legislation are relevant. One aspect of the Education Act 1981 was the emphasis upon parental involvement in a child's assessment. It might be worth considering how the family work in clinics and elsewhere could perhaps provide a base for such involvement.

An approach to a different use of testing, developed in the USA and still of interest although not, so far as we know, duplicated elsewhere, is provided by a number of publications by Fischer (e.g. 1979). She describes a way of using tests in order to increase the testee's own understanding and suggests how the report-writing may be a shared activity. Fischer encourages the client (she works with adults and children) to relate events that occur during the test performance to experiences in other situations. These discoveries then become shared material which can be used to examine the client's approach, which may then be seen to be applicable elsewhere. In a chapter on personality and assessment (1979) she gives an example of a report on a school-age boy. The report was written first for the parents as a letter, with concluding suggestions which could then be discussed with them, modified and sent to the boy's school. The detail of the report goes beyond generalization and overall recommendations to reflect the actual process of the assessment interviews. There was also, of course, appropriate discussion with the boy himself.

Another more explicitly systems-oriented approach to assessment is provided by Burden (1989). He asks the question, 'If traditional assessment techniques are to be criticised for their concentration upon within child variables at the expense of any interactionist perspective on the learning process, what is to be put in their place?' He further makes the point that taking the whole school as a unit for analysis is not necessarily the best way to build a picture of the school's ethos. He goes on to offer a critical examination of a technique for examining teachers' and pupils' perceptions of each other and how they feel about the interactions involved, on the basis that 'educational psychologists who do not want to spend all their time giving children intelligence tests need not opt out altogether from the business of assessment'.

Whilst a critical attitude to the routine use of intelligence testing in particular remains it seems that new approaches to assessment are being pursued by psychologists. It also remains the case that some children with educational problems, and their families, will continue to be referred elsewhere, in spite of the efforts made by the schools and the educational psychologists to contain more of such problems within the school or classroom. It is proposed now to look at ways in which psychologists might be involved in families where a child has an educational problem. In such cases this is frequently with a request for assessment.

CHOICE AT REFERRAL STAGE

It may not be clear at the point of referral that the child referred with a problem is necessarily the starting-point for intervention. There may be a considerable amount of work to be carried out beforehand, in order to discover where the problem lies. The referrer may be asked for a clarification of information, be invited to become involved in a joint approach to the family or to work in parallel with the psychologist, the family and the school. It may appear that the referral is more a statement of the referrer's needs, if, for example, this is one of a series of referrals from the same person or agency. Do they indicate a referrer's personal difficulties in coping with some current pressure? Are there general feelings in the agency of discontent or concern about the worker's position, or of underlying difficulties with seniors? Has a worker recently left? Are there organizational difficulties? Is there a feeling that the situation is hopeless, because everything has been tried, and this referral is the end of the line? A brief focal piece of work at this initial interface between referrer and clinic or SPS may lead to a more informal and/or appropriate intervention with the family.

Where the parents have themselves referred a child for assessment they may make it clear that they have no wish for the whole family to attend. Some initial exploration may be necessary to help to clarify their position before complying with their request. For instance, have there been other assessments which were considered unsatisfactory? Are there differences of opinion as to the nature or cause of the problem? Is it important to obtain the consent or co-operation of a separated or divorced parent before proceeding?

The range of options available at this point may lead to clinic-based interviews or joint interviews with parents and teachers at school or elsewhere, including the possibility of domiciliary visits. Whenever the decision is to include an assessment of the child then the question of feedback to the family is of crucial importance.

FEEDBACK TO FAMILIES

The importance of the assessment process to the family seems especially great when the problems presented are about progress at school or learning failures. Even careful feedback of results can be misunderstood, distorted or forgotten. Parental feelings can be at least as intense as those of the child, and frequently more so. It is clearly useful to consider how the psychologist can help the parents to make better use of any assessment, as well as in general ensuring that they feel adequately informed.

Some of the important issues raised by assessment include the nature of the differing expectation between two parents or between parents and child or school; attitudes to success and failure; notions of authority and feelings about being evaluated.

SUCCESS AND FAILURE

Judith was the only daughter of successful parents who had settled in England some years previously. In the course of some family interviews the parents asked for an assessment of Judith as she was making a very poor adjustment at nursery school and they were worried about her transfer to primary school, due shortly. It was understandable that her parents should be ambitious for this bright little girl, and it was clear that the results of any assessment would be seen as very important.

After some discussion it was agreed that the parents would be present during some age-appropriate testing and Judith was invited to solve some attractive puzzles in an informal atmosphere. The easygoing pleasure which she took in the tasks changed dramatically when she became stuck in attempting to put together a moderately difficult jigsaw-type puzzle. Attempts to prompt her only led to her becoming more rigid in her response, producing the same solution over and over again, even though she was aware that it was wrong. Helping her to start again from the beginning finally broke the deadlock. Later, however, Judith retaliated for her experience of failure by setting tests for the psychologist to do and acting very harshly, declaring every answer wrong, and refusing to offer clues or any help. In this way she seemed to show how devastating the experience had been.

For their part the parents had taken surprisingly little pleasure in their daughter's success and the paralysing effect of failure upon her perform- ance was equally devastating for them. Apart from the implications this had for future schooling it was also clear that the experience of failure for this family needed clarification. The experience of observing had enabled the parents to see the effect of failure on their child in a very vivid way, and led to an opening up of issues around the fear of failure which, it became clear, was destructive to their own coping and this had been mirrored in Judith's behaviour. This became an important topic in the subsequent family sessions.

A different approach to success was demonstrated by 7-year-old Sally, also an only child with a single mother bringing her up alone. Sally had been described previously as a 'gifted child'. Her mother felt rather intimidated by this assessment and daunted by the thought of managing this clever child. Watching a video of her daughter performing some tests lessened these feelings, put a more realistic perspective on this 'cleverness' and allowed Sally's mother to share more in her daughter's enjoyment of success and achievement.

A FAMILY TASK AS AN EXAMPLE OF FAMILY INTERACTION

Family P offer an example of how the setting of a family task can offer new perspectives on the family structure by providing samples of family inter-action, especially when the referral is about schooling problems.

The family's view of themselves was summarized at the point of referral as follows: Frank, 12 years old and the older of two children, was refusing to go to school. At home he spent much of his time alone in his bedroom. He was unpopular with his classmates and his mother found him difficult to manage.

Mrs P expressed an opposite view of Tracey, their 8-year-old daughter, describing her as a happy child with no problems. It was not surprising that Frank was doing badly at his school work and that the referral, in part, was for an individual assessment of his abilities. The school had suggested that Frank should be seen by the psychologist and the family had requested a referral to the clinic. This virtual self-referral made it rather easier to ask them all to come and talk things over in the first instance, and this they agreed to do.

During this first meeting the focus was firmly on Frank, with his mother listing many complaints. The parents were in agreement that success at school was important and they therefore had been trying to help Frank at home. This only led to quarrels, however, with Frank refusing to make any effort.

Throughout this discussion both children expressed boredom and made only desultory replies if questions were directed at them. Frank said he was also bored at school and, when asked about the different subjects there, he said he didn't like anything much, often they were too easy, except for maths which was too difficult. Earlier it had appeared that all the family disliked maths, but when this was now described as something common to them all it was denied and firmly made Frank's problem.

The children were asked how they assessed themselves. Frank said he was about average, Tracey rated herself as quite clever and the parents said they did not know how to compare them with other children.

In this context it seemed that singling out Frank for assessment would further identify him as *the* problem. The psychologist considered that this would not be useful in understanding the problem the parents had over working with Frank at home and it was suggested that they might all be interested to try out some intelligence test material so that they could discuss it afterwards. Matrices were produced, as being relevant to all the family members, and there was immediately keen interest from each of them in trying to solve the matrices for themselves.

A marked change in the atmosphere in the room followed. The children became lively and interested, listening keenly to what they had to do. The whole family worked separately for some time. However as the items became more difficult and they were less certain of their success it was proposed that they should work in pairs in order to compare their solutions so far. The parents were also asked to help the children over particular difficulties, Mother working with Tracey and Father with Frank.

Many aspects of family interaction became apparent. In summary, these included a vivid picture of Mother's competitiveness with Father, the children's difficulties in accepting help from their mother, who frequently intervened in the discussion between Frank and his father, in order to point something out, and the whole family's tremendous investment in the task.

Frank's alleged slowness was not borne out; he worked at least at an average pace until he found it impossible to make a definite choice of the right solution. At this point he refused to guess, arousing his mother to a frenzy of impatience. He in turn was exasperated by her attempts to press him to a decision.

In contrast Tracey spoiled her results by her hasty approach; she guessed wildly, and became sulky when she discovered that she had made a mistake or when any attempt was made to help her. Attempts to draw attention to the contrasting strengths and weaknesses of the two children's approaches was initially taken by their mother as confirming Frank's faults. In Tracey's case, however, her speed and certainty were seen as signs of her high intelligence and their potential hazards were not accepted. When their results were compared it was clear that Frank had in fact been more successful, even after allowing for his age, whereas Tracey had given up quite early.

Discussion of the parent's results also produced some interesting indications of the family interactions. Mrs P's delight in her performance was very noticeable, especially in relation to Mr P, who did marginally less well. The competitiveness between the parents led to discussion of Mrs P's resentment at having given up a promising career after the children were born and it became clear that this was an important part of the family constellation that had not previously been acknowledged. Their mother's investment in the children's success was exacerbated by her need to prove that her sacrifice had been worthwhile.

In spite of his own success Mr P showed surprising diffidence and uncertainty about what he had done, and was therefore not easily able to help his son either. It was noted that Frank sought certainty at all costs, contrasting with his father's uncertainty, and Tracey allowed speed to monopolize her performance, thus avoiding censure through her mother's impatience with any slowness or uncertainty.

Much work remained to be done by the family but the focus on Frank had been shifted in a way that would have been unlikely had the request for an assessment been met in the conventional way. Indeed, individual testing would have been more likely to reinforce this focus and would not have uncovered the potential for work difficulties which Tracey now showed.

The concrete nature of the task and the use of video recording of the session to illustrate points made, provided an enrichment of the family sessions and allowed us to make discoveries and to face the task of understanding mutual perceptions, and of the restructuring which the family needed to do in order to reach its shared aim for success.

Frank became more confident and returned to school. As a result of the family's acknowledgement of Mrs P's ability her image in the family was enhanced. Mr P was able to make a new alliance with Frank and was encouraged to help him with his homework. Since it was clear that their different approaches to work made it very difficult for his mother to help, his father was able to be more sympathetic to Frank. An acknowledgement that Tracey's impatience might lead to work problems was made.

Commentary

Reintegrating Frank into his school was effected only with the essential understanding and open attitude of the staff. One of the risks which can arise when a child is referred out of the school system is that the school transfers an important part of its responsibility for that child, maybe with relief, or resentment or some combination of both. Retaining the active involvement of the school, which had backed the referral, was an important part of a holistic, systemic approach, which not only kept his teachers informed of the work in the clinic but ensured that the psychologist respected their ongoing responsibility, rather than appearing to take Frank over and return him 'cured', which, of course, he was not. The shifts in the family system, including the alliance between Frank and his father, less disapproval from his mother, and a greater acceptance by all the family of Frank's ability, enabled Frank to return to the school with more confidence.

In Chapter 7 more consideration is given to the ways in which clinic and school may relate over individually referred children. The aim in this present chapter has been to focus on the relevance of the family system to a school-related problem that was initially firmly located in one child.

In the next case-study the link with the school was more remote, and largely maintained through its education social worker. In a sense responsibility had already been handed over by the school, but the importance of bearing in mind the total context in which the child functioned was no less great.

A LONG-TERM SCHOOL REFUSER

Linda was referred at the age of 10 by the education social worker (ESW) of the school she was supposed to be attending, although she had not done so for over a year. The ESW was in regular contact with the family and the information given on referral was therefore quite detailed.

The family was described as one in which there was considerable depression, with a long history of failure to attend school. Attempts to engage them in any plans had been unsuccessful and the department was requested to make an assessment with a view to placement in a special unit. The ESW offered full co-operation, but showed little optimism as to what might be achieved.

The themes which emerged from the referral were:

1 Feelings of hopelessness from school and social worker. The school staff considered that everything in the way of trying to accommodate the family had been tried and failed. It was clear that the ESW was feeling that she had been left carrying the despair.
2 The possibility of involving the whole family still seemed preferable, although they were reported to be unwilling to accept family therapy, and the two older sons refused to be involved.
3 There was a need to discover what strengths there were in Linda and in the family as a whole; all the information about them tended to be negative, yet they had remained an integral family which seemed caring and affectionate.
4 Individual assessment would be difficult as Linda was said to refuse to leave her mother in any unfamiliar situation.
5 Many other agencies had been involved in the past, including clinics, the local Social Services department, other social work agencies and a special unit. None of the workers felt they had been used really constructively.
6 There was one school which the parents thought Linda would accept but the headmistress was unwilling to take her.

It is not altogether unusual for the Tavistock Clinic to be at the end of the line after a great deal of effort elsewhere, and this must be true for other agencies also. The indications in this case were that workers had been used by the family to take a great deal of responsibility for them, and when attempts were made to ease this dependence the parents had become disillusioned and resentful. Currently the ESW was acceptable to the family and very keen to offer support by bringing the family to the clinic, and by acting as an intermediary, with messages and persuasion.

With these factors in mind I wrote to both parents asking them to bring Linda 'with a view to seeing how she was getting on'. In consultation with the ESW it was agreed that she would discuss the appointment with the family, but would not offer to bring them in the first instance. The family was given a map and precise instructions for reaching the clinic.

The first interview

In the event the parents and Linda came in good time for their appointment, without the ESW. As expected Linda clung to her mother's hand and sat closely beside her when they reached my room. Her father came a little behind and sat separately.

I welcomed the family and turned to Linda, who gave several sobs and buried her face in her mother's lap. I pointed out that the whole family would stay together throughout; Linda would not be made to separate from her parents and I sought agreement on the aim of the meeting. This was described as wanting to know what Linda could do, that this was necessary before thinking about other schools, and that they would all be given a chance to discuss any outcome in full.

Linda was asked to write down her name and birthday. She sought prompting from her mother, claiming that she had forgotten her birthday. The significance of this, in the light of Linda's babyish behaviour, was noted but no comment made. However, as the pattern was established of her mother answering the questions for Linda, this was remarked upon. The parents were asked, even when it was difficult sometimes, not to answer for Linda, and at the end of the session they could say whether they felt she had or had not done herself justice.

As her parents sat quietly Linda was drawn into answering some moderately easy questions, and when the blocks for the WISC block design item were scattered on a nearby table, she left her mother's side and began to work at the table. She began to show pleasure in her success, an interest in the test material, and gradually to respond without reference to her mother. By the end of the session the change in her behaviour was remarkable. She looked and worked like a very normal 10-year-old, and I found her co-operative and pleasurable to work with.

The importance of the experience for Linda, of being allowed to perform independently, was clear; she skipped across the room at the end of the session and willingly agreed to return. The significance for the parents was also considerable, since they had observed her as a normal child, working independently and enjoying her success. Her underlying strengths were emphasized: her good concentration, her attentiveness and motivation to succeed. We agreed that she certainly had a need to make up for her lost schooling, but it was possible to be confident that she could do so in an ordinary classroom with some extra help. An interactional approach would lead us to bear in mind the effects of improvement in one individual on the rest of the system, and this becomes apparent in a significant way later.

There were, of course, many other things happening in the interview which have not been covered here, but the parents' real pleasure in observing their daughter coping and behaving naturally was especially marked. This shared picture of an ordinary 10-year-old Linda became an important feature of the subsequent sessions with the family. These were held up as the mother became ill and I had to keep hold of my own anxiety that if Linda got better her mother would suffer. To some extent this indeed turned out to be the case. However through letters, telephone calls, and with the help of the ESW, the need for a further interview to discuss Linda's results was kept in front of the family.

Feedback session

A few weeks later the family returned. I thanked them for their helpfulness during the initial session and acknowledged their concern for Linda. During this session of careful feedback Linda was asked to move away from her mother and sit with her father, and much more reference was made to him and his relationship to Linda than previously. Formerly workers had focused on Linda's relationship to her mother, placing the responsibility on her mother to give up this close relationship and 'to let Linda go'. Now, however, it became clear that Linda's father was concerned and unhappy about the situation but unwilling to act. At one time, before his work prevented it, he had successfully taken Linda to school. Later it seemed that he had gone along with her non-attendance and this now produced an acknowledgment of his realization of his wife's intense need to have someone at home with her.

I agreed to act as an advocate to the headmistress of the preferred school and her father agreed to organize himself in order to take Linda to school. Linda agreed to this. Her mother was close to tears, and for the first time spoke openly of her agoraphobic symptoms.

Network contact

There was also, alongside the work with the family, negotiation with the ESW, who was being asked, in a way, to give up the family. She was kept fully informed of the appointments offered, the decisions made, and was encouraged to get the family to take as much initiative as possible for themselves. The work with the ESW was essential as was her willingness to change her approach, which went well beyond superficial co-operation. The importance of keeping in mind the referring person is well expressed in Palazzoli (1980), although in this case the referring person was not included in the initial family interviews. Palazzoli's practice was to include them where there was considerable enmeshment, and this may indeed be appropriate in such circumstances.

Discussions with the head teachers of the two schools involved, together with the local authority educational psychologist, now became the main focus of the work with the aim of altering the perception of the family as helpless and hopeless. The head teachers mutually agreed that Linda should be allowed a trial term at the school she preferred, 'in order to give her a fresh start'. There was every indication of a good investment by the school, supported by its EP, in making this work.

Contact was kept with the family and the school during the subsequent arrangements. Linda made a successful start in her new school and a month later the family came to the clinic together again. The family and the ESW were reluctant to accept an appointment on a school day, saying that it was more important to keep Linda at school. My own view was that it was important for the family to keep an undertaking that they had made (at our last meeting) and that we should not go along with the notion that Linda's school attendance was so fragile and uncertain. The family was offered a date with a clear acknowledgement that this would mean Linda coming out of school. This was also discussed with the school, the reasons explained and their support requested.

Relocating the problem

There was perhaps some risk in this approach, but I considered that the responsibility was now with the parents, and that some testing out of the situation was realistic. Parents and daughter again came by themselves. Having established that Linda was now going to school by herself and pleasure in this having been shared, the discussion again turned to her mother's fears of being alone. At this point I suggested that Linda need no longer stay, she could go to the waiting room where she could find things to do, as her parents were now talking about their own worries. An escort was offered but Linda agreed and went easily on her own. After she had left her mother said, 'I suppose I have let her off the hook'. This now seemed possible because father's renewed involvement had in a way let mother off the hook also.

The task for the clinic staff changed from this time to one of addressing the parents' own problems. However Father's new involvement had already made some change to the situation, so that although in a sense Mother was worse, she was now able to seek help for her fears in a more appropriate way. The parents were also genuinely glad that Linda was back at school. This side of their ambivalence had been successfully engaged and without this positive aspect, present from the beginning, the outcome might not have been so generally successful. The careful work in the initial phase and the close monitoring of all the network around Linda were also essential.

Six months later Linda was continuing to attend school regularly, the teachers were pleased with her progress in work and reported that she was making friends. Her trial term had been successfully completed.

CONCLUDING REMARKS

The referral of a child to a clinic, or some other external agency, to some extent dictates the possibilities for response. In many cases the adoption of a systemic approach will be expressed through an offer of family therapy. The work with Frank and Linda's families are largely accounts of such an approach. The focus within the family, however, was determined by the educational and school-based nature of the problem presented. In both cases a shift in the parents' perception of their child's functioning was a significant step towards change which was directly relevant to the family's interaction with the school. The attention to the family system could not be exclusive; it was still essential to keep in mind the entire context of family, school and related professionals.

The punctuation in these instances took place within the clinic, because that was the route chosen by the referring person and the family. The application of the concepts would be held constant wherever the punctuation was made, for instance the emphasis on total context, the focus on interaction rather than individual pathology, the importance of feedback, the clarification of differences in perception and on facilitating communication.

There are many other areas of clinical work which may be relevant to children referred with problems, for instance a range of family therapy approaches, plus other longer-term case work, counselling and psychotherapy as well as consultation to other organizations. Longer-term work with children who continue to fail to respond to efforts to teach them the basic skills, especially reading, is offered in the form of educational therapy. This pays particular attention to the emotional aspects, feelings of distress or hopelessness for instance, which can accompany such failure to learn. A full account of educational therapy is given in Barrett and Trevitt (1991) and a brief introduction is in Osborne (1989).

The examples given in this chapter are of brief work with families, focusing on the problem presented. Too often clinic based work is seen as remote, separated off because of the demands of confidentiality. The concepts which have been outlined are considered still to be of practical use in the success of this individually based work. The reader is again referred to Chapter 7, where these issues are discussed further.

NOTE

This chapter is based in part on a chapter in the previous edition of this book, written jointly by Barrett and Osborne, entitled: 'The child, the family and the school, a clinical perspective'. I gratefully acknowledge the permission of Muriel Barrett to make use of some of this joint material.

4

TAKING THE CLINIC TO SCHOOL

A consultative service for parents, children and teachers

Emilia Dowling

Over the years I have been concerned with developing an understanding of the interaction between the family and school systems, particularly in relation to disturbing behaviour in children. I refer to *disturbing* as opposed to *disturbed* behaviour, as, with Jay Haley (1976), I believe that a statement about someone's problem is also a statement about someone else's difficulty to handle it.

The location of the problem in a particular context often determines who owns it, and also who is responsible for its origin, its maintenance, and its resolution.

Families often feel very strongly that if only their child were taught properly all would be well. Likewise, teachers feel equally strongly that a child's learning and behavioural difficulties could be improved if only the family circumstances would change.

In Chapter 1, I outline three familiar scenarios that occur when children present with an educational problem:

1 The family blames the school for the problem and places responsibility with it for resolving it.
2 The school believes that it has done all it can but, given the family circumstances, there is very little hope of change.
3 The family and the school agree that the child 'needs help' and they set about looking for an expert who will provide it.

Any of these three perspectives may result in a referral to a school psychological service, a child guidance clinic or a child psychiatric department.

My interest in recent years has extended from the relationship between families and schools to the way they relate to and view professional systems.

It is a common observation of teachers that those children and their families who are most in need of help are the very ones least likely to ask for or receive it, and Child and Adolescent Services are well aware that they are not reaching a sizeable sample of the population. Failed appointments or failure to attend after a first interview suggest a difficulty experienced by many families in following through or in finding the contact sufficiently promising to come again. Dupont and Dowdney (1990) have recently described the dilemmas of referring school-based problems to other agencies.

The project to be described, which has been named 'The clinic goes to school', was sparked off by two primary schools with a long-standing association with the clinic. Over the years they have referred for individual, family and educational therapy. However, school staff, whilst appreciating the service offered, felt it was only appropriate for a minority of the children at school and, even when attendance at the clinic was successfully established, they hoped and wished for closer liaison and more help with the management of the problem at school. Therefore, an outreach, school-based service was set up by a team of two psychologists and a teacher from the clinic, based on two suppositions or assumptions:

1 That the service would attract a population who would not normally make use of conventional clinic-based services.
2 That such a service would have a preventive function. Parents and teachers would seek consultation about the difficulties presented by children before they became sufficiently serious to warrant referral to an outside agency.

A detailed description of the setting-up process has been published before (Taylor and Dowling, 1986), but I would like to outline the key elements, as I see them, which need to be borne in mind when setting up an outreach service:

1 Sanction from the supra-systems. It is extremely important and time is well spent communicating the objectives of the service and ensuring that everyone who *needs* to know is informed and the appropriate management structures approve and support the idea.
2 Ongoing communication. Review meetings with the key people concerned, i.e. educational psychologist, education social worker, and provide opportunities for feedback and deal with issues relating to boundaries, who is doing what, etc.
3 Getting acquainted with the system (Burden, 1981a). A period of informal, less-structured contact with the staff, coming into the staff room, observing different classrooms, joining an assembly, will all provide an opportunity to get a feel of the culture of the school and to be seen to be there and interested in the everyday life of staff and pupils.

4 The service needs to be available both to teachers and parents so that the concerns can be thought about in the dual context of home and school.

5 Publicity about the service. Detailed information must be given to the staff, preferably in a staff meeting with opportunity for discussion and questions, and a strategy must be planned with them about the way to inform parents of the service.

6 A support system for the workers. Schools have a different culture from a clinic; life is hectic, there are often difficulties in terms of keeping the boundary around time and space and the worker can easily feel disqualified or even undermined and isolated, if arrangements change at short notice or it seems as if a particular activity has taken priority over a carefully planned observation or consultation.

Those of us who work in schools will recognize the bewildering experience of arriving to observe a child and finding that the very time that was carefully selected for this purpose has been designated for a play rehearsal or a film to be shown by the police! Having a team to go back to, to share experiences, plan interventions and generally keep one's head above water, seems to me an essential requirement to sustain an efficient and well-co-ordinated service.

Since the initial project was set up in the early 1980s three more schools (two primary and one secondary) have benefited from the scheme. Over this period we have learned from the different experiences and modified our practice accordingly (Dowling and Taylor, 1989).

In this chapter I would like to describe the work I am currently doing at another local infant school, highlighting the lessons learned. Particular attention is paid to the changing role of the head teacher and how the consultative process has had to adapt to the changing context of the work.

TERRITORY

One of the most important requirements was a place, however basic or small, which would reliably be made available to see parents and teachers in an uninterrupted, private way. Despite the fact that in theory this had been seen by all concerned as an essential feature of the service, we found in the previous schools that competing needs for space often put tremendous pressure on the head teacher to make this space available for other purposes.

In my present school it has been possible to have a room which is consistently available at the designated times, and is identified as the place where I meet parents or teachers.

THE CHANGING CONTEXT

During the last twelve months the pressures of the changing environment have resulted in a change in the service I provide both in terms of my time and the focus of the work. I have been visiting the school on a monthly basis and the focus of the work has been to offer consultation to the head teacher in her role as manager.

I will begin by describing the service as it was originally offered (Dowling, 1990), and will then move on to describe the co-evolutionary process which has led to the present way of working.

TIME AND FREQUENCY OF SERVICE

For the first three years of the project I went to the school once a fortnight for two and a half hours on Wednesday afternoons. My time was divided between a regular slot with the head teacher at the beginning of the afternoon and a drop-in service for parents and teachers. Occasionally it may have been necessary to observe a child in the classroom or during playtime, to increase my understanding of the difficulties as viewed by a teacher, parent or both.

THE DROP-IN FOR PARENTS

Our experience of this kind of service is that it is possible to facilitate some change within the context of brief work. The drop-in service consisted of a maximum of three sessions for each family of approximately half an hour's duration. The first session usually took place at the suggestion of the head teacher. The parent would bring his or her concerns in the knowledge that this was a resource available to all parents at the school and therefore the stigma and fear of labelling attached to referrals was minimized.

Concerns brought by parents ranged from sleep and eating difficulties to problems of discipline, difficulty in making friends, unhappiness at school, unsettled behaviour usually related to some significant event in the family's life cycle, e.g. birth, death, moving house.

Using this model of brief consultation, the first interview would be spent defining the problem and the context in which it occurred: asking questions about what made it worse or better, what had happened before, what followed, what effects problematic behaviours had on other family members, but also thinking about what would be the consequences if things got better. Often in the course of this first interview particular patterns were identified which contributed to maintaining the problematic behaviour.

After the first interview, and using on the information obtained, a task might be set, or a discussion with the teacher and an observation of the child in the classroom might be arranged with the parents' consent.

A second interview would usually follow about four weeks later, and a third interview arranged for six to eight weeks later to follow up the outcome of the intervention. This last session would provide an opportunity to consolidate progress and to identify areas of competence but also to hear of any new concerns that might have cropped up.

The feedback from parents has been very encouraging. They often report that the consultation gave them confidence to try something different, or enabled them to stand back and see how they had got stuck into a particular way of reacting. The emphasis of these consultations has been on the reinforcement of parental strengths whilst acknowledging the anxieties and difficulties inherent in the parenting task.

SOME CLINICAL EXAMPLES

Sonia: different belief systems

Sonia was a 5-year-old girl and the third of four children. She had two brothers aged 13 and 9 and a baby brother of 4 months.

Mother described Sonia as very small but 'quite able to stand up to her brothers'. She thought Sonia needs help at school.

The teacher complained about her lack of independence and would try to get Sonia to do things by herself. She knew she could do this but at the end of the day, when Father came to fetch her, 'It's all back to square one'; he would do her coat up, put on her mittens, etc. The teacher felt very strongly that Sonia needed to grow up and this could happen only if the parents would co-operate.

At first interview it became apparent that Mother felt very strongly Sonia should be helped to grow up. She felt guilty, as Sonia still drank milk from a bottle at home. However, Mother felt hopeful that the baby brother would help Sonia grow up. She also mentioned her mother-in-law, who lived with the family and thought that adults are 'in such a hurry for children to grow up. They are only babies at 5.' I positively connoted the pace of growth at home for the time being, but introduced the idea that we may need to find a different pace for Sonia in order to manage at school. I suggested I observe Sonia in the classroom prior to our next meeting.

When I arrived in the classroom I found Sonia at the painting table with three other girls and it soon became apparent how skilful Sonia was at getting the three other girls organized to help her, passing on the paint pots and getting brushes to her. When I asked their names the three others took responsibility for telling me theirs *plus* Sonia's name.

Talking to the teacher, who saw her efforts undermined by the family, I explained and positively connoted Sonia's ability to get help organized for herself and talked about different views and beliefs, introducing the notion of Sonia's loyalty to the family's belief system.

After my observation I met the mother and the teacher and decided that in order to manage at school a certain level of autonomy had to be evident, particularly when Sonia moved up to the next class. It was acknowledged and emphasized that the family's belief about girls growing up had to be respected. The emphasis was on the shift from a perspective which defined the school's view as right and the family's as wrong, to finding a way of working together to enable Sonia to cope with school (which the parents wanted anyway) and to support the school's efforts towards her development.

We reached agreement in finding the right pace for Sonia. At follow-up, the teacher was satisfied and I observed a physical education lesson where Sonia's competence and autonomy was evident.

Tim: different perceptions of a situation

The head teacher expressed concern about Tim, whom she described as a 'very odd child'. Discussion with the class teacher revealed she was not as concerned as the head but somehow 'felt she ought to be' as Mother came in quite regularly to complain to the head that Tim was being bullied. I suggested that as there did not seem to be a major problem in the classroom I should observe Tim at playtime as Mother's concern was bullying in the playground.

I came out at the same time as the children and my attention was immediately focused on this child, who looked larger than the rest, and who came out with his fists clenched ready to attack. As he paced up and down the playground, it seemed to me that he was looking for a target. I noticed how the children passed by and for the most part either ignored him or kept out of his way. However a couple of children made feeble attempts to relate to him and did so by pulling his coat in order to draw his attention. Describing this situation to the mother produced a very surprised reaction. Tim had been complaining about the children pulling his coat. She had got so worried she had asked Tim's older brother, who went to secondary school down the road, to come up and look over the wall at playtime 'just in case'.

Exploration of the family situation revealed a belief that life was dangerous outside the family, therefore you had to protect yourself or be protected. Tim had learned to behave in this way and needed to be helped to develop sufficient trust in people to allow them to come close to him. This had to be done cautiously and his brother's monitoring was encouraged 'until such time as James [Tim's older brother] feels he is entitled to his own lunch break'.

Change must not be introduced by knocking down or disqualifying a family's perception of reality. Therefore it was important to acknowledge the family's reasons but at the same time introduce the idea of an alternative view.

THE DROP-IN FOR TEACHERS

In the present climate of constant changes in education and increasing demands on teachers to adapt to change, it seems essential to create a context where teachers can express their concerns without being labelled 'a teacher who has a problem', which could be decoded as 'a teacher who can't manage'. We know how difficult it is for teachers, particularly in primary schools, to do anything other than teach. We also know how unsatisfactory it is for both the teacher and the consultant to have to snatch a few moments in the classroom or while on playground duty to talk about a difficulty, or to resort to intruding into the very much treasured break-time in the staff room.

The time for teachers to drop in was carefully negotiated with the head teacher so that she was able to cover during the consultation. This ensured forward planning, as it was the responsibility of the individual teacher to use the drop-in and arrange cover, and again, as with the parents, the fact that it was a service available to all staff minimized concern about being labelled. As with the parents' drop-in, there was a maximum of three consultations of approximately half an hour each. After the first session when the problem was explored, a visit to the classroom was usually arranged, with some exploration for a new strategy to be used.

Teachers expressed some ambivalence about being observed. On the one hand it felt like being 'exposed', particularly if they were already wondering if they were handling a situation badly. On the other hand, the opportunity for a second session after the observation provided a chance to talk about it. The teachers often found it a relief to hear another view, one which recognized the difficulties involved whilst suggesting a different course of action. For example, Mary consulted about Adam, a 6-year-old whom she found 'increasingly demanding and difficult in class'. She said she had run out of ideas and saw him as a very spoilt child. During the consultation it became apparent how Mary, a very gifted, secondary-trained teacher, had recently come to teach in this infant school and was finding it very difficult to adapt to young, demanding children. Adam, who was the youngest of several children in his family, was particularly sensitive to Mary's attitude. The less response he had from her, the more his demands increased, and this pattern escalated to the point where the interaction between him and his teacher was mainly of a confrontational nature.

A second session after a period of observation in Mary's classroom provided an opportunity to empathize with Mary's difficulty in adjusting to the needs and demands of children at a much earlier stage of development than she was used to. Mary experienced great relief at not having been seen as a bad teacher (she had feared that had been my conclusion after observing her class). We planned together a different structure to her day which would include a nurturing time, possibly reading stories sitting on soft cushions where the children could be physically close to her. She was delighted to feel free and empowered to try such a thing which she didn't see as proper teaching, when she saw how such an activity was not only age appropriate but also conducive to learning.

At follow-up not only Adam but other difficult children had become more manageable for Mary.

WORKSHOPS FOR PARENTS

In our experience of the service, it soon became apparent that somehow a parent had to have a problem or at least a concern in order to use the service. So an opportunity was provided about once a term for parents to explore stages in their children's development and recognize the hazards in each without having to define them as problems.

Informal meetings for parents to discuss issues over a cup of tea were organized about topics such as starting school, coping with separation and feeling safe in a dangerous world. This provided opportunities for lively discussion where parents themselves shared with each other their strategies and experiences. The emphasis was on empowering the parents to use their own resources to help each other.

CONSULTATION WITH THE HEAD TEACHER: CHANGING ROLES IN A CHANGING CONTEXT

Preserving a regular time with the head teacher has proved an essential aspect of the project. A head in a primary school has a pivotal role in maintaining and developing the relationship between parents and teachers. An opportunity for consultation and exploration of her concerns has been much valued and appreciated by the head teacher. It has also provided an opportunity to hear the school's view of some of the problems that will be brought by parents. This information has proved invaluable in planning a strategy of intervention which takes into account the staff's as well as the parents' perspective. However, in the current climate, rapid and demanding changes in education are taking place: National Curriculum, local management of schools, standard attainment tests (SATs), to name a few. In this context the role of the head teacher is changing and their preoccupations and responsibilities are increasing.

The impact on these changes has been acutely felt as head teachers see their roles shifting from being in charge of curricular and developmental aspects of their schools, to a much more managerial job, one which has involved developing new skills as responsibilities previously held by the local education authorities move towards them.

Under local management of schools (LMS) head teachers are responsible for budget holding, allocating resources, making appointments, etc. There are different lines of accountability, more direct contact with the governors, and different relationships with the parents and the rest of the staff.

It is in this context that the role of the consultant had to be examined, as the consultative relationship is constantly co-evolving in relationship to the changing position of the consultee.

The head teacher and I reviewed the work done so far, referring back to the two premises on which we based the outreach service, namely, that families and teachers would find it easier to use a school-based resource and that the service would have a preventive function and therefore contribute to a reduction in referrals to outside agencies.

The first assumption has been confirmed by increased demand and feedback from parents and teachers, who found a school-based service much less daunting and more accessible. In addition, although no formal evaluation has been carried out, it has become apparent that when difficulties are detected and dealt with at that early stage in the school context, a brief intervention seems sufficient to promote some change. The second assumption, the reduction in referrals, has been confirmed by the head teacher, who has experienced this resource as a useful container of anxieties, and has felt particularly supported in her pivotal role in maintaining a constructive relationship between home and school.

She has also developed her abilities and skills and feels more able to deal with difficulties between parents, teachers and children which she previously might have chosen to refer to the service.

We agreed that the next stage needed a change of focus in the work and for the last twelve months I have been consulting to her on a monthly basis, focusing on her management role and its implications for the task of running the school and relating to the wider community.

The following notions have been helpful to me in developing the consultative relationship with the head teacher.

The task of the consultation

As I understand it, the consultative process consists of creating conditions for the consultees to utilize their inner resources and potential: (1) to make their own decisions and (2) to build resources to live with the consequences of those decisions.

In the consultative relationship, the responsibility for the decisions and their consequences remains firmly with the consultee. The task of the consultation is to enable the client or consultee to do his or her job more effectively, and to help bring awareness of the anxieties and irrational forces that may get in the way.

Another useful concept is the concept of *boundaries*. Setting time and space boundaries conveys a message that the consultant takes the task seriously, is reliable, and that the consultee deserves respect. If time and space boundaries are respected, consultees gradually develop the notion that the space for their concerns is worth having.

It is important to have a *territory* where the consultation takes place every time. The continuity in territory gives a message that there is also continuity in the work, that the consultant is keeping it in mind from one consultation to the next. In this particular school, the head teacher has been very meticulous in creating a clearly defined boundary of the time and space designated to her consultation with me. There have been no interruptions and it has been possible to treat the work seriously and to encourage the development of a trusting relationship. Changing times and space boundaries may convey the message that the mental space to think about the work is not worth preserving, that it can be chopped and changed, and it will inevitably lead to the consultee having doubts as to whether it is right to take up the time of the consultant. Reliability and continuity ensure that the consultee gradually builds a model of her own worth and the right to think about her work in order to be more effective.

It is very useful to ask questions about the *beliefs* of the school or organization in which the consulting takes place. What is the meaning of the consultation for the organization? What are the expectations about the consultant's involvement? Who will lose or gain by his or her presence? Thinking about the consequences of this presence in the rest of the organization and the 'ripples' it may cause is very important in securing a type of contract that can be accepted and not sabotaged by the rest of the organization.

In the case of this head teacher it was crucial for the rest of the staff to know that they also were entitled to have a one-off consultation with me if they so wished, provided they negotiated it with the head teacher. It was important to explain to them how the head in her role as manager of the school needed a space to think about her management role and her leadership in relation to all aspects of the school development.

The consultant needs to be aware and understand the possible mixed feelings and different views and beliefs that might develop in relation to his or her presence in the school, particularly if there is an exclusive relationship with the head teacher. In this instance, the effect of the consultative relationship on the rest of the school is constantly monitored by the head teacher, who is able to use the consultation to clarify and explore her relationships with the staff as well as with the parents, governors and members of the wider system.

The relationship between the consultant and the system is referred to throughout the book but particularly addressed in Chapter 10.

5

JOINT INTERVENTIONS WITH TEACHERS, CHILDREN AND PARENTS IN THE SCHOOL SETTING

John Dowling and Andrea Pound

The central function of both schools and families is the nurture and education of children, a common task which should ensure their close co-operation and mutual support. When a child is developing well, both socially and educationally, this is indeed usually the case. However, when he or she has social or educational difficulties, is unhappy or disobedient or slow to learn, each side of the school–family partnership can relieve its disappointment and sense of failure by judging the other to have been deficient in its task. Instead of pooling their resources to solve the child's problem, the stage is then set for a deteriorating relationship between them, in which each, while doing what is considered to be the best for the child, undermines the authority and effectiveness of the other. The child is left either very anxious because previous sources of support have demolished each other so neither can be depended on, or uneasily powerful because the child can manipulate the authority figures in his or her life and reduce them to angry helplessness. Such misunderstanding between school and family may lead in the long run to school refusal or truanting, behaviour problems leading to exclusion from school, or failure to make academic progress consonant with ability.

Children and adolescents need to see parents and teachers engaged in a co-operative enterprise on their behalf, as they need to see their parents co-operating with each other, if they are to develop the capacity for impulse-control, sustained attention to a task, and tolerance of stress such as will confront them daily in the school setting. All too often such problems come to the attention of the mental health professional or school psychologist too late in the day to offer much opportunity for effective intervention. Often the family and the school have a long history of dissatisfaction with each other and with the child, who may in any case be nearing the end of his school career, so there is little motivation on anyone's part to achieve constructive change. Where such problems can be identified earlier, whether presenting in a child psychiatry clinic or in a school psychological service, joint school–family sessions may prepare the ground for future co-operation between both systems, to the benefit of the child.

The notion of parents and teachers as partners in children's education and care is not new and it is now generally accepted that families and schools cannot operate in isolation without detrimental effects to children (Kaplan, 1971). However, it is often the case that good home–school liaison in the primary school tends to wane after transfer to secondary school. In a national survey of parents of children in maintained primary schools, which was carried out for the Plowden Committee, only 8 per cent had had no real talk with the head or with their child's class teacher (Schools Council, 1968) whilst in their own survey the Schools Council found that when children were in the third, fourth or fifth years of their secondary schools, 37 per cent of the parents had no real talks at all with the head or any of the child's class teachers at the sampled schools. After this report much effort went into improving contact between parents and secondary schools (McGeeney, 1974). Nevertheless, parents often recall their children's time in the primary school as a period when they found communication with the teachers much easier, and the school seemed more accessible.

This perceived distance between the home and school can lead to interactions between parents and school staff characterized by defensiveness, lack of co-operation and, at times, open aggression and conflict. Such interactions are likely to occur when the parents are asked to visit the school because the child has a relatively severe problem. If a relationship of confidence, friendliness and mutual support has not been previously established, such parent–teacher meetings can become a confrontation rather than a dialogue held for the benefit of the child. Alternatively, mutual suspicion or fear can lead to a bland, empty discussion in which neither parents nor teachers dare honestly describe the problem as they see it or express their real feelings.

Tucker and Dyson (1976) have pointed out how a feeling of alienation between parents and teachers can leave the child with the burdensome role of the primary 'communicator' between home and school, carrying information, messages and values between the two systems. They suggest that the role of message bearer may take a heavy toll of the child physically, emotionally or academically.

Of course, it is not only between systems but within systems that feelings of isolation and poor communication can occur. The staff of a school may find that there are few opportunities to meet, pool resources and work co-operatively on their difficult problems. There are sometimes dynamic processes within staff groups that interfere with sharing and supporting behaviour between teachers. Similar difficulties occur in families.

Although the contextual complexity of school-related problems for children is broadly understood by professional workers, there are few reported attempts at a multi-system intervention. In the United States some responses to children's family–school dysfunction have been the application of 'ecological strategies' (Hobbs, 1975) and family systems theory (Tucker and Dyson, 1976). Other accounts of interventions taking account of the complex web of systemic interactions are given by Aponte (1976) and Freund and Cardwell (1977). All these writers express the following common views: facilitating collaboration between home and school is the mainstay of a successful approach; one should avoid prematurely identifying the child as a patient and elicit the commitment of the family and the school staff to a joint problem-solving effort; the joint resources of teachers and parents should be used to try to find solutions rather than to dig for causes of trouble, which can be experienced as blaming or scapegoating. Another point emphasized by Taylor (1982) and Freund and Cardwell (1977) is the importance of taking the presenting problem seriously and limiting one's therapeutic boundaries to those issues concretely identified with the problem. Difficulties may arise here when parents and teachers, either because of different cultural norms or different tolerance levels, do not share a common perception of the nature or severity of a problem. Such differences of opinion, however, are more likely to reflect negative attitudes between the two systems than irreconcilable viewpoints.

EXAMPLES FROM CLINICAL PRACTICE

One of the most common presentations of a school–family problem arises when a child's difficult behaviour in school is denied by the family, who see the school staff as scapegoating the child in a heartless and unsympathetic way. The school in turn is likely to see the parents as irresponsible towards the child and aggressive in their response to the school's complaints. Parents naturally tend to identify with their children and see the world from their point of view, and their fierce defence of their offspring, however mistaken, should be taken as a sign of love which demands some respect, and which can be put to therapeutic use in the child's interest. Furthermore, many parents of children with school problems themselves had negative experiences in school, of scholastic failure or exposure to harsh discipline, and may expect or even covertly (and usually quite unconsciously) encourage their children's failure and rebellion in school. The child who fails to exceed his parents' school attainments may be demonstrating a deep loyalty to them even though they are at the conscious level angry and disappointed with him as well as with the school (Taylor, 1982). Some children in this situation will add to the disorder between the systems by misrepresenting each to the other, criticizing the family to the school and vice versa. The split between them, like that between warring parents, enables such children to avoid taking responsibility for their own behaviour. While this may in the short run reduce their anxiety and tension, in the long run it makes them less able to solve their problems because of the weakness of their introjected authority figures. Failure to heal the breach between family and school can presage delinquent development and a persistent paranoid attitude to authority and to outside institutions.

Case one, Mark S

An example is the case of Mark S, aged 5, whose parents referred him to a department of child psychiatry when the head teacher threatened to exclude him from school in his second term there. His mother had heard from a neighbour that his teacher had said, presumably at an unguarded moment, that he was the most difficult child in the class and should be in special school. Appalled and angry, she had approached the headmaster who, while not condoning the teacher's indiscretion, had confirmed that he was extremely disobedient in class and got into constant fights in the playground. If matters did not improve he might have to be excluded and recommended for special education. When he was seen at the clinic it was difficult to imagine how the situation had arisen. Mark was a bright, lively child and clearly strongly attached to his parents. They were also a devoted couple, though both reported unhappy and deprived childhoods and stormy school careers. They were living in damp and dilapidated rented accommodation and were engaged in a battle with the resident landlord over repairs and maintenance. He had a large family and obviously wanted to evict them but, lacking legal recourse, was resorting to harassment and intimidation. Both were enraged at the school for its attitude to their only child, whom they reported to be a model son, sympathetic to their misfortunes and particularly quick to comfort his mother, who had a history of depressive illness, when she felt especially low. It was noticeable in the initial family interview that every time the parents became upset over their current difficulties, Mark created a diversion by drawing an amusing picture or telling a joke to brighten them up, like a court jester in times past. The overall impression was of a fragile family clinging together in the face of a hostile world, reducing the danger of internal conflict by projecting all the bad things on to the external environment. The therapist (AP), concerned lest the threat of exclusion from school be carried out in earnest, suggested that the next meeting should be in the school, since she was confused at the discrepancy between Mark as they knew him in the family, and Mark as he had been described at school. An appointment was made by telephone with the headmaster, who turned out to be a sympathetic and concerned man, very anxious to improve relations with the family, but also convinced that they were too defensive and hostile to co-operate with the school in any useful way.

The interview began in an atmosphere of suspicion and mistrust. When the class teacher arrived Mrs S glared at her as if she could have gunned her down on the spot. She exploded with fury while describing how she had come to hear of her son's difficulties and berated the teacher for not having told her more directly how he was behaving. The teacher, who was young and inexperienced, tried to explain that she had attempted to, but had not felt Mrs S really heard her, and she had finally inadvertently let out how she felt when a parent complained, not for the first time, that Mark had attacked her child and torn his coat. The therapist came in at this point to point out the puzzling fact that Mark was not like this at home, and it had therefore been very difficult for the parents to believe he could be difficult in school. On the other hand, they had made clear to her that they were under a lot of strain, and it was possible that Mark was showing *his* strain at school, rather than burdening his parents with it at home. She also voiced some sympathy for the teacher's inability to talk honestly about Mark, for the simple reason that Mrs S loved him so much and so got very upset at any suggestion of his having problems. Both the teacher and Mrs S could accept this account of their misunderstanding, which showed respect for both, and with the air cleared, the parents were able to share with the staff their worries about their housing. The staff had not realized how difficult were the family's circumstances and listened sympathetically while they were recounted. The headmaster undertook to write a letter in support of their application for rehousing, and the therapist suggested a weekly meeting at a regular time between Mrs S and the class teacher to discuss Mark's progress. The meeting ended on a note of optimism and goodwill, and there was a very rapid improvement in Mark's behaviour over subsequent weeks. Through the weekly meeting with the class teacher Mrs S became drawn into the life of the school and helped in the classroom and on outings. Some months' later they were rehoused and the case was closed.

This case illustrates how even a caring family and a concerned school can come into bitter conflict under certain conditions, and how a joint meeting under the auspices of a therapist can reveal to each the virtues of the other, and in particular the concern for the child which each feels. It also shows how failures in communication can be made good in a joint interview, and in particular how knowledge of home-based stresses on a child can recruit sympathy from teachers who then feel less threatened by misbehaviour and can deal with it more effectively. Likewise parents are more able to hear the school's complaints when made in a calm and supportive atmosphere and to engage in joint problem-solving with the school in their child's interest.

A second not uncommon presentation arises when the split between family and school mirrors a split between the parents themselves. One parent may collude with the child's symptomatic behaviour for reasons concerned with his or her own unresolved childhood conflicts while the other is prevented from dealing with it because of withholding of salient information, or for fear of disrupting the marriage because of the close identification between the first parent and child, as in the following case:

Case two, John C

John was nearly 10, a pupil in the third year of junior school. He had been referred to the educational psychologist in his previous school a year before for provocative behaviour to other children, which led to his being unpopular and bullied, and for his refusal to engage in written work, although obviously above average in intelligence. The father had his own business and worked long hours, so he had not been involved directly in any of the discussions with the psychologist or teachers, but had accompanied his wife to see the psychiatrist to whom the boy had been referred by the psychologist. Both parents were unimpressed by all the professionals involved, and saw the school as entirely to blame for their child's problems. They refused treatment and moved him to another school. Two terms later, this school also referred him to the educational psychologist, but the parents referred themselves instead to a child guidance clinic. They reported John to be strong willed but fairly well behaved at home, and the mother in particular seemed almost to admire his resistance to authority at school, seeing it as independence and high spiritedness, unlike her own meekness and compliance as a child. When the therapist telephoned the school, she was surprised to hear how seriously the school viewed John's behaviour problems. He was coming up to secondary transfer in a year's time and the school could not anticipate his surviving in a large senior school.

Several more family interviews were held in the clinic at which little progress was made. It seemed impossible to hold on to a sense of the seriousness of the situation because of the casual attitude of the family, and especially the mother's amused tolerance of the boy's bad behaviour, which they both managed to make seem quite delightful and comical. The father followed her lead and tended to agree the school was exaggerating, though he was more concerned than she about the boy's future prospects if he did not make better scholastic progress. They seemed to be a happy enough family, with unremarkable backgrounds, and there was little explanation in the history for the severity of the problem. Finally a joint interview at the school was suggested. The teachers there reported extremely disturbed and disturbing behaviour on John's part. He screamed and cried when asked to do work, tormented other children and then complained of being bullied when they retaliated, and was generally unpopular with staff and children. The deputy head as well as the headmaster and two class teachers told the same story. John was hardly containable in school. Mr C was visibly horrified and ashamed of his son's behaviour. He had never realized it was so bad. Why had his wife not kept him better informed? She pleaded that she had not intended him to know the truth because she got a vicarious pleasure from John's rebellion and did not want his 'courage' broken.

The parents then proceeded to negotiate with the school as to how to deal with the problem, and at the therapist's suggestion a daily report system was instituted, with evening television contingent on good reports. Both school and parents co-operated meticulously in writing and signing the reports and within several weeks there was a great improvement in class behaviour. As John became less disruptive he began to get on better with other children, helped by discussions within the family sessions at the clinic. Within several months the only outstanding problem was his continuing academic failure, which was diagnosed as arising from an unsuspected specific learning disability. It had been masked by the behaviour disturbance and was treated by intensive remedial tuition, with which John co-operated well. He was more mature and realistic about himself and his world and seemed to have grown up several years in a few months.

His case illustrates the great importance of involving the father as a respected person in the school–family interview, who can ally himself with the school in expecting age-appropriate behaviour from the child. This may sometimes be in opposition to the mother's wish to keep him as an indulged and omnipotent infant who functions as an extension of herself and acts out her unfulfilled desires (Lacan, 1977). The importance of the joint interview as a means of conveying accurate information between family and school on which realistic problem-solving can be based is again illustrated by this case. It can be seen as increasing the permeability of the joint boundary by holding both systems within a third system created by the therapist, who guarantees the integrity of both by his respect and concern for them and for the child. It also shows how conflict between home and school can lead to mounting acting out by a child. By adding fuel to the fire he diverts attention from his real difficulties which neither school nor family can deal with unaided.

Families may also feel threatened and distressed by complaints from school about a child which they have no immediate means of putting right. An example of this follows.

Case three, Angela T

This concerns a 12-year-old Afro-Caribbean girl at a Catholic comprehensive school. Right through primary school and now in secondary school her parents were told she was withdrawn and isolated and resisted communication with her teachers, however friendly they tried to be. When referred to a child guidance clinic they revealed that she had been sent back to the

West Indies as a small child when they were living in poor accommodation and the mother was working full time to raise money for a house of their own. On her return she was quiet and withdrawn, especially outside the family, but was also very helpful and motherly to the younger children of the household. The parents felt criticized and judged by the school, like 'bad parents' who had failed to socialize their daughter so that she would be acceptable at school. The family was seen together and, although almost silent in the session, Angela took a lively interest in her siblings and supervised their play. She reluctantly complained of being teased at school in explanation of her isolation and unhappiness. Enquiry revealed that Mrs T had herself been a very shy girl, who had taught herself in later life to cope with social situations and to stand up for her own and her children's rights. Her father also said he had been teased as a boy at school, but now had a responsible job which involved supervising other people and he had learned how to deal with such things. The parents were congratulated on having overcome their own earlier difficulties, and it was suggested that they were therefore the best people to help and advise Angela now regarding her shyness and sensitivity to teasing.

Times were set for them to talk with Angela about her problems at home, and a joint family–school meeting arranged for a month later, as there was still a climate of distrust towards the school, which the therapist feared could militate against their best efforts if left unchanged. At the school, the form tutor announced some improvement in Angela's social behaviour over the past week or so, which was attributed by the therapist to the parents' work with her. The parents were seen by the school as caring and constructive rather than angry and defensive as they had been before, and the school likewise emerged as genuinely concerned for Angela rather than merely persecutory of the parents as they had seemed to be in the past. Arrangements were made for half-termly meetings between parents and form tutor, so they had accurate information on which to base their 'teaching' at home. Angela made excellent progress, joined the school choir, and made several personal friends in her form over the following term.

The therapist in this case can be seen as providing a *problem-solving context* for family–school communication, so that instead of being heard as complaints and criticisms, difficulties can be seen as problems to be overcome by joint action. It is particularly important in dealing with minority-group families to take account of their likely experience of prejudice, and the difficulties both for families and professionals in discriminating between racial bias and other problems which need to be dealt with rather than defended against.

A cautionary word needs to be said, however, about the possible dangers of joint family–school meetings. While most families and most schools are devoted to their children, a very few can be downright hostile and destructive. Confronting such a school with such a family may only deepen the rift between them, as they observe the obvious nastiness of the other. In other words, while most paranoia is neurotic, some suspicions are totally justified! A case in point is that of Ben.

Case four, Ben W

He was a boy of 9 whose school wanted him designated maladjusted because of his restless, irritable behaviour and disobedience at school. He remained absolutely still and silent in the family interview, never touching the play materials or speaking unless spoken to. His parents were formidable people, the mother especially being extremely forceful and dominating, and Ben seemed quite frightened of her. He was obviously kept on a very tight rein at home, never allowed out and expected to do a lot of work in the house. Because of the anger with the school a joint meeting was arranged, and to the therapist's horror the headmaster turned out to be as intolerant and inflexible as the parents, using the session to pour out a stream of invective about the child. Since neither system could be influenced in any way, as they were now even more convinced the problem was in the other, individual therapy was arranged for the boy, but with little effect, and he was finally sent back in disgrace to his father's family in Nigeria. It may be wise therefore to have some contact with both school and family, and feel in some sympathy with both, before setting up a joint meeting. While usually a most valuable intervention, it may in a small minority of cases increase the difficulties under which the child is labouring.

A SCHOOL–FAMILY INTERVENTION PROJECT

The common approach, indicated by these examples and previous work reviewed above, is for a school-based collaborative intervention involving school staff and families, aimed at assisting children who are experiencing difficulties in the learning situation because of maladaptive behaviour. Normally, children with such problems are referred to an educational psychologist. However, the traditional response to a referral has been to gather information from teachers, see the individual child for an interview which may well include psychological testing procedures, discuss the situation with the parents (often with the mother only) and finally review the findings in a written report and discuss the recommendations with one or more representatives of the school. One of the authors (JD) had been working for two years in a large girls' secondary school along these lines. Dissatisfaction with the effectiveness of this approach led him to review his work in the school and consider an alternative method.

Most of the referrals from the teachers were of third- and fourth-year girls with severe behaviour problems usually considered so serious that there was no real belief from the teachers that they might be able to help. Many of the girls referred had histories of difficult behaviour going back to the first year in the school and in some cases back to their primary schools. Relationships between the parents were frequently distant or strained. Teachers often reported that the parents of these girls were uncooperative or apathetic, whilst parents experienced the school as remote, impersonal and unfriendly. Teachers complained that the parents seemed unconcerned by their daughters' behaviour whilst parents complained that they had not been told about the problem before or they were tired of hearing the same complaints. These observations do not imply that teacher–parent relationships were generally poor nor that the school was comparatively less interested in home–school liaison than other secondary schools. But in the case of many of the girls referred to the educational psychologist, trust and confidence between home and school was all but gone. In these circumstances, the notion of a constructive family–school interview, 'as an instrument to learn about the presenting problem, the relationship among the people who contributed to the problem, and the ways in which these people can bring about change' (Aponte, 1976, p. 304), seemed unrealistic. Such attempts that were made were sometimes acrimonious and usually unproductive.

In some cases it was possible to get parents to agree to attend a NHS child guidance clinic or hospital child psychiatry department. But without the genuine motivation to get help that comes with a mutual understanding between parents and teachers about the nature of the problem, referrals tended to result in poor attendance and failed appointments. Even when there was an acceptance and understanding by families of the need for help there was often resistance to being seen in an unknown psychiatric agency because of anxiety about visiting such clinics and the stigma sometimes felt by families about receiving psychiatric treatment. In those cases where girls were attending child guidance departments, problems of home–school communication were often considered minor by the teachers compared with the difficulties of liaising with the professionals involved at the clinic regarding treatment plans, educational implications and management advice. So, lack of intersystem co-operation of one kind was replaced by intersystem problems of another kind.

Another dissatisfaction felt by the educational psychologist arose through the lack of contact and involvement in problem-solving by the form tutors. The form tutor is the first-level pastoral figure and 'arguably the most important person in the school' (Marland, 1974, p. 74). Marland goes on to say that

> a school creates good tutors by the degree they are taken into its confidence and the degree of responsibility they are given. It is these

two factors that lead to concern, and from concern comes ability. I have observed tutors performing markedly better and relishing their roles more when they have been put more into the picture and given more responsibility.

(1974, p.76)

Practically, it makes sense that form tutors should be more involved. In an eight-form entry secondary school such as this one, it was extremely difficult for a year tutor to know all the pupils directly and maintain the sort of quality and frequency of contact with parents that was necessary to establish a good working relationship. More direct contact between educational psychologist and form tutor in discussions about girls experiencing problems seemed another way of increasing their responsibility. However, with increased responsibility there is an increased need for support and it seemed reasonable that form tutors should have this from their form tutor colleagues, and the year head, as well as the educational psychologist.

Against this background and guided by the work of Tucker and Dyson (1976) the educational psychologist (JD) decided to offer a different sort of service contract to the school with the following aims: (1) to work in a more preventive way through concentrating psychological support on the first year in order to monitor, identify and, when appropriate, intervene regarding girls showing early adjustment problems; (2) to promote more understanding and co-operation between parents and teachers; (3) to improve liaison between the school and a local child guidance clinic; and (4) to strengthen the pastoral role of the form tutors. In order to provide this intense service and bring the sort of special skills required in approaching family-based school problems, a clinical psychologist (AP) with experience as a family therapist, agreed to work in partnership with JD in the school. It was also reasoned that as the clinical psychologist was a member of staff of a local child guidance clinic, this would make for more constructive and continuous communication when families were referred to the clinic for help.

The plan presented to the head teacher was for the two psychologists to visit the school for one afternoon a fortnight. During our visits we proposed to meet the first year head to consult about pupils causing concern and also, after school, a meeting with the first year head, form tutors, education welfare officer, school nurse and the teacher in charge of the school's adjustment unit. We also proposed that during our visits we would, when appropriate, see girls with their families and that the year head and/or form tutor would normally be included in the interviews.

In exchange, the educational psychologist had to negotiate with the head teacher for a reduction in the amount of support provided to the rest of the school; there would be less frequent, monthly visits to consult with year heads and only exceptionally to intervene directly. This was accepted by

79

the head teacher as the plan offered hope of preventing some serious problems developing and, by bringing parents into school at an early stage, there seemed the prospect of home–school relationships that could withstand the possible pressures of a later crisis.

It was very fortunate that the 'target' first year was headed by a very able teacher who was already involved in developing her own pastoral work as well as planning the role enhancement of her form tutors through a training programme in development work in tutorial groups (Button, 1981). She was very receptive to the service input we had planned and had her own plan for improving home–school contact through a social evening in the first term, when the girls and their parents would be invited to meet their form tutor. We agreed that this should be early in the term when parental hopes are high and curiosity strong about the aims and purposes of secondary schooling. We also agreed that the evening should be used as an opportunity to introduce the support professionals, including ourselves, to the parents and girls. The attendance at the evening was very high and our presence proved very valuable. We met informally several parents whom we later interviewed. The evening acted both as an icebreaker and a demystifier in that there was no difficulty, as is sometimes the case, in arranging to meet any parents later and on some occasions there had been sufficient discussion at the social evening for the psychologist already to be a little informed about the family and forewarned of the problem.

Initially, the meetings with the form tutors had the primary aim of monitoring the girls' behaviour in order to identify early those girls showing difficulties and discussing with them how the problems were being managed. Although the psychologists found this function of the group valuable, some of the younger teachers did not find the group satisfying and the group was clearly not fulfilling another function, that of giving support to the tutors. One teacher complained that the discussions in the group seemed to be based on limited evidence and in some cases little more than gossip. Others excused themselves from the meetings saying they were too busy with more concrete, competing demands on their time and they saw little value in discussing girls with problems that were not their own. These feelings, although genuinely felt, seemed to mask other factors. The group was obviously experienced as very threatening by some of the teachers. This was probably due mainly to the unfamiliar invitation to share perceptions and difficulties with other teachers, some of whom were of more senior status and greater experience. The discomfort was probably compounded by the fact that the form tutors and year head did not meet together on any other occasion, so the meetings were also experienced as frustrating because there were business and policy matters which could not be discussed.

Another early problem was the apparent discrepancy between the year head's and form tutor's commitments to developing pastoral skills.

Although we felt there was tacit consent from the form tutors to attend the meetings, it seemed later that they felt that they had little choice in the matter and they had been rather swept along by the year head's enthusiasm. As the beginning of these meetings also coincided with the commencement of their developmental work in tutorial group training, those teachers who were also involved in curriculum development work and who needed to give a lot of time to lesson planning, were feeling under great pressure.

After about three meetings of the group, when these difficulties became apparent, we renegotiated the contract with the group, stressing its voluntary nature. The emphasis on monitoring shifted more to joint problem-solving. The resulting smaller group became more diligent and felt more supportive and cohesive. Those younger teachers who were disaffected initially remained outsiders, only joining the group for occasional meetings when they needed advice regarding a particular child or issue. One particularly useful meeting is recalled when a relatively inexperienced teacher asked for help in managing a form of girls that she found very troublesome. Some of the more experienced teachers who taught the same form joined the group for this meeting and were able to work together constructively in suggesting to the teacher management techniques that she could try.

As time went on the psychologists and teachers were able to contribute at the level of feeding back to the group observations and feelings about interviews that had taken place with families. Out of these discussions feelings of empathy towards the parents seemed to develop. It proved constructive for teachers and others to know that the parents were puzzled and often pained themselves. Gaining increased insights about the child's family circumstances can lead teachers to a new view of the child's behaviour, typically a freeing from a feeling of being persecuted by the child. This alteration can then bring about a change in response to the child which, in turn, alters the child's responses in the classroom.

SCHOOL CASE EXAMPLES

Christina S

One of the first cases brought for discussion to the tutors' meeting was a bilingual girl of Greek Cypriot origin who was discovered on entry to the school to have a reading age of 5 years 8 months. The year head contacted the parents and asked if one of the psychologists could see her for a full assessment, to which they agreed. She presented as a very attractive and likeable child, but the assessment revealed a severe deficit in linguistic ability (Wechsler Intelligence Scale for Children, revised, Wisc-R Verbal Scale IQ 55), while her practical and visuo-motor abilities were in the normal range (Wisc-R Performance Scale IQ 90). Her parents were then seen with the year head; they explained that they had been concerned about Christina's slow progress for a long time, but the primary school staff had always been reassuring and made them feel they were being unduly anxious. Mrs S had tried to help with her reading, but did not really know how to go about it. She saw Christina as being much happier in the current school, and felt more was being done for her there than in primary school. The parents' great concern for and excellent upbringing of Christina was acknowledged, and it was explained that given her considerable learning difficulties she would not have made as good progress without such good care on their part. It was agreed that the school would do all it could to help her remain there, and that the parents should be closely involved in the programme.

A later meeting was held involving the teacher in charge of the learning support centre, where the mother was instructed in ways of developing Christina's expressive language at home, by not speaking for her, encouraging her to describe events in the school day as well as by listening to her reading each evening as the teacher would direct. Mrs S was also invited to visit the centre at regular intervals to discuss Christina's progress and work out with the teacher how she could continue to help her at home. Further discussion in the tutor group occurred from time to time about curriculum issues, such as whether she should take French or whether the time would be better employed in extra English. She is now near the end of her second year and progressing quite well, with no further concern being expressed over her placement in the school.

Anita G

Anita was also mentioned early in the tutors' meeting because of poor attendance and anxiety in school, manifesting itself in running out of lessons in an agitated state for no apparent reason. She had been a poor attender in primary school, where she had taken a long time to settle in, and had cried and clung to her mother in the mornings. The family was invited to a meeting with the psychologists and the year head, where it emerged that mother had always 'spoilt' Anita, especially since her younger sisters (aged 8 and 2½) were born, because she herself had been jealous of her siblings as a child. She also identified with Anita's fear of school, and often had stayed at home herself.

Father was less indulgent and often felt very angry when he got home from work and found Anita had not attended school that day. His own father had left home when he was aged 5, and he had then been sent to boarding school, which he hated but had no choice but to attend. The session focused on the mechanics of getting Anita up and out in the morning, and mother's need to resist her crying and tantrums and firmly send her off to school. Father's view of the importance of Anita's education was strongly supported, and his status as a working man who understood the value of such things in later life was given weight to counterbalance mother's indulgence and home-centredness. The main difficulty emerged as Anita's crying and tantrums when about to leave for school, which Mrs G found impossible to resist, especially as she was also trying to cope with feeding the youngest and getting the middle child ready for school. Anita was asked to practise crying *after supper* each evening when her mother had more time to attend to her, and would therefore be able to work out better ways of dealing with it. Father was to look after the other children for the fifteen minutes' practice time.

When seen again one month later, Anita was reported not only to be attending regularly but to be much happier at home and school. She had given up crying in the morning after two evenings' practice, each of which had culminated in mother and daughter convulsed with laughter. However, three months later, after a period of illness, she was missing school again. In a further family session, Mrs G was more open about her need to have her children at home, and her dependence on Anita as a helpmate. She was told what a good mother she was, and how she understood that her daughter needed to learn from her about mothering. She would know intuitively when she had learned enough and could return to school to develop her other talents. Both parents thought this absurd, and were sure she had had plenty of opportunity already to learn from her mother.

Again, Anita returned to school for several months after this intervention, until the family moved house at around the beginning of the next school year. This time the parents reported that they had kept her at home on several occasions to help with the move, and to look after the younger child. The cost of the move had also left them short of cash, and on several occasions there had been no money for fares and lunches. Anita never cried about school now, but instead would get involved in long interesting conversations with her mother over breakfast, with neither of them realizing she should have left long ago for school.

At this point it was felt that not only was the mother too indulgent, but so were the psychologists and the school staff, and that perhaps we should have used Berg's approach (Berg *et al.*, 1977), and invoked the power of the court from the start to back up father's authority in the family. We pointed out that unless Anita returned to school promptly the divisional director would institute court proceedings, and an agreement was made for Anita to have her conversations with mother at night rather than in the morning. This worked for a while but she again went absent after a few months and a court warning was issued. Almost immediately the parents arranged transfer to another secondary school very close to home and so legal action was not pursued. This could be seen as an attempt by the family to find a compromise solution to the pressure to restructure their family system or alternatively it might be seen as an avoidance manoeuvre to resist change.

Several other girls were seen with their parents and teachers because of unruly behaviour and disobedience in school, with a view to strengthening the authority of both home and school by helping them work out a joint strategy for containment. The method usually involved setting up daily reports plus regular meetings with the tutor or year head, and was very successful with several girls. One girl, however, with a very disturbed background and a stormy relationship with a new stepfather was finally recommended for special boarding school, after all efforts on the part of school and the child guidance clinic (to which mother had referred herself after the first consultation with the psychologist) had failed.

Another girl, the youngest in a large family who had all in turn truanted from school and several of whom had been in trouble with the law, was referred for poor attendance, stealing, and aggressive behaviour in school. She lived some distance from the school and was the only one in the family who needed to get up in the morning, the older siblings being either excluded from school or unemployed. She had also persuaded the year head not to inform her mother about the stealing, as she would then be beaten by her older brother. A number of school meetings, home visits, and contacts with other agencies were carried out on behalf of this family, including several discussions with a solicitor who knew them well. He undertook to persuade them not to use corporal punishment as a way of dealing with the stealing, so that the school would feel confident in sharing their concerns with the family, which we expected would be a far more effective means of social control. Extra funds were also made available from a local charity when it was discovered how small the family income was after various debts had been met. Though there has continued to be anxiety about this girl, the stealing seems to have stopped, and attendance to have improved.

It is interesting to compare the school-based with the clinic-based interventions both in terms of process and outcome. Interviewing on the school's territory rather than our own, often with a member of staff present who may or may not take charge of the session, and with frequent interruptions from the telephone or small girls entering the room on 'messages' from other teachers, at first made us feel rather incompetent. It took time to establish a workable pattern in which each of us played an appropriate part, and which strengthened the alliance between school and home rather than invested too much hope in the psychologist's magical skills to effect change via an assessment or consultation with the child.

In retrospect, we felt we could have been more successful in the case of Anita G, for example, if we had worked more closely with the year head on the case, using simple behavioural techniques, e.g. negotiating a clear contract between school and home regarding the management of absences.

As soon as one moves into a style of work which has a more complex theoretical rationale, the teachers feel excluded and their management skills can be put to only limited use in the conduct of the therapy. It was also useful to us to realize how our interventions were only part of a process of change within the family and school which continued long after we had seen the family and child. There was less sense of a piece of work leading to a rapid 'cure' and discharge, and we were forced to come to terms with some short-term improvements which did not hold because of further life events which militated against a successful outcome, or other problems (e.g. within the marriage) which our intervention had left untouched. On the other hand, we did develop a lively sense of the rich resources of families and schools, and their potential for supporting and guiding children through the difficult years of early adolescence when they work in harmony together.

There was a parallel gain from the experience of joint work between the educational and clinical psychologist. At the outset we were inhibited and awkward together, and it required lengthy discussion to discover that the major difficulty arose from mutual projections about the training and expertise of the other. The educational psychologist was felt to know all about schools, the clinical psychologist to know all about families. Over time we realized that neither was as expert in the one area, or as ignorant in the other, as we had first imagined, and we were able to supplement each other's contribution with growing confidence.

CONCLUSIONS

In the second year of the project we began working with a new first year but continued to be involved with the second year. Trying to provide a similar service to the first two years proved very difficult and the loss of time available to the first year detracted from the thorough monitoring and family–school work to which we were originally committed. We therefore reverted to intensive work with just the first year.

As was found by Tucker and Dyson (1976), the present *modus operandi* of the educational psychologist we have described was far more satisfying than focusing an assessment in that change was brought about by spending more time with all the people connected with the problem: year head, form tutor, subject teachers, pupil and family members. Testing and other evaluative techniques were used more discriminatingly to provide data when they had a direct relation to the problem.

From the point of view of the clinical psychologist, who had previously worked largely alone or with other mental health professionals, the project brought an increased respect for the skills and talents of teachers, both in their educational and their pastoral roles. It became clearer why clinicians are so often felt to be omnipotent and exclusive by schools and other agencies, because of their assumption of an esoteric knowledge and their frequent lack of regard for the human relations skills of other professions. It seemed that over the course of the project this view of psychologists was modified and most of the school staff involved were able to share realistically with us in the school–family work without undue anxiety or stress. Particularly in the management of school behaviour problems, the practice of working exclusively within the clinic walls with no more than a telephone call or brief written communication with the school began to seem increasingly inappropriate. In most cases, joint work with the school and the family reveal large areas of mutual concern and shared values, whereas in the clinic the split between them may become an abyss as the family members attempt to persuade the therapist that the responsibility for the problem is entirely with the school, or alternatively that they have no influence whatever on the child's behaviour in school. Both these views are likely to be strongly and sincerely held and are difficult to modify except in the school context; here, the reality of the staff's concern for the child, and the genuineness of their desire to co-operate with the family has to be acknowledged, as does the family's wish to do well by the child.

Formal evaluation of the approach was not attempted but there were signs that the work had been effective. Through regular, frequent meetings with the tutors, there was early warning of the girls with incipient problems, and meetings between the teachers and the parents and pupil, or between the psychologists and the family, were conducted in an atmosphere of shared concern and mutual goodwill. The developmental work in tutorial groups seemed to have complemented the other efforts made towards building bridges between home and school. The year tutor found the joint interviews with psychologists and parents very useful not only for developing insights into the family dynamics and the child's problem in context, but also through learning techniques of interviewing that avoid power conflicts, make use of empathy and mobilize co-operation from parents.

The psychologists felt that essentially the form tutor group as a support group had failed. However, the year tutor considered that the group provided the basis for improved communication between tutors and that the group had evolved so that the tutors were more able to trust and help each other. Certainly, the psychologists' expectations of the group at the outset were unrealistic in that they overestimated the degree of openness that the teachers might show in offering observations and sharing their thoughts and feelings about work difficulties with colleagues to whom they did not feel affiliated and with outside support staff with whom they had little or no previous contact. [A more recent project has used trained internal facilitators for staff consultation and support groups with some success (Stringer et al., 1992).] The dual purposes of the group, i.e. monitoring, and consultation and support, further added to the initial problems.

However, in spite of these difficulties, in general these form tutors did become more committed, involved and skilled in their pastoral work.

It was not possible to carry out a follow-up study of the project but it was hoped that an intense service during the first year would prevent more serious problems arising later. All whom we worked with except one girl were functioning satisfactorily in school one year after the end of the project. The exception was a child with serious behavioural difficulties who had been transferred from a special school. Apart from this case all the families had been helped in the school situation and no other referrals to the child guidance clinic had been made. In the few cases where there were some remaining problems, generally positive interactions were maintained between the family and the school in trying to find solutions.

It may be important to note that the project was carried out during the 1980s before the NHS reforms came into effect. We were able to negotiate time for the school–family work on an informal basis. An NHS-based psychologist or family therapist would now probably need to negotiate a contract with his or her purchasing body before commencing a project of this kind. Similarly, in some education authorities, educational psychologists' work has become largely confined to fulfilling statutory responsibilities. However, we feel that collaborative work of the kind we have described is still possible within the present public service context, and within a statutory framework. We would see it as a useful model both on grounds of clinical effectiveness and of the professional development of all the staff groups involved.

6

PARENTS AND CHILDREN
Participants in change
Neil Dawson and Brenda McHugh

For the past ten years, the Marlborough Family Service Education Unit has operated as a context dedicated to the application of a joint family and school systems approach (Dowling and Osborne, 1985). The unit, located in a Health Service managed institution, is run by three teachers who are also trained family therapists. Their aim has been to develop a model of practice which forms a bridge between the health and education services in order to make a family-based intervention acceptable and useful to more people (Dawson and McHugh, 1986a, 1986b, 1987, 1988). The population targeted for help has been families thought to be reluctant to seek, or welcome, professional intervention, particularly in those situations where the original presenting problem is a child showing difficulties at school. To this end, the model has been designed to reduce the feelings of failure, blame, anxiety, anger and fear, often associated in people's minds with being referred for help to psychiatric, psychological or other mental-health-based services. This has been achieved by using the two roles of teacher and therapist to create a classroom context in which parents, or carers, and children are encouraged and enabled to try out ways of being different with each other and to develop new, more successful approaches to managing at school or at home. The role of the therapist gives access to the family and the role of the teacher gives ready access to the school system; the two together afford the potential for significant joint systems interventions.

When a child behaves in a way that is considered inappropriate or unacceptable, it is common for the adult deemed to be 'in charge' of that child to feel in some way responsible for his or her behaviour. This can apply for parents, carers and teachers in relation to their role acting *in loco parentis* whilst the child is at school. If children continue to behave in ways that worry, disturb or annoy people with whom they come into contact, it is very common for the adults involved to feel as if they have failed (Haley, 1976). When people feel as if they have failed it is extremely common for the idea of responsibility to switch into blame, with a concomitant search for a scapegoat. This feature of blame is nearly always present in situations

88

when parents and teachers are forced to talk to each other, because a child that they both have responsibility for is not behaving as one or other, or both of them, think he should. Parents feel blamed ('Wouldn't it be better if you gave your son a good breakfast before he came to school?' or 'Have you thought of buying her an alarm clock so that she can get up in time for school?'). Teachers feel blamed ('She tells me everything that goes on in your lessons. She says nobody ever listens to you or does any work. She says you are always picking on her.' or 'I see children from this school in the local shops and at the bus stops; they are so rude, always pushing and fighting. There's no wonder that Stephen's doing what he does. There's no discipline in schools anymore.'). Interchanges such as these often lead to increased distance between parents and teachers with the result that the original reason for needing to talk becomes obscured and the child's way of behaving does not get discussed within a constructive framework. The task of the teacher-therapist is to talk with both teachers and parents in such a way that mutual blame can be minimized; the distance between them then becomes decreased in a safe way and new solutions can be explored on the child's behalf.

Being teachers, who actually teach and deal with very difficult children every day, and who have all had experience of the stresses and strains of teaching in mainstream primary and secondary schools, has helped the teacher-therapists to gain a degree of trust with their colleagues in schools. The skills and knowledge gained from training as family therapists (Cooklin, 1982; Minuchin, 1974), together with ten years of experience of working with hundreds of families, have helped to develop practice which has the intention of removing blame as a feature of conversations with parents and children.

Learning difficulties often accompany emotional or behavioural difficulties. Being teachers able to provide a classroom, able to help investigate a child's specific areas of difficulty with learning and able to design appropriate curricula has helped parents to see that their child's best interests are central. This in turn has helped to foster a climate of trust which has made it more likely that the adults would start to share some of their worries, either about their children or about other important relationships in the family. At the same time, by encouraging and enabling the children to see themselves as something other than academic failures, the teaching component of the model has been central to the development of the overall package.

REFERRAL AND INITIAL CONTACT WITH
CHILD AND FAMILY

Intervention by the Education Unit is designed to offer an alternative referral route to the more usual medical or social services method of accessing help for families. As a result, referrals are from schools, either made directly by teachers or, at one remove, by educational psychologists or education welfare officers. The child showing difficulties at school, or not attending, is the basis of all referrals. A full range of problems from attempted arson of a primary school through to straightforward disruptive behaviour have been dealt with in the unit.

The initial discussion with the professional colleague looking for help on the child's behalf is made with the aim of hearing about the problem, finding out who is the most closely involved with the child and deciding on when and where to meet the family (Anderson *et al.*, 1986). The preference is always for visiting the child and the parent(s) or carers at home. This has several potential benefits; many parents have said that they were 'sick of going to school to be told off' for what their child had done wrong in school. Many have described that awful feeling of being picked out in the playground by other parents or children and told to 'do something about' their child. Lots of parents have not had positive experience of schools and teachers themselves, and find that the whole atmosphere of school rekindles old memories, sometimes leaving them feeling intimidated or foolish. Having the meeting at home is intended to create the possibility of different kinds of discussions without the inhibitions which can easily be inherent in meetings held at school.

From the point of view of the family therapist it also offers the opportunity to see a different picture of the child and the family from the one that would be likely to be presented if the family had simply been invited to a meeting at school or at the Education Unit. Lodgers, for example, have on several occasions proven to be significant contributors to key relationships within the family. The willingness to 'put oneself out' to visit someone at home can help to support the idea that the current difficulties are being taken seriously as well as enabling the teacher-therapist to adopt a relatively impartial position. Given that many referrals are made at a stage when the relationship between teachers and parents is tense, it is important to be able to hear both parties' explanations about how they understand the problem. If the parents or other family members are likely to talk about their worries, they need to believe that their concerns will be listened to without too much bias. This is a difficult mediating position to maintain as the teacher-therapists cannot be truly neutral because of their position as professionals employed by the education service; as a consequence it has been important to compensate for this imbalance by making every effort to try to understand the family's predicament, sometimes at the expense of being seen to be unfair to the school's position. The power differential between schools and families, particularly as perceived by families that may feel themselves locked in a struggle with a school, makes it vital that the move to compensate on the family's behalf should be positive, obvious, and recognized as such by the family members (Andersen, 1987).

Kim A was the mother of three boys; Kevin aged 10, Andrew who was 7 and Jason who was 5. The teachers at the primary school attended by the boys were desperate because all three of them were constantly in serious trouble. Kevin was described as likeable, even though he was always in fights, both in the playground and the classroom. When he had calmed down after a fight he would invariably be very sorry, would admit that he had been in the wrong and would promise never to do it again. Andrew was said to be the most worrying of the three because he would fight with other children and would continue to lash out when teachers tried to restrain him. After a recent incident of this kind he was said to have kicked his male head teacher and shouted, 'You're not my dad, you've got no right to control me.' Jason had not been in the school very long, but he was already starting to terrorize the reception class by hitting and biting other children.

The head, his deputy and the three current class teachers had all spoken to Kim on many occasions about her sons. They had usually found her to be concerned about what was happening at school but seemingly unable to effect any change in the boys' behaviour. The teachers were despairing about the situation because they felt condemned to suffer the boys' violence with little hope that they, Kim or anyone else could get them to stop fighting. Kevin and Andrew had regularly been sent home for one, two or three day exclusions from school, after fights. Privately, the teachers were quite angry with Kim because they felt that she must be at least partially responsible for the boys' behaviour. They had even speculated that she might be hitting them herself or was allowing them to be hit by someone at home. Although they had no evidence that the boys were being hurt, the teachers could find no other acceptable explanation for her ineffectual handling of their violence. They felt irritated and let down by what they felt was Kim's lack of real concern for their worries about the children. They were also very angry about the damaging effect of the violence on the other children in the school.

At the meeting in Kim's flat she was warm and welcoming and talked openly of her worries about the children. She was also despairing about the situation because she didn't have any idea how she could get her boys to stop fighting at school. She was irritated and angry with the teachers because they kept sending them home when they had been in fights. 'I shout at them and send them to their room. Andrew's already grounded for a month, but it doesn't make any difference. What do their teachers expect me to do? Sending them home isn't going to do any good, why can't they deal with them in school? They love it when they get sent home, they can watch the video. I try to stop them but they creep downstairs and say they're sorry. What am I supposed to do?' Kevin, Andrew and Jason were present throughout the meeting. They fought with each other, squabbled continuously and didn't stop when Kim shouted at them. Jason went regularly to his mother and got a kiss or cuddle. She shared the teachers' view that Andrew was 'the worst' because he didn't have the same charm as Kevin nor was he as loving as Jason. She said that she dreaded going to school to pick up the children because she knew that she was never going to hear anything good about them.

After talking about the boys in school, Kim started to relate some of the things that had happened to her family over the previous few years. The boys' father had left three years earlier; he had been violent throughout the relationship and had beaten her particularly badly when he had forced his way back into the flat just over two years ago. All the boys had witnessed their father punching and kicking their mother; Kevin had eventually managed to escape and call the police. Shortly after that, her then partner had been murdered in a local pub. Kim described how, after these events she had been extremely depressed and had drunk too much. She also said that at that time she had attempted to commit suicide by taking an overdose. She was now living with a new boy-friend called John. She said that they got on well together and the only major rows they had were about the children. John thought that she was too soft with them, whereas Kim said she didn't like his telling them off because they were her responsibility.

Clearly, from a family systems perspective, the issue of violence and Kim's management of her three boys took on a very different meaning. With the new information gained from the home visit, it was no longer at all appropriate or helpful to think of her as ineffectual or in any way responsible for the boys' violence at school. It was more relevant to consider the whole family as one that had experienced a number of highly traumatic events and that help could be offered, both collectively and individually, so that the process of recovery be supported and the pattern of violence interrupted as soon as possible. At the same time it was necessary to be alert to the possibility of helping the newly forming stepfamily tackle the many issues it would inevitably face, the most pressing appearing to be the one concerning parental authority and how that could be managed between Kim and John. It was particularly important to recognize that John was not actually a parent and to help Kim think about the degree to which she could ask him to support her authority in relation to the children or at times delegate some aspects of control to him. This is difficult enough in more 'normal' stepfamilies but with Kim and the boys' previous experiences of men and violence it had the clear potential to be very difficult for them all. How this could be handled would, in its turn, be likely to have implications for the development of Kim and John's relationship as a couple.

After this first meeting Kim accepted an invitation to visit the Education

Unit with Kevin, Andrew and Jason. She said she would try to persuade John to come as well.

THE CLASSROOM, THE FAMILIES AND THE
ENGAGEMENT PROCESS

Isolation is a recurring theme spoken about by the majority of parents who have attended the Education Unit. ('I never thought that there was any-body else with the same problems as me.') Families where there are children with severe emotional or behavioural difficulties are often unpopular in the local community. If the children play out, they either bully other children or are equally as likely to be bullied by them. In both situations the experience of contact with others is likely to be negative. Similarly, the parents are very frequently shunned by other families in response to their children's behavioural problems. The overall effect is often to turn the children and families inwards on themselves, with the result that the 'outside world' gradually becomes considered to be danger-ous and hostile.

The first visit to the Education Unit is always arranged at a time when the education component is functioning so that the prospective new entrants can see the sorts of things that actually happen. This takes place on four mornings each week during the normal school term times. The aim of this second contact with the child and the family is to extend the ideas discussed during the meeting at home and to give them the opportunity to talk to other parents and children who are currently attending the unit. At a second meeting it is very unlikely for trust to have been well established between the professional and the family members, especially in situations where, to date, this relationship has frequently been one characterized by tension and open hostility. People generally feel much more comfortable talking informally to others who might be in the same sort of predicament; everyone who attends the Education Unit has at least one thing in com-mon: they are all struggling with their children who are having difficulties with school in one way or another. If parents visiting the unit for the first time hear from other parents that attending the place with their children has been useful and that things have started to change for them, it is a powerful message which gives some hope that things can be different. In situations where both parents and children have often experienced years of unhappiness and usually seen themselves as failures, giving hope that change can happen is a vital component of the whole model. To hear such a message from people who are actually going through the changes is much more convincing than hearing professionals telling any number of stories about people who have been helped in the past.

When parents who are already attending are encouraged to talk to others it can have the bonus of highlighting the progress they have made.

Talking about successes and ways that have been found to overcome difficulties can have a positive effect for the speaker as well as the listener.

Lubna B had only been in Britain for two years, after leaving Beirut as a refugee. She had been forced to leave her husband behind in the Lebanon and escape to London with her two children, Mohammed aged 10 and his sister Farah, aged 7. Mohammed had been permanently excluded from his primary school because of his repeated and dramatic violent attacks on other children. The teachers in the school were sensitive to the family's plight but felt incapable of containing Mohammed and at the same time maintaining the safety of the other children. Lubna spoke only minimal English and, despite the help of an interpreter at the home visit, remained extremely anxious and wary about becoming involved with the Education Unit. She did however, visit the unit with Mohammed and spoke to another parent who had left the unit some months previously but who had been willing to come back and talk to Lubna and Mohammed. Being a Muslim who also spoke Arabic, she was able to talk freely with Lubna about her experiences in the unit and also to hear what was making her feel particularly anxious about pursuing a place for Mohammed. She was able to help Lubna explain her worries that Mohammed might be defined as 'mad' if she were to let him attend the unit. Once this had been openly discussed and she had seen the other children and parents attending on that morning, she visibly relaxed and asked if she and Mohammed could start as soon as possible.

Mohammed was helped to talk about his feelings, both about missing his father and his belief that as the 'man of the family' he had to take care of his mother. Lubna was eventually able to explain how there was greater significance to Mohammed's behaviour and beliefs than could be understood by simply attributing them to the natural consequence of the physical separation of a son from his father, even in such traumatic circumstances. She described how her marriage was very happy but that she had never been accepted by her husband's family as they were from different religious groups who should not intermarry. Nobody from her husband's family had gone to their wedding celebration. In Lebanon, Lubna had worked full time and Mohammed had been brought up almost entirely by her mother-in-law. In view of the rift in the family, Lubna told how she had felt deliberately excluded from being allowed to care for her son and that Mohammed had even been given specific instructions by his grandmother not to pay any attention to his mother. This was initially how Mohammed behaved towards Lubna when they were together in the unit; he showed her no respect, frequently shouted abusively at her as well as physically intimidating her on several occasions. With a great deal of support from both families and staff, Lubna was able to establish her objective: to help Mohammed distinguish when it would be appropriate to take on adult responsibilities and when to do so would cause him problems. To achieve this there would need to be a change in the relationship between the two of them so that Lubna could start to feel confident in her position as Mohammed's mother and Mohammed could start to feel more secure and be reassured that he need not feel so responsible for the family's welfare.

INTERVENTIONS IN THE CLASSROOM

Therapeutic interventions in the classroom are based on family systems principles; the aim is to make connections between the child's behaviour and the other relationships in the family, to make sense of the behaviour and to introduce the notion of change (Cooklin *et al.*, 1993). Two basic routes to change are used. First, attempts are made to understand the family's beliefs and to explore with them where their ideas might be resulting in their getting stuck. Different information, designed to challenge the family belief system, is introduced in many contexts; in formalized family interviews, in multi-family discussions during the morning education programme, as well as in individual or couple interviews (Palazzoli *et al.*, 1980; Watzlawick, 1974). The other route to change is to help people have an experience of doing something different as an event is happening. The aim is to encourage people to have a new experience of each other which in turn should start to challenge established beliefs (Minuchin and Fishman, 1981). The first belief that is usually challenged is the idea that things are unchangeable. This is particularly relevant in relation to children, where there is very often a deeply embedded belief that everything is hopeless and that nothing can make any difference.

Neither route to change is thought of as working independently, the one is intended to feed the other. Informing the family belief system can be the forerunner of behavioural change and helping the family members to have a different experience of each other can help them to think differently about themselves. For example, there was a 13-year-old girl who was thought of as being totally incapable of doing anything on her own initiative; her parents and teachers were all agreed that she was lazy and incompetent. At the meeting where her failings were being catalogued the girl suddenly sneezed loudly; within three seconds there were about half a dozen handkerchiefs being thrust towards her by parents and teachers alike. The belief that she was incapable was supported by the evidence that she couldn't even manage to take care of her own sneeze. The behaviour of so many people offering her handkerchiefs highlighted how little need she appeared to have for competence; why bother when others will do everything for you? Commenting on this pattern and helping both family members and professionals to curb their unhelpful helpfulness was the starting-point for changes in perception of how this girl was thought about and how she could be encouraged to behave in more age-appropriate and competent ways.

It is a serious decision to have a child removed from mainstream school and so a number of guiding principles have been developed. The central belief is that children should be out of school for as short a time as possible and that every attempt should be made to reintegrate them into their original school, or if this is considered impossible, to help them find an alternative, appropriate, permanent, full-time placement. The intention is that actual attendance at the Education Unit should be for no more than approximately three months; there are occasions when this restriction is not rigidly adhered to, usually in situations where there are worries that undisclosed physical or sexual abuse have happened, or are happening, whilst the child is attending. The period of contact with children and their families is quite commonly for much longer, either prior to entry to the unit, or after the child has returned to school.

The attendance at the unit is part time, for up to four mornings each week. This is designed to counteract the tendency for children who behave inappropriately at school to be forgotten about once they have been required to leave the mainstream classroom. Intervention by the teacher-therapists in the Education Unit is intended to be a catalyst for change, with the wish that any change in behaviour that starts at the Marlborough is tried out and reinforced in the mainstream school. Again, this is not always possible, as many of the children referred to the unit have been permanently excluded from school before the referral was made. If a child is attending school and the unit it is much easier to do effective joint system work, connecting the child and the parents to the actual difficulties the child is experiencing at school, at the same time as, or soon after, they happen.

Approximately twelve children attend the unit with one or more adult family member on any one day. Who attends, and for what number of sessions, is negotiated with the family and the teachers in the school. This is always a difficult negotiation because of the potential stress that taking time to attend the unit might place on individuals in families. Every attempt is made to accommodate the needs of the parents or carers, particularly in relation to employment; they are told clearly however, that the more people attend, the more likely it is that change will happen quickly and be more effective. The children who attend are all of school age, from 5 to 16. There have been many occasions when all siblings have attended the unit, either all together or one at a time.

If possible the children should follow a curriculum set by the teachers in their own school when they are attending the Education Unit. This has the potential of aiding reintegration as an active possibility; if the child's academic performance can be maintained or improved during their absence from school it is more likely that their teachers will look favourably on a return to the mainstream classroom. By doing the same work as the rest of their peers in school, the children in the unit find it easier to go back to school in the afternoon without feeling that they have become even more of an outsider because they have not been able to keep up to date with their work. If teachers are being continually asked to set work and then to record it, it has the effect of always keeping the child under active consideration. As with the brief period of attendance, this feature is intended to keep the child in the forefront of everybody's mind so that the urgency of the need for change doesn't become dissipated. Similarly, the child's experience of the Education Unit should be supportive and nurturant, but not to the extent that they become disconnected from the everyday realities of full-time school with its wider capacity to provide a broad and balanced education within the National Curriculum. The aim is not that a child should become capable of managing in a small education unit setting, rather that their experience of being there should help them to be better equipped to manage in the most appropriate full-time school.

Many children referred to the unit arrive with terrible reputations; Jack C fitted into this category very well. He was 8 years old and it was impossible to find any teacher at his school who could say a good word about him. It seemed that he not only behaved extremely badly but the teachers felt that he was in total control of his behaviour and calculated his actions so as to cause the most damaging and disruptive effect in the classroom and playground. He was said to leave a trail of chaos behind him wherever he went; he was described as bright but unwilling to settle to any activity for more than a few minutes at a time. His teacher complained that Jack always wanted to argue with her over even the most trivial details and to negotiate every step of the way before he would agree to do any work. She said she was worn out by trying to contain Jack at the same time as managing the rest of the class and was seriously considering handing in her notice because of the stress that she was suffering, which she directly attributed to having Jack in her class.

Both the class and head teachers had talked to Jack's mother and stepfather, Jane and Mike G, on numerous occasions. Even though they were said to be very worried about Jack's behaviour, conversations between parents and teachers had made little or no difference to the situation. Jane and Mike G had been married for five years and had known each other for six since Jane's divorce from Jack's father. They both worked and took it in turns to take time off to bring Jack to the Education Unit for three sessions each week. During the early family meetings it became clear that Jane held a belief that she had somehow emotionally damaged Jack by divorcing from his natural father. For herself she had no regrets because, she said, the marriage had not been successful and she was very happy in her relationship with Mike. Mike's relationship with Jack was described as good and even though he sometimes felt despairing about the complaints about Jack's behaviour Mike was said to be very tolerant and understanding. During one meeting Jack suddenly spoke out and said,

'Mummy, sometimes I get a bit confused because it's like I've got two wires in my head, a green one and a red one. The green one is Mike and the red one is my real daddy.' Everyone was rather stunned by this statement until Jane explained that Jack often said the same, or similar things usually at a time when he was about to be told off for something he had done wrong. She described how she instantly felt guilty and incapacitated whenever Jack came out with such statements and instead of continuing to feel cross with him would kiss and cuddle him to reassure him that she and Mike loved him. There were several issues that needed to be sorted out, particularly in relation to Jack's contact with his natural father which to date had been sporadic and unreliable, mainly consisting of occasional large presents at birthdays or Christmas. Jane and Mike successfully managed to adjust the arrangements so that Jack was able to see his father at more predictable intervals. Just as important, they were able to say to Jack that they took his feelings of confusion about 'fathers' seriously, but that there was an appropriate time and place for discussing such things. They told him clearly that an inappropriate time was when he was being told off or when he was being asked to do something he didn't want to do.

On one morning in the Education Unit when it was Mike's turn to be with Jack, Mike said that he and Jane had been talking on the previous evening and that they had both agreed that they were fed up with Jack always wanting to do what he wanted to do without any compromises, and that they wanted to tackle Jack on this issue. As the morning developed Jack was supposed to be reading his book from school and Mike was sitting with him to help him if he got stuck. Jack had on previous occasions shown himself to be a competent reader who was capable of reading the particular book he had with him. After two minutes Jack announced that he didn't want to do reading and that he wanted to paint instead. Mike insisted that Jack continued reading but said that he could change activity when he had finished reading the page that he was on.

The teacher-therapist was close by throughout, talking and supporting Mike as the event developed. The following extract from the transcript of the ensuing twenty minutes illustrate how parents are sometimes encouraged and supported to go beyond the point when they would normally give up with their children. Jack would normally expect Mike to capitulate quickly and allow him to switch activities as and when he wanted.

All Jack's speeches were shouted and Mike's were in a calm, reasoning but firm voice.

Jack: You're so cruel, too cruel for words. You know that Dad, you're so cruel. I bet you're cruel to other children as well.

Mike: I know that, but you've come here to learn. I don't mind taking time off work to come here with you and Mummy doesn't mind either but you're not doing your part. Now come on, I want you to read this page. Look you've already read three lines, you've only got eight more to read.

Jack: Eight, God. This book's too easy. I want to read the other page. You're too horrible, just disgusting, really disgusting.

Mike: You can say what you like to me but I still want you to read this page.

Jack: I wish I'd never come here with you, I wish I'd come here with Mum. She'd be different. You're really horrible, too horrible for words.

Mike: Mum wouldn't be any different. We want you to learn. This is what the teachers are complaining about. You're not doing what you should. I'm not going to let you get away with this, and Mummy wouldn't either.

Jack: She would.

Mike: There will be no pocket money and certainly no trips to Brighton. Now come on Jack, I want you to read this page. You want to be like the other boys and girls at school, don't you. You can read this page easily, now come on.

Jack (spoken very slowly and deliberately finishing up with his face only inches away from Mike's nose): I WANT TO READ THE OTHER PAGE ARE YOU DEAF?

Mike: Look I've had enough of this. Turn round and sit up straight. Now read this page.

Jack (shouting again): OK I'll read it, I'll read it. But only if you'll take your whole hand off the book.

Mike: There's no deals here. This is what you do all the time. I'm asking you to read this page, something which you can do very easily and you're choosing not to do it. There will be hell to pay when Mummy hears about this.

Jack: You're really cruel, really, really, really, really, really, really cruel.

Mike: I know but no matter what you say we are going to stay here until you've read that page.

This style of conversation continued for approximately twenty minutes until Jack started to calm down and asked Mike for a cuddle. In their discussion on the previous evening Mike and Jane had accurately predicted to each other Jack's tantrum-style responses but they had not expected that he would ask for a cuddle. Mike maintained his position of wanting the page to be read and said to Jack that he could have a cuddle after he had read the rest of the page. Slowly Jack started to read the page and with Mike's help finished it in about thirty seconds. He got his cuddle and Mike was congratulated by the teacher-therapist for being so persistent in helping Jack to be successful in a situation in which he had failed so many times before. Jane was thrilled when she heard what had happened and seemed instantly reassured that things could be different with Jack, that he wouldn't 'break' if challenged and that he wasn't permanently emotionally damaged as she had previously thought.

After this event in the Education Unit Jack's behaviour changed dramatically to such an extent that shortly afterwards his teacher in school, who had been so desperate about him, asked if he could return to school full time as soon as possible because she was worried that he was missing too much by being out at the Marlborough. This example demonstrates the importance of developing a systemic understanding of the problem so that the child's behaviour becomes explainable within the context of family relationships and beliefs. It also shows how understanding is not always enough and that sometimes change in the here and now has to be encouraged and supported in order to challenge long-established unhelpful habits and behaviour patterns.

INTERVENTIONS IN TWO SYSTEMS: RELATIONSHIP WITH A CHILD'S SCHOOL AND TEACHERS

Working together with colleagues in schools in order to evolve a shared perspective on a child presenting difficulties is a crucial component of the whole intervention (Plas, 1986). In order for change to have a chance a child's behaviour needs to be understood in a different way, not only within the family but also by their teachers in school (Aponte, 1976). Without a common framework it is very difficult for a child to change unilaterally, often because of the pressures in the class and school contexts for them to remain the same. Throughout the whole period of involvement with a child and family regular meetings are held in school with the child, the parents or carers and the key teachers in order to monitor change, to share new views and to develop fresh strategies. A simple report booklet is created for each child which details the things that child, parents and teachers want to change during attendance at the Education Unit.

It was particularly important to work closely with the teachers of Kevin, Andrew and Jason whose family predicament was described at the beginning of this chapter. Kim's experiences of being the victim of marital violence perturbed several of the teachers and raised many questions about responsibility for violence and the basis of the power relationship between men and women. When Kim was beaten up by her new partner, John, these issues had to be discussed urgently, not only with Kim but also with the teachers, who were all women. Taboo ideas were talked through: what was it about Kim that every relationship that she had with a man ended up with her being badly hurt? Was she responsible in some way for provoking the men in her life? Without raising and rejecting such ideas they would have almost certainly lingered around and helped to fix Kim as a hopeless case who always brought trouble on herself. After John's assault on Kim there were further disclosures of abuse that other women in Kim's family had suffered in their relationships with men in the past. Developing new frameworks for understanding Kim's dilemmas was not only important for her, individually, but was also vital for her and the teachers together, so that she could be helped to prevent the habit of male violence passing unchallenged to the next generation – Kevin, Andrew and Jason.

DISCUSSION

The model of practice described in this chapter is on the one hand very simple in that it seems obvious to get together the relevant people to help when one person, usually in this situation a child, is unhappy, is getting stuck or is in a mess. On the other hand the model is extremely complex in that to work on the above premise seems to go against many fundamentals of how problems are conceptualized in society. In historical terms, using systemic principles as a basis for thinking about problems is a relatively recent phenomenon; over the last twenty or so years these ideas have started to have increasing influence in the psychiatric and social work fields. The application of systemic principles to work with families and schools particularly in an educational context has been even more recent, a view supported by the relative absence (this book and its previous edition being an exception) of relevant literature in this area. As a result the Marlborough Family Service Education Unit is very different from any-thing else currently available in the education context. This difference has enabled the practice of the teacher-therapists to develop in many creative and exciting ways. Many families have been helped to change over the last ten years, most from significantly unpromising beginnings. However, as a note of caution, the benefits derived from being different have not come without a potential price. To be too different from the rest of the surround-ing context can be problematic (Auerswald, 1985) and much work has to be done to explain and demonstrate the potential benefits of implementing a systemic model of practice in an education unit. With the development of local connections and through taking care not to be too different the Education Unit has so far managed to continue to exist and to evolve its practice. There needs to be more training and dissemination of systemic ideas before a unit such as the one described here can develop securely or before similar units can be set up in different parts of the country.

7

THE TEACHER'S VIEW
Working with teachers out of the school setting
Elsie Osborne

It is common practice for most of the work with teachers to take place in their own school settings. This applies to projects described in this book (see for example Chapters 5, 8 and 10). When professional workers are concerned with one or more children in a school, they usually meet there with the teachers, for instance when a child is referred to a clinic or some other outside agency. Local school psychological services are based on their school contacts and the work with individual children is most likely to be carried out on the school's premises. The educational psychologist will often interview parents in school, and Chapter 5 describes a project in which whole family interviews took place in school. Gorell Barnes (1975) describes the advantages in using the school as a place for community-based meetings with teachers, as a way of working with parents who are reticent in the face of clinic settings. Emilia Dowling describes a later development in Chapter 4, in which the school is used as a more accessible base for consultations with parents and children as well as teachers.

The advantages of such school-based work are self-evident: the work of the school is minimally disrupted, observations can be made in a relevant background, children's work and records are to hand, other staff can be approached as necessary, and the teacher(s) can be relaxed on home ground.

Consultation or general discussion with groups of teachers is described in Chapters 8, 9 and 10. That there can be problems, in spite of the advantages described above, becomes apparent in some of these accounts. For example Dowling and Pound, in Chapter 5 on joint interventions with teachers, children and parents in the school setting, describe how incompetent the psychologist could feel when there were interruptions from the telephone, or from children coming in with messages, and how it took time to establish a workable pattern.

This chapter is a brief exploration of those occasions when it can be useful to hold a meeting with teaching staff outside the school, for individual discussion, for a meeting with parents on 'neutral ground' or for discussions between teachers from different schools.

THE NATURE OF THE SCHOOL SETTING

Schools are busy, active communities, and their primary tasks are educational and social, and only incidentally therapeutic. Most teachers would probably agree with Hoyle (1969), who sees the teacher's role as one of instructing, socializing and evaluating children. The teacher works with autonomy and in privacy, and exposure to parental pressure is usually rather carefully managed.

In contrast, the head teacher's role is usually oriented towards the external world; whilst supporting and guiding his or her staff, the head teacher must also pay attention to demands from parents, governors, social workers and psychologists, apart, of course, from the requirements of the education authorities, including government ministers. To sit in a head's office is inevitably to be made aware of this. As commented above, children and staff call in, the telephone rings, representatives arrive and queries are raised about school events. The policy of easy entry to the head's office can help to diminish staff anxieties, but can make the opportunity for sustained and detailed discussion difficult in practical terms. It can also make prolonged attention to one child or family seem extravagant, alongside the clamour for other problems or requests to be considered.

These obstacles to reflective discussion can be overcome, and often are, but the experience described highlights the conflict which is implicitly present in any school between the needs of the school community as a whole, and the needs of an individual child or a worried parent. If the conflict is between a teacher's and a parent's view, then the head teacher has the task of holding the ring between them. Since the head teacher has the ultimate responsibility for the implementation of decisions about the running of the school, then it is clearly appropriate that he or she should generally chair the meetings within it.

A CLINIC-BASED MEETING WITH FAMILY
AND TEACHER

In contrast to the school setting described above clinics are usually organized in order to allow quiet, private and confidential discussions with families, individual members of families and other workers. The discussions relate to individual requests for help, time is allowed for them to develop and interruptions are generally kept at bay. The closed door is respected. The climate is therefore likely to be more intense, on the one hand raising anxieties about revealing problems, but on the other hand, providing time and space to take account of these problems, within a therapeutic orientation. Where the problems revealed include conflict between school and parent, it is now the clinic worker who must maintain a non-judgemental, exploratory stance in order to mediate.

An instance of such use of a clinic as a base for a meeting arose with Mr and Mrs W whose son, Lawrence, was in difficulties at school. The parents asked for an assessment by a psychologist. Lawrence's reports showed a steady worsening in achievement since transfer to secondary school at 11. Now at 13 he was seen by his teachers as no longer applying himself to anything, and not having established himself socially. The comments on his work were sour and of the 'it is time he began to realize . . . ' kind. Neither his parents nor his teachers doubted that he had plenty of potential ability, but beyond that there was considerable disagreement. The parents felt that the school's teaching methods were dull and conventional. The teachers thought that the parents should pay more attention to Lawrence at home. These views had been expressed to me as the psychologist in separate meetings, and I discovered that they had not been revealed by teachers or parents to each other.

The only bright spot at school was in technology, where Lawrence continued to produce some good work. He liked this teacher, who gave him a great deal of freedom to develop his own ideas. He disliked all the rest of his teachers, according to his parents and Lawrence himself. His teachers responded by finding him surly and uncooperative, as well as liable to lead others into misbehaving.

An assessment session revealed an intelligent boy with a great need for expressive outlets for his considerable creativity, combined with a preference for working under his own control. He showed a liveliness and originality of mind, but also how he had to divert this into coping with occasional but quite important gaps in basic skills and information.

During a family meeting at the clinic the parents were considerably taken aback when the extent of their son's unhappiness at school became apparent. The parents had perceived Lawrence as losing interest, as well as blaming the school, and were concerned that he did not care. Lawrence saw his parents as being on the school's side in trying to press him to work, and as not appreciating his feelings of being dragooned and having no freedom of choice. Although the perceptions of each other shifted quite a lot as a result of this discussion, leading to more accord within the family, it seemed that this was now leading to a more unified opposition to the school as bad and unhelpful, and the family sought an alliance with me against the school.

At this point I suggested a joint meeting at the clinic, if the school would agree, as a way of exploring what was possible in the way of help there, and to describe together to the year head the findings of the assessment so far. The school and the family agreed on this same basis. It seemed important that the parents should know what was being said to the school about

Lawrence, and that the parents and year head should think about his work together. Equally it would provide a chance for the year head to put the school's point of view directly to the parents in a situation where mediation was possible.

In the event the meeting began with a long statement from the year head about the school's disappointment with Lawrence. My attempts to describe Lawrence as an intelligent boy, caring deeply about his inadequate achievement and with reference to his enjoyment of creative work, led into a direct confrontation between parents and year head and away from the latter's attack on Lawrence. In particular, it now focused on where the responsibility lay for Lawrence's present discouragement and poor performance.

The anger was controlled on both sides, but criticisms were explicitly made to each other for the first time, together with demands for the other side to do more to stimulate Lawrence. The year head suggested projects should be initiated at home, the parents requested more independent work should be organized at school.

It was now possible for me to point out how much concern they all had for Lawrence's progress and greater enjoyment of work, but to recall how Lawrence himself had described his feelings of being dragooned and to add that he seemed to experience their concern as pressure. Some of Lawrence's more positive aspects were raised and his father in particular spoke with appreciation of many of Lawrence's qualities, and rather wistfully recalled some of his own school-work problems.

The heated atmosphere subsided and there was some agreement that Lawrence might be given a bit more space and choice both at school and at home.

Two or three months later, during a visit to the school, the year head commented that the decision taken at our meeting to ease up on Lawrence had been right, and that he was now working well and there were no real problems. At home it was reported that his father was sharing more activities with Lawrence and this had brought the two of them much closer together.

The fact that this meeting had been held in the clinic seemed useful in a situation where parents and school had been unable to communicate their views adequately, because of the anger this might expose. The clinic setting put the psychologist into the chair, where it was possible to mediate with an authority which was relevant to the problem. The quiet, undisturbed setting allowed time for all the participants to express their views, but also to reflect and develop them thoughtfully. It may also have made an easier climate in which Father could speak of his own recollections of school difficulties. It is interesting to note that the year head took away the message to ease up on Lawrence, although, in fact, no direct advice to this effect had been offered during the joint meeting. The year head's view was drawn from his own interpretation of the discussion, and this may have helped him to take it back to the school with some conviction and to gain the co-operation of some key staff members.

SHARING INFORMATION WITH TEACHERS

There are other occasions when the clinic has been seen as offering an appropriate setting for one or more teachers to discuss a child. That is to say it provides a quiet, neutral setting, free from the pressures of other duties and where the focus on the individual child arises as a natural expectation. Usually these are one-off meetings, in the context of other meetings held at school. In an example of this given later there was video material of work with a child, which the family had agreed could be shown to the child's teachers. In the clinic setting the confidential nature of such material is easier to maintain.

A visit to the clinic may also facilitate an exchange of information about the work of the clinic, and may even help in demystifying what may be a comparatively unfamiliar setting.

The following example refers to Bernard, aged 9. His background was a very troubled one and he had been in care for some time. He had commenced individual sessions with a psychotherapist about 18 months previously and he was now in a class with a different teacher from the one who had participated in his referral to the clinic.

On a routine school visit to check on Bernard's progress, his teacher reported him as doing quite as well as most of his age group. However there were two themes apparent during the visit that could not be satisfactorily dealt with at the time. One was the hostility to his clinic attendances implied by the teacher's comments. The other was the psychologist's realization that the teacher was aware of gaps in her knowledge of his background but this could not be shared in an open staff room, which was where the meeting was taking place.

The teacher readily accepted an invitation to come to the clinic and fixed a time to come after school. In the clinic's atmosphere of confidentiality it was possible to put the facts of Bernard's family situation, the breakup of his parental home and his uncertainty about his future, into a coherent whole. These factors could then be related to the problems that had brought him to the clinic. The teacher went on to share her own observations in more detail, which contributed to building up a picture of a boy whose obsessional striving for perfection could seem encouraging, but which resulted in most of his work being left unfinished, sometimes, indeed, collapsing into an untidy mess.

On her visit to the clinic the teacher commented that she had taken particular note of Bernard's behaviour in the playground, where she had found his relationships with the other children to be very insecure. This was in contrast to the classroom situation, where it seemed that he could manage when supported by a clear structure.

Discussion of possible ways of helping Bernard led on to a sharing of information about the context and role of the clinic and an increased feeling by both participants of being included in a full sharing of information.

The teacher subsequently found that Bernard participated well in drama sessions in the classroom and in turn invited the psychologist to join her class one day. This arrangement was agreed with the head teacher and with Bernard, who was given the task of introducing the psychologist by name to the class and telling her about the work the class was doing. Together they enjoyed his good work in the class; the psychologist noted his poise in presentation and his much more relaxed approach than when seen previously.

It seemed that as the work of the clinic became better known to the school Bernard himself was freed from the questioning about his clinic attendance. Bernard was reported as still spending much of his playtime alone, reading, but was also developing a friendship with the boy he sat next to in class. His teacher had clearly remained alert to his social difficulties and was helping him with these.

This reciprocal joining of each other's subsystems for a brief time seemed to have been to the child's benefit. Rather than blurring roles it had allowed for a sharpening of perception of the relevance of each other's settings and demonstrated respect for the distinctive view and contribution of the teacher.

In another instance the sharing was highlighted by inviting a group of teachers from a primary school to watch (with parental permission) a video film of an assessment session with a very intelligent 5-year-old. The school staff who came included the headmistress, the current teacher and the teacher who was due to take over the class in the following year. The session was towards the end of the school year.

There was relief for the current class teacher in seeing that the psychologist also had some difficulty in managing a bossy little girl, and this helped to create a relaxed and friendly mood. The lessons of the video tape could be shared, including the child's impatience, her failure to listen to instructions, and the way she tried to take charge. These all meant that she often missed the real purpose of a task and helped to explain why such a bright, eager little girl should seem so difficult to teach.

The class teacher was thus given an opportunity to discuss her teaching difficulties with the headmistress, who could respond sympathetically, and together they could offer helpful comments to the new teacher. The interest and the perceptive comments of the headmistress strengthened the links between the staff group. In this case the video itself provided a safe and informative basis for observation, available for comment from all the group. The material was relevant to the teacher's work, but relieved her of the need to start from the point of discussing the difficulties in the classroom that had puzzled her and made her feel something of a failure.

This way of working is not intended to replace the more usual school-based consultation with teachers. It may, however, supplement it on occasion, with useful results. Some indications for externally based meetings include a situation where there is friction between parents and the school as a whole, or where an alternative meeting place provides a safer or more acceptable base for the parents. The clinic or other external agency may also provide the venue of choice where it can conveniently present its own data or where confidential information can be exchanged more easily.

In the examples given I have hoped to demonstrate that by inviting the teacher to become part of the clinic system for a time the understanding of the differing roles of clinic and school may be enhanced, whilst emphasizing the shared concern for an individual child.

WORK DISCUSSION GROUPS WITH TEACHERS

Other work with teachers which takes place out of school takes place when staff from a number of schools come together either for in-service training or in some other way to discuss their work and to look anew at their everyday problems. An account of a course of this latter kind, including work discussion groups of teachers from a range of schools, in different roles within them and from many areas of the country, is given in Salzberger-Wittenberg et al. (1983).

These mixed discussion groups provided opportunities to compare ways of handling many of the difficulties which arise in the classroom, for the members to learn from each other, to sharpen their observation and modify stereotypes of children and of other schools. A new perspective on individual teachers' own schools, their place within them and their relationship to their own staff groups were obtained, and difficulties, even failures, were more readily acknowledged and addressed than might have been possible in each one's own school setting.

During a year of weekly meetings these work discussion groups each developed their own identity, offering an additional reference group and source of support for the individual members. Such a group may be particularly valuable when a school is going through a period of turmoil or change. It may be useful in allowing a new teacher to reflect in a setting removed from immediate pressures, or, on the other hand, in giving permission to a well-established teacher to explore where mistakes might still be made.

In the course of one of these regular discussion groups, meeting weekly, a teacher from a school which at that time was designated as one for 'maladjusted' children, found that the group, to whom she had presented a case-study, had great difficult in sustaining any discussion. The psychologist leading the group found herself locked in an exclusive dialogue with the presenting teacher, and also unable to stimulate any liveliness in the group. When the psychologist asked what the label 'school for maladjusted' meant to them, the group members immediately became more lively, describing a quite horrifying place, to which the rest of them sent their failures, and in which they said they would find it impossible to work. It became clear that they could not therefore share the presenting teacher's experience, nor accept responsibility for suggesting any action. There was agreement that they felt such children were the job of a psychiatrist or psychologist, yet they observed for themselves that the psychologist had no easy answer. In this livelier atmosphere the discussion was able to turn to the nature of the stereotype of a 'maladjusted school' that members of the group held and they could begin to look at the aspects of the teacher's situation with which they could identify.

We may suppose that the policy of mainstream integration for many children with emotional and behavioural difficulties may have made such an example of stereotyping outdated. However the tendency to separate off our most intractable problems in some way or other is most unlikely to have disappeared completely, and the above example may still serve as a useful reminder of how blocked we may become when this defensive approach is challenged.

There is a great deal of consultative work with teachers taking place in the schools, which would share many of the principles outlined here. A good example of a consultation model with groups of mainstream teachers is provided by Hanko (1990). In particular Hanko pays attention to the context of the whole classroom group and to the nature of the teacher–pupil interaction, including the teachers' understanding of their own reactions to pupils' difficulties. The intention now is not, however, to present a general discussion of consultation groups but to describe how teachers meeting away from the school setting can be encouraged to take a new perspective.

Sometimes the task of the work discussion group can be extended to look at the processes within the group itself as they affect the content of the discussion, as in the example of the 'maladjusted school' above. A further development is to involve the group primarily in the study of its own behaviour. There is now a considerable body of literature on group work with other professional and occupational groups (see for example Miller, 1976).

Wynn Bramley (1990), in an article on staff sensitivity groups, explores the use of experiential groups with professionals in order for its members to come to a better understanding of the relationship between themselves, colleagues, clients, their job and the wider context in which they operate. Although overlapping with other kinds of support, supervision, consultation, therapy and education, such groups are seen as distinctive. An example is given of a clinical psychology trainee group. Thompson and Kahn (1970) also contrast group discussion, in which the group process is the focus, with group therapy and group counselling, but nevertheless see it as a helping and educative technique.

Work with teachers where group processes have been the main focus have been comparatively rare with the notable exception of Richardson. In her book on group study for teachers, Richardson (1967) describes the part such groups can play, amongst other kinds of seminar and tutorial groups, in the training of teachers. Maybe she was optimistic when she said, 'teachers are coming to realize that an understanding of the dynamics of personality may not be enough . . . since the group itself has an identity that is puzzling and elusive and that cannot be understood simply in terms of the identities of its individual members'. Richardson describes how a small group 'can become something more than the forum in which opinions and ideas about educational practice are exchanged and scrutinized: it [the group] can become the crucible in which a sample of educational experience can be studied while it is actually taking place'.

As with much of the work with groups at the Tavistock and elsewhere, the foundation of Richardson's work with small groups is obtained from Bion's pioneering studies (1961) and his theoretical account of group behaviour. His theory related to the two aspects of group functioning, the work group which is defined as seeking a structure which makes learning possible, and the basic-assumption group which seeks to escape into an easy or painless way out of its task.

In the course of the work discussion groups with teachers noted previously (Salzberger-Wittenberg et al., 1983), a number of themes were raised which illustrate the importance of understanding group functioning in school. These included the effects of various splits in a school's staff, issues related to the special position of a head teacher, conflict between a special unit and its related school, the problems arising for a school counsellor in relation to other staff, and the effects of school changes on the classroom. The teachers expressed appreciation of the chance to air such topics in a neutral setting, where consideration could be given to whether and how, most productively, they could be opened up in the school setting itself.

When, in addition, a group had been given the opportunity to experience and study its own functioning as a group, including the quality of relationships that formed, the feelings that could be evoked and how learning could be hindered by group tensions, or helped by co-operation on a shared task, then the individual teachers could look at the way in which the learning that resulted could be taken back to the classroom or staff room in their own school.

CONCLUSIONS

It seems reasonable to suppose that most of the work psychologists carry out with teachers will continue to be in the schools, and there is no question that this is convenient and appropriate. Whether the work is to do with a child's adjustment to school or the school's arrangements for a child, or with a family, support and consultation for teachers, or related to the school system itself, the school is the likely base for meeting.

In this chapter I have attempted first to identify some of the occasions when there seem to be advantages in working with teachers outside the school in connection with the children and families they are concerned about. I then look at the way in which groups of teachers from different schools may work and learn together, taking themselves, for a time, out of their own school system, in order to understand it better, to their own benefit and that of the children they teach.

8

SOME ASPECTS OF CONSULTATION TO PRIMARY SCHOOLS

Caroline Lindsey

INITIAL CONSIDERATIONS

The school context

A first step in consultation is to recognize the wider and local community contexts which define the nature of the school, which is also part of the national educational system and hence constantly affected in its practice by government policy. Each primary and secondary school will be defined by factors such as its place within that national system, in the private, grant maintained or local authority sectors; by religious denomination; by being single sex or co-educational; by the ethnic balance in the population served by the school; by its urban or rural location and by its own physical resources as well as the level of material endowment in the local community. The nature of the primary school because of its size, close identification with small geographical districts and the age of its pupils, is likely to be particularly affected by the community to which it belongs and of which it is, in a sense, a subsystem. This will be reflected in the ethos, policies and aims of the school, as well as in the kinds of concern that are the subject of consultation.

The tasks of the school

Although there may be differences of emphasis related to the school's context, all schools have two main, interrelated tasks: to educate and to provide care and nurture. Whilst both tasks apply to primary and secondary schools, in primary schools care-giving is such an essential part of schooling, that without it little or no learning is likely to take place. The development of the pupil's learning is greatly influenced by the nature of the care-giving. But, also, since the primary school years are those most significant in respect of the formation of relationships with adults and peers outside the family, the quality of the care experienced by the children will be a key influence in their social and emotional development.

The educational task

The school provides an introduction to learning within a formal structure. The children absorb a great deal of information about learning from the methods of teaching which the school chooses to use. The teacher's beliefs about learning as reflected in her classroom management will, in turn, influence the pupil's learning about how and why to learn, including how, whether and when to listen. Pupils imbibe the attitudes of teachers towards achievement, success and failure, competition with self and others, experience the incentives and rewards for learning, for example the satisfaction of curiosity, and the ability to read, the emulation of older siblings and the gratification of parents and teachers. The learning of social skills continues to develop with opportunities for a wide range of possible new relationships with adults in distinct roles: teachers, welfare assistants, dinner ladies, school nurses and secretaries, and play with older and younger children.

The care-giving task

In order to learn, children need to have experienced parenting that has been good enough to meet their individual needs for love and attention. A child coming from such a home can be expected to make the necessary transition from the more or less individually tailored responses by parents to reasonable physical and emotional needs and wishes, to the school, where sharing, postponement of gratification, frustration and self-care are to be expected, to a far greater extent than before. This is achieved with the help of teachers, over the period of the first few years of nursery and infant school life. The transition needs to be made smoothly, a need reflected in a comment made by an experienced nursery school teacher who said that the highest compliment she could be paid by a child was to be called 'Mummy'. For the teacher, this meant that she had been able to provide a secure setting for the child, although at the same time she recognized that her role and relationship with the pupil was new and distinct from that of the mother. This need for smooth transition is met by the teachers' willingness to have physical contact with their pupils: with cuddles, sitting on laps, by talking in circles rather than at desks, and by hearing the daily news from home. The increased recognition of child sexual abuse may make teachers feel vulnerable and inhibited about physical contact. Nevertheless, it remains important for the relationship between young pupils and their teachers that there is appropriate physical contact.

For the teacher, the function of care giving involves talking and listening, giving and receiving affection, helping with the tasks of eating, dressing and toileting and maintaining the vigilance needed to maintain safety.

It requires sensitivity and understanding of the emotional experiences of the child in school and at home. To this end, many junior schools request that parents inform them of all major events in the family's life including 'comings and goings"to which younger children are particularly sensitive. For example, parents going away on business or holiday, grandparents' visits, illness and hospitalization, separations and divorce, births and deaths. Knowledge of these events enables teachers to anticipate and understand the consequent behavioural manifestations in the classroom such as withdrawal, tearfulness and aggression.

Teachers of children from emotionally deprived homes are faced with pupils whose most pressing needs are for nurture rather than teaching. Some attempt has been made to alleviate this deprivation, both in the pre-school years and in the infants' department of many schools with nurture groups (Boxall, 1976). A notable example of such an attempt was the unit set up in Langtry Young Family Centre, by E. Holmes (1982) with the specific intention of preparing children for school. Despite such input, teachers working in deprived communities have continually to balance the task of meeting emotional needs with the demands of formal teaching. By contrast, sometimes the teachers' experience of the children's deprivation leads them to make assumptions about the limitations of their learning potential, with low expectations, which in turn may deprive the children further. Even in communities where the children come from materially well off homes, teachers may find that, because of family size, the nature of the parents' work and parental delegation to au pairs, the children have no one to listen to them. The capacity of these children to listen and learn in school is disrupted by their intense need to communicate about their daily lives, before, during and after classes. One useful intervention has been to suggest offering the child a regular time for a brief, private chat with the teachers, which may not always be used, but which serves to contain the desire to communicate, diminishing the disruption of the classes.

Overlapping concerns for parents and teachers

There is, in addition, an important area of overlapping concern for both parents and teachers. This is to do with personal aspects of children's lives that impinge on school life, over which teachers can potentially exert some influence directly or indirectly, for example concern with health, adequate sleep, appropriate clothes, hygiene, eating habits (food faddiness, table manners). The extent to which teachers are allowed and allow themselves to be involved in these matters varies with the inclination of the teacher, the orientation of the school and the acceptance of the parents and with the degree of privation and deprivation of the families. For some children, the discrepancy in child-rearing practice between home and school is a reflection of differing values; it may lead either to an undermining of the parents in the child's eyes (an anxiety sometimes expressed by teachers) or, more likely, to an undermining of the authority of the school in the eyes of the child, which may result in disruptive behaviour at school. The consultant may need on occasion to support teachers in exercising authority in an appropriate way with the parents, in order to achieve the respect of the children. At other times, it may be necessary to facilitate an understanding of the family's perspective. In one case, the school policy regarding medication was that all medicines had to be given to the child by a member of staff. This created intense anxiety in an asthmatic child, who was worried that she would not get access as rapidly as she needed to her medication; her parents and doctors wished her to take as much responsibility as possible for managing her illness. Here, safety precautions were resulting in an experience of lack of safety for the child and responsibility being taken for her, instead of by her. For other children, who have disturbed, neglectful or abusive home backgrounds, school may represent the only secure, safe place they know and teachers may be the only adults who show them concern. In my experience, these children may be regular school attenders, contrary to what might be expected, even to the extent of attending school when on the run from home.

The pupils and their families

The nursery school child aged 3½ and the child entering the reception class at the age of 4 plus are being asked to undertake the complex task of moving each day between the family and school systems. During the first few years of life the children will have experienced their own family's attitudes towards learning, if only in an informal sense. A younger family member will also have had opportunities to observe the approach of parents and siblings to the task of formal learning and therefore will enter school with some pre-existing attitudes and expectations of learning. Children will also have developed a limited understanding of personal relationships based on their experiences with parents, siblings and extended family, which will include sharing, rivalry and competition for parental love and attention or of exclusive relationships in the case of an only child. Children also bring a set of values about acceptable and unacceptable behaviour and accompanying rewards and sanctions. It is self-evident that the more compatible the social and educational values of the child and family are, the less conflict will arise in the children in their daily move from one to the other, and the less will learning be impeded. Children, of course, gain from the differences they experience in the two settings; it is when ideas and values are presented in opposition to the extent that the conflict cannot be resolved, that serious problems arise. However, in many schools, the children come from varied ethnic, religious and cultural backgrounds, with a first language other than English. Often one or both parents do not speak English at all. Lack of familiarity with the child's family traditions and practices may make understanding and communication even harder and this may impede the management of a child with learning and behavioural difficulties. Where schools do not have a teacher or assistant who speaks the family's language the use of interpreters may facilitate consultation between school and family.

Problems may arise in relation to differences of beliefs about child-rearing practices arising from cultural and class differences. This tends to focus on issues of discipline and attitudes to learning. In relation to discipline, parents who come from a culture where there are very high expectations of children's conformity to adults' requests, reinforced by physical punishment, often use coercive methods at home; they see the difficulties the teachers have in controlling their children as consequent on their failure to use similarly punitive and restricting methods. This may result in the question of abuse being raised, whilst the parents see themselves as acting in the interests of their children. The need arises to reconcile what may be their culturally accepted patterns of discipline with the rights of the child and the framework within which British schools work. By contrast, parents who believe that they should place few constraints on their children and give them a chance to become independent, or feel unable to exert their authority, often allow for more freedom than most teachers would find acceptable. Such children, for example, stay out late, watch television programmes designed for adults, and are left to decide whether to do their homework or not. Children with this kind of experience often reject the attempts of teachers to control them in the classroom or playground, and become disruptive.

Conflict may also arise because of the teacher's view that the family has a negative or ambivalent attitude towards learning and study and consequently does not seem to provide stimulation and reinforcement of learning at home. This may stem from a family history of school failure or from a sense of inadequacy because of the parents' lack of education. Assumptions that the school may make about the likely attitudes of a family coming from a particular housing estate to learning may prevent a co-operative attempt to facilitate the parents in participating in their child's learning.

Even when the family and the school are in tune with their values and attitudes towards life and education, parents and teachers alike have care-giving, educational and socializing roles which require the development of a shared approach. Co-operation, mutual trust and understanding of their aims, goals, wishes, ambitions, hopes, fears and values need to be established. It is in this area that there is both potential for a mutual relationship which can enhance the life of the child and also maximum opportunity for the development of conflict which militates against learning. It is in this interface between parents and teachers that the consultant to a primary school can potentially play a part.

The developmental stage of the junior school child and his family

The transition of the child from his family into the nursery or infant school marks a major stage in the family life cycle. It is the first step that the child takes in the outside world towards eventual independence and is frequently felt by child and parent alike as an intense emotional experience; as with all key life cycle events, it is accompanied by a sense of loss as well as gain, of regret for lost intimacy as well as anticipation of potential growth. This transition is accompanied by a widening of the nuclear or extended family context to include the community of families of school-age children; by the opening up of possibilities for employment outside the home for the hitherto home-bound mother; and can potentially alter the balance of the marriage or change the life-style of the single parent. It brings the influence of relationships with other significant adults into the life of the child and the first steps in the gradual move from the family-based system towards membership of a peer-based system.

The way in which the transition is felt by the child and his family will be determined in part by the historical, inter-generational experience of the family of separation and movement from one context to another, as well as by the family's attitudes towards school. In some families, the transition is eagerly anticipated as an exciting opportunity for growth and learning; in others, it represents a loss of relationship, perhaps the re-experiencing of loss by death or separation in current or previous generations; it may be seen as an invasion of an antagonistic outside world, a legal imposition of a hostile or alien culture and environment. Those factors will obviously determine the way in which the child enters school and may affect his ability to attend and learn.

Subsequently, many other transitions will be made in the child's life, from class to class, from school to school and eventually from home to the outside world. (See Dowling, 1980, for a study on the adjustment from primary to secondary school.) How these subsequent transitions will be experienced may be influenced by the way the initial transition from home is made, as many of those who pause to consider the significance of their own first day at school will agree.

Something important for a consultant to a primary school to consider is the way in which the school recognizes the significance of this life cycle stage and prepares children, parents and teachers for it. For example, in one school a pamphlet designed to look attractive to a young child is provided before school starts. It is written in language that can be under-stood by children as well as parents and is aimed at helping parents to prepare their children for the first days at school, and anticipating the

117

expected behaviour and responses from children new to the school day. The pamphlet is in conjunction with an introductory visit to the school as well as a more formal interview with the parents and the child. Throughout this school, the children are introduced to their new classroom at the end of the summer term, in anticipation of the next year, and where possible they will have the experience of being taught by next year's teacher, even though they may already be familiar with her in school. The lesson includes a 'trailer' of what might be expected from next year, in an attempt to diminish anxieties about unknown demands and pressures. For example, in one year a great deal of emphasis on the transition from infants to junior school at the age of 7 plus gave rise to worry about the possibility of very much harder work than before. This was allayed without diminishing the challenge of the transition. Parents are also affected by their child's experience of the move from one class to the next. Another school seeks to answer the spoken and unspoken questions by a meeting at the beginning of the school year (distinct from open evenings) in which teachers meet the parents, outline the intended academic programme for the year and give them a chance to voice their concerns about the curriculum and other general matters. In this school too, at the end of the summer term, a staff discussion of those children likely to be particularly sensitive to the move from one class to another, enables a sharing of previous observations of the same children and others to take place and alerts staff to their potential need for additional help. It also highlights the experience of transition for the teachers, who in varying degrees feel a sense of loss of 'their children', as well as having the challenge and opportunity for a fresh start. Recognizing this enables them to be aware of the feelings of their pupils and the parents.

This practice contrasts markedly with other schools, where no such arrangements are made, where there is a cut off at the school gate between parents and teachers, and where the child only knows who the new teacher is on the first day of term. This may be explained as a way to avoid anticipated conflict with parents about the choice of teacher. An appreciation of how a child experiences belonging both to a family and a school may reduce the conflict that can arise from the inevitable tug of loyalties between the two.

The departure into school may be marked by no more than a kiss and a wave goodbye, to the chagrin of many a tearful mother. But for others, there may be a range of behaviours on the first days, such as crying, tantrums, clinging, withdrawal and silence. Staff may need help to appreciate the many ways in which the move into school is experienced by a child so that this behaviour is not simply perceived as oppositional, naughty, attention-seeking and to be ignored – although eventually the latter is what may have to happen. An attempt has to be made to understand the meaning of going to school in a particular child's family; to identify important factors such as particularly significant relationships for the child with a mother or father, a sibling at home, a grandparent or a pet; the coincidence of starting school and the birth of a sibling; the fearfulness of the child in unknown situations, which proves difficult to allay and is possibly being influenced by parental experience and attitude. There is also a need to acknowledge that not all children may be sufficiently physically and emotionally mature at 3½ to cope with separation. This presents nursery school teachers with a sensitive task, that of helping parents understand that it is their son or daughter who may not yet be ready, not the nursery who is unwilling to have their child. Most nursery and infant schools encourage parents to stay for a while in the early days, which enables children to separate at their own pace. But there are others who advocate 'throwing in at the deep end', which gives the child no opportunity to come to terms with the separation.

There may, of course, be children who are exceptions to these general statements and for whom the tears represent something other than the current separation from home. For example, a consultation was requested by a reception class teacher and headmaster when, after several weeks of term, a little boy was still crying for long periods, whether his stepmother was in the classroom or not. The usual techniques for coping with problems of initial separation had not so far succeeded and his distress was painful for all around him. Information from his parents, in an interview with the headmaster, suggested that going to school may have evoked the child's late-infant experience of the death of his mother. It became apparent that his family did not recognize the significance of the loss to him, although her death had been mourned in the family as a whole. They felt unable to help the child with his distress. During the consultation, the suggestion was made that the child's tears were for his mother and that he needed permission to weep, rather than to be consoled. The teacher was asked to tell the child, 'It is all right for you to cry . . . you can cry for as long as you like . . . how long do you think you will need to cry for today?' This was an attempt to reflect both that he needed to mourn for his early loss and that it need not go on for ever. The intervention resulted paradoxically in the diminution and cessation of the crying over a period of a few days. It also reframed the child's pain for the teachers as a positive expression of his loss and thus contained their distress.

Another issue arises in schools where the class of the child is always determined by chronological age. Teachers and parents face the often opposed social and academic needs of children who for a variety of reasons have a slower or faster rate of maturation than the norm for children in that school. This generates anxiety and intense feelings of responsibility for decisions about the wisdom of delaying or accelerating moves from nursery to reception and within and between infant classes and junior classes. The staff may need help in identifying the most significant factors in such a decision, taking into account the individual child, in his or her family, in this particular class and school.

The slow evolution of a school over time is punctuated each year by the arrival of a new class and the departure of the oldest class, and less predictably, by teachers joining and leaving. Particularly in primary schools, this experience is parallelled by the growth of many of the families of junior school children by the birth of siblings and consequent changes in the balance of relationships in the family. The experience of the mother's pregnancy, the birth of a sibling and its aftermath may be so significant in the life of a child as to produce changes both in behaviour and in academic performance. Inevitably, some of the children will also experience the effects of family breakdown, separation, divorce and remarriage, which also has an impact on their learning and relationships in school.

SPECIFIC ASPECTS OF THE CONSULTATION PROCESS

Setting up the consultation

Certain questions are crucial to the successful establishment of a working agreement between the potential consultant and the school. These include: how has the choice of consultant arisen and with what purpose in mind; by whom in the school is the consultation being set up and for whom and with whose agreement? The request to an individual for consultation often follows a single, helpful experience in relation to a problem with a child or class. The problem may not have been fully resolved or the consultation may have been set up to resolve underlying difficulties which had come to light. Very often, the intention is also to continue discussion of specific problems with other children. It is crucial to the success of the consultation that it is apparent to the teachers and those parents involved that the consultation is linked to the needs of the individual children with whom they are concerned. Even when it is apparent to the consultant that the problem being presented has wider implications for the school or family, it is important that the discussions and solutions are clearly linked to the original request for help for a child, class or teacher. The consultant is then subsequently able to set the problem within the context of the school and family systems. (I have also consulted to a new school, where the task was seen as facilitating where possible the healthy growth of the school as an institution. This is, however, most unusual.) It is also important to consider the warning of Palazzoli (1982) to recognize that the person who calls in a consultant to help is often in the position of the 'loser' in the situation, attempting to strengthen his position in the 'game'.

Following a request for an ongoing consultation the consultant needs to ascertain the significant staff relationships within the school's hierarchy, who is being involved, who is being excluded, and whether participation is voluntary or not. Within the context of the consultation, following requests for help about specific children, definition of the problem includes finding out who is experiencing the problem in the school and its effect, and about similar and differing experiences amongst teachers, ancillary staff and parents. Thus, the consultant acquires information either about the effect of the perceived difficulties in the school or about the effect that the presenting child's problems are having on interrelationships between pupils, pupils and teachers, and between teachers and the head teacher. Hypotheses can then be made about the significance of the problem for the school system and, if there is sufficient information, about the school–family system. The decision to offer an intervention, and to whom, will be informed by these hypotheses.

An area of interest to me as a child psychiatrist is the impact that the discipline of the consultant has on the way that problems are formulated. It is generally known that the presentation of referrals to different 'helping' agencies is influenced by a knowledge of the kind of problem that the agency is accustomed to handling. Members of the same family may present with a child's behaviour disturbance to a child guidance clinic, with backache at the GP's surgery, as a problem of feeding to a health visitor, or as a housing problem to social services. In my experience, there has been a tendency for teachers to discuss individual disturbance in a child with an emphasis on contrasts of pathology and normality, talking for example of 'strange, bizarre, abnormal, peculiar, unusual behaviour', or of a sense of unease in the presence of a child which may be influenced by their knowledge that the consultant is a psychiatrist. Similarly, psychologists may be asked to test the child, produce solutions to behavioural difficulties and solve the riddles of a failure to learn. This tendency diminishes when an effort is made to shift the orientation towards developmental and systemic considerations in understanding the child's behaviour in the joint contexts of school and family.

Another issue which may arise in the course of a consultation is the discussion of material which suggests hitherto unrecognized physical, emotional or sexual abuse of a child. The consultant may then be in a position of having to enable the school to follow recognized procedures, taking on a role other than that which was contracted. The recognition and management of abuse in schools raises many concerns for teachers, affecting their relationships with the children and their parents, including concerns about themselves as individuals, which may benefit from consultation.

The tasks of the consultation

The setting up of the consultation will have involved an attempt to define the aims of the participants, which may be targeted at the school as an institution, a section of the school, a class or a pupil. As referred to previously, any move which tends to reduce conflict in the school system, whether located between school and managers, within the staff group or within the family–school system, will enhance learning and prevent or reduce referral to other agencies such as child guidance. It is helpful to introduce early on the notion of the significant systems that impinge on the child in school and how these can be taken into account in understanding and finding solutions to difficulties. This should not be understood as an exercise which results in a difficulty being explained away by a child's problematic home background, a personality clash between child and teacher, or a hostile relationship between parent and school, about which nothing can be done. Rather, it should be seen as a dialogue in which ideas can be exchanged about the nature of the reciprocal relationships in the school, between children, teachers and parents and their mutual influences on each other – in class, between the pupils, between pupils and teacher, between teacher and the staff as a whole, and between the teacher and the child's parents and siblings. It includes an exploration, as far as is possible, of the family's relationships to the school and teachers, experience of education in general, and the child's position in the family, including the sibling subsystem. In thinking about the boundary between the family and school, family attitudes towards education, history of learning difficulties, attitudes towards authority and possible interaction with the authority structure of the school, and the educational background of the parents, all need to be considered. The concept of the problem determined system (Anderson et al., 1986) may be useful, in shifting the emphasis from the problem being located in the child, the family, the class or the school to the notion that the problem creates a system around it, made up of the people who need to participate in the (therapeutic) problem-dissolving system.

The parents' views about the child's learning performance, achievement and potential, and their compatibility with the teacher's aims and ambitions for the class in general and her assessment of the potential ability of the child in particular have to be discussed. The quality of the relationship between the parents and school in their joint venture is also considered. Does it seem that the family is supporting the teacher's work with the child or are they subtly or even blatantly undermining her efforts in the presence of the child? For example, a chronic case of school refusal was undoubtedly fuelled by the child's appreciation of the parents' dissatisfaction with the schooling she received. Her refusal to attend school regularly served to make them more dissatisfied with the school, confirming the child in her conviction that her parents agreed with her that home was the best place to be. On the other hand, the school must be asked to examine whether it recognizes and respects the wishes of parents for active participation in their child's education. If these wishes are frustrated or appear to be resented or blocked by teachers, antagonism may be generated. This may present as critical comments about reading schemes, the learning of multiplication tables, homework, poor discipline and so on.

The consultant may enable the teacher to recognize and welcome the positive aspects of potential and wished-for parental contribution to the child's education, so that the parents' energy can be channelled into a creative contribution in line with the school and pupils' needs. Teachers are enabled to become curious about the parents' perspectives on the problems rather than to be threatened by them. The consultant may also enable the teacher to present herself to the parent in such a way that the parent no longer needs to hold on to a previously undermining stance. The teacher could be shown how on occasion to adopt a respectful, one-down position in relation to the parents, thus diminishing their sense of competition and rivalry for the child. For example, an ex-teacher mother made demands for extra homework for her son who was thought by his teacher to be making adequate progress and therefore not to require it. She became more and more insistent, as the teacher and then subsequently the head refused her request. The child became involved in his mother's dissatisfaction with his progress. It seemed possible that the mother regretted the loss of her previous successful career and experienced an urgent sense of rivalry with the teachers of her son as a consequence. When asked to work regularly but briefly with her son throughout a school holiday, she was able to recognize his ability to learn at first hand. Subsequently her academic demands diminished appropriately while she maintained an active interest in his continuing progress.

In the same way, the consultant needs to help the teachers to recognize the positive aspects of the child's learning or behavioural difficulties, so that they in turn can help the child to find alternative behaviours out of a sense of choice rather than coercion. A restless, active, intelligent girl from a family with ambivalent attitudes to school was regarded by all who taught her as a fidget and a chronic disturbance to those around her. When it was suggested that this child was seeking a way to conform to the demands of a formal school structure entirely alien to her family and in which her own mother had previously been seen to have failed, the teachers were able to endure and hence ignore her behaviour and recognize that she was attempting to find a solution to what was for her and for them an inescapable situation. As she became engaged in the learning process, her disruptive behaviour diminished to a more tolerable level.

In some situations, the consultant has to counter the tendency to view the child in the context of the school system only. This often arises in schools where the individual needs of children, and family patterns and values, are secondary to the overall goals and ambitions of the school for the body of pupils. In such a school, the children with a different rate of maturation, a minor handicap, or emotional and learning difficulties may experience school as a place into which they cannot fit, from the word go. This affects their expectations of learning from then on. The consultant in such a school may only be able to ensure that those children who do not fit in have their needs met (possibly as a result of a statementing of their needs procedure) separately, within the school context. This kind of response is becoming increasingly common as schools compete with others for pupils and for places in league tables based on academic achievement, the worst result being the rising rate of expulsion.

Techniques of consultation

The consultant needs to be aware of the tendency to be cast in the role of expert on the one hand, and to be decried as inexperienced in the practice of teaching on the other. A non-authoritarian, respectful, encouraging and wherever possible non-judgemental stance is taken; language used in discussion is preferably jargon-free and non-technical; an attitude which conveys curiosity about the views of all participants in the discussion and that the consultant's contribution is only one way of seeing things, facilitates the development of an ethos which values multiple perspectives. Through the appreciation that there may be more than one explanation, alternative solutions arise, providing the potential for change. This attitude of respectful curiosity applies to discussion with parents and about them.

It is at times extremely difficult to maintain neutrality and to avoid 'taking sides' in a conflict. This can be addressed by the consultant discussing the consultative work in a workshop or supervision context.

In setting up the structure for consultations, there is an opportunity to provide a working model for open communication within the school, by encouraging teachers and heads to meet with and without parents, in different groupings, depending on the task, without secrecy but with recognition of the needs for appropriate boundaries and confidentiality. Thus, there can be no hard and fast rule for who should be present at such consultations. Some staff find group work particularly difficult; if it is expected that all staff attend, then this requirement should be part of their initial contract.

In-service training days may provide an alternative context for the exploration of institutional processes, team building and discussion of topics such as a whole school approach to discipline, learning support, racism and so on.

Inevitably, questions about referrals to outside agencies arise. Detailed discussion of this aspect of the work is beyond the scope of this chapter. It can, however, be stated that the aims of consultation in a school may include the attempt to prevent the need for referral, and, where it becomes appropriate and necessary, to facilitate the process of referral so that it is experienced positively by the staff, parents and pupils. Preparation and timing are all important, informed by an appreciation of the meaning for the pupil, the family and the teachers of the involvement in their lives of yet another associated system.

Dual personal and professional roles in the school setting

So far I have primarily considered some of the issues that arise as the child moves between two systems, from family to school, from a role as son or daughter to pupil.

An important factor which must be taken into account in consultative work is that of the effect of dual roles held by adults in the school. For example, there are many schools where governors, teachers, assistants, dinner ladies and secretaries also have children in the school. It is necessary to consider how the 'wearing of two hats' affects, in particular, the work of teachers and their relationship with other parents (as parent and teacher), their colleagues' behaviour towards them and their children and their relationships with pupils and their own children. Similar factors may also affect the consultant, for example, in terms of personal ideology, consulting to a state school whilst sending his or her own children to a private school and vice versa, an agnostic consultant working in a religious school, and the common predicament for professional parents when asked for help by a school which their own child attends.

It is usually unrealistic to adhere to the strict rule that boundaries should never be crossed and that personal and professional lives and attitudes be kept totally separate. It may be necessary for the consultant to help the staff of the school to recognize the effects of the dual roles and to help them to work out ways of managing the boundaries and limits of involvement. In several schools I have known of some highly disruptive or underachieving pupils being the children of staff or governors. It became clear that the way the child, the staff and the mother or father as teacher, assistant, etc. were behaving was partly a function of the confusion in the definition of relationships between the child, parent-teacher and the rest of the staff. For example, in one school the daughter of a governor said, 'You cannot tell me what to do, this is my daddy's school'. In other cases, the pupil would know that the parent-teacher would learn about 'bad' behaviour more quickly than any other parent, and depending on the response this could lead to inhibition or escalation of normal boisterous behaviour. Staff have constantly to be aware of 'which hat' is being worn at any one time. In these circumstances it has been helpful to have people state, 'Right now I am talking to you as a parent' or 'as a teacher'. It has been useful to clarify channels of communication. For example, the teacher might explain to the pupil that what happens in the classroom and playground is nothing to do with his parent, unless it merits discussion with parents, which will only be done with his knowledge. The teacher will report to the head when necessary and not directly to the parent-teacher. The need for restraint on staff room discussion in the presence of a parent-teacher should be respected.

Consultation may prove an invaluable tool in the struggle with the loss of objectivity and the effort to maintain a balanced view.

CONCLUSION

In this chapter I have attempted to address some general and specific issues for the consultant in a primary school. Fundamental to the consultancy is a working knowledge of the school's context and hierarchy, including the definition of areas of responsibility and decision-making and the channels of communication. Whilst working systemically, the consultant needs always to bear in mind and acknowledge the preoccupation with the individual. An important difference from work in secondary schools arises from the developmental characteristics of the life cycle stage of the primary school child and family. This is reflected in the need for teachers to achieve a synthesis between the teaching of academic and social skills and of care giving, in a co-operative partnership with one another and the parents. In my view a major task for the consultant is to facilitate this process by attempting to define areas of conflict and assist in their resolution, thus enhancing the learning process for the children.

9

SCHOOLS AS A TARGET FOR CHANGE

Intervening in the school system

Denise Taylor

A HISTORICAL PERSPECTIVE

In most of the world the vital contexts for a growing child are the family and the school, with the neighbourhood community implicit in both. The relative importance of the influence on the child of family and school have been much debated by professionals, with opinions being influenced by the results of researches exploring the subject from one angle or another. Thus the reports by Coleman (1966), Jencks *et al.* (1972) and Plowden (1967) all concluded that the family and neighbourhood subculture was the decisive influence, with the implication that school could only ameliorate or develop, but not make a vital contribution, by the quality of experience it offered. This seemed to be confirmed by the disappointing results of compensatory education and the many studies attesting the powerful influence of home and neighbourhood, such as those by Douglas (1964; Douglas *et al.*, 1968).

From another point of view, Hargreaves (1967) and Lacey (1970) studied social relationships in secondary schools, demonstrating their power to influence individual performance. They also showed that the internal organization of schools could significantly affect attitudes and expectations of teachers, and thus the behaviour of pupils. What proved to be much more difficult was to control the nature and quality of a school's intake of pupils, evaluate the outcome and compare this with that of other schools. An early attempt in this direction was the study of Power *et al.* (1967) which, setting aside the nature of the intake and catchment area, simply examined the delinquency rates for boys in twenty secondary schools in one London borough. They found the rates in their sample ranged from 0.9 to 19 per cent and that these figures remained stable over a six-year period, and argued that such differences could only be accounted for by factors within the schools themselves. Further research on these lines, however, had to wait until the educational climate had become more positive and robust in facing such a challenge.

From the mid 1970s studies such as those by Gath *et al.* (1977), Reynolds (1976a) and Rutter *et al.* (1979) continued to tease out the variety of factors affecting the within-school experience of pupils and teachers which could be seen to affect outcome, such as academic performance, behaviour and personal satisfaction. It became clear, as Rutter found, that schools have a greater effect on children than children do on schools. It had taken a long time for this to be stated about schools as compared to other organizations. Goffman (1961), nearly two decades earlier, had drawn attention to the way the organizational structure of large institutions, like mental hospitals and prisons, affect their inmates. Argyris (1964) made a similar point concerning workers in industrial organizations.

R. G. Owens traces the history of organizational theory over the last century or more, from an American perspective. He refers to the changes in direction since the mid-1980s with particular relevance to schools. He highlights a collapse in traditional thinking, 'based on the conviction that bureaucratic structures, top-downward exercise of power and centralized control have demonstrably failed to produce the organizational results that advocates of traditional organizational theory had claimed it would' (Owens, 1991, pp. 37–8).

By the mid-1980s it had become evident that organizational culture is a fundamental factor in determining the quality of educational organizations.

Schools and change

These swings in professional opinion, somewhat comparable to the long-standing debate of nature versus nurture, must be seen in the context of society at large, where religious bodies, political factions and governments have always recognized schools and the education process as a potentially powerful influence which had to be kept under surveillance and control. A consequence of this recognition has been government sponsored attempts at educational reform which have been criticized as 'social engineering'. As Bernstein (1970) pointed out, 'education cannot compensate for society'. However, education remains the main route to social mobility and schools can and do make a difference. The fact that some schools are much more successful than others in certain important parameters, has been a spur to looking at schools as worthwhile targets of change. The change implied by these researches is one that would affect the school as a whole, i.e. at the level of the organizational system, and it would aim to achieve a school culture or ethos, to use Rutter's term, which was conducive to the optimal functioning of its members.

However, large systems are no more welcoming of well-intentioned offers of help to change 'for the better' than are families or individuals. To the inbuilt resistance to change of any system some additional forces working against change in schools must be considered. One is the fact that the educational system has long held a position as part of the establishment. As such it has been easier to criticize it in general terms, for example that the selection of pupils is divisive, rather than to comment on the particular, for example that some schools appear to foster and others to prevent delinquency in pupils (Power *et al.*, 1967). Schools have therefore either been deprived of specific feedback from outside the system or overwhelmed by it, and this has tended to push schools nearer the 'closed' rather than the 'open' balance from a systems point of view.

A more promising possibility for change would arise if teachers themselves, individually or corporately, came to perceive certain aspects of their job performance or school organization as unsatisfactory. However, in a corollary position to schools, teachers represent authority. As such they are the recipients of the projections and the expectations of society that they should be wise, just, capable, competent and knowledgeable. It is therefore understandable that the teaching profession should find it hard to acknowledge a difficulty and ask for help – except when this is put in terms of help for a pupil in the light of the tension between these expectations of society and its desire to control or lessen the school's power.

The other force militating against change is the healthy conservatism of head teachers. In Great Britain head teachers of schools have traditionally had more autonomy than perhaps in any other country. In recent years this has been increased on the one hand by the local management of schools legislation, whilst on the other hand new constraints have been introduced by the National Curriculum and standard attainment tests. Nevertheless schools in this country are still likely to reflect the philosophy and persona-lity of the head teacher. Able and strong head teachers, in fact, are the most effective change-agents in their schools, as anyone will bear witness who has ever had the privilege to observe a new head teacher revolutionize an indifferent school. Not unnaturally, heads look on their school as their territory and do not wish to see others interfering with the operation of the school or the attitudes of the staff on their behalf. A too eager proselytizing for change by those who are still 'wet behind the ears' has created a good deal of negativism and a cautious resistance on the part of head teachers who have to carry the full responsibility for managing the organization, and are only too well aware of its wide-ranging influence on the lives of the individuals within it. It is clear that change will be possible only when there is a wish for, or at least an openness to, the possibility for change by the actual people involved. The great advantage of the action research approach to organizational changes – to be described in greater detail later – is that any change or innovation is self-directed by the staff and moves at a pace which suits the particular organization.

Once a system has been in operation for some time, subsystems and individuals tend to become caught up in it, so that conformity and with it the homoeostasis of the system is preserved. Indeed, the dynamics of systems are such, that those who do not fit in are either excluded or isolated and rendered ineffectual. This applies to staff and pupils alike. It is therefore very difficult, if not impossible, for self-generated change to occur. What is needed is some fresh input into the system. Leaving aside the possibility of this coming from a new organizational leader, who is to supply this input and how? The rather indeterminate answer to this question is that it must be a change-agent from outside the system, who, with the authorization and co-operation of the head of the organization, takes on a consultative role. This outside change-agent is usually a professional specialist and his or her team; in industry, for example, this may be a management consultant, a technical or a financial consultant.

The proliferation of the specialist is a by-product of the technological revolution of our time. Thus we have seen the rise of the big industrial corporation with national or worldwide networks, the growth of central and local government administration, the expansion of the National Health Service and Social Services and the incorporation of smaller schools into large comprehensive institutions, all with an accompanying diversification and multiplication of specialists. The rapidity of change (Toffler, 1970) and the increasingly complex and 'turbulent' environment (Davis, 1977; Emery and Trist, 1965) has led to a great emphasis on the fact that survival depends on adaptability – avoiding the dinosaur syndrome exemplified in the decline of large organizations such as General Motors and IBM in the late 1980s and early 1990s. General systems theory, true to its biological roots (Bertalanffy, 1950), explains this increasing differentiation as an inevitable concomitant of growth (Katz and Kahn, 1969) and pinpoints the system's capacity to adapt to environmental change as a basic requisite if entropy is to be avoided, i.e. if the organization is to survive.

As always, industrial and commercial organizations exposed to harsh economic realities in the environment lead the field and are responding by reorganizing into networks of smaller semi-autonomous work groups within more decentralized general structures; the latter continue to provide overall co-ordination, control and support, including a pool of specialists. In education, decentralization is reflected in the education reforms leading to local management of schools (LMS). A parallel process has taken place in the National Health Service, with devolution of power from the centre and the creation of self-governing trusts and general practices' self-funding. The organizations are not exactly comparable with industry and commerce, however, since at the same time overall control has become more centralized, in the greater specification by central government of curriculum, or treatment, accountability and appraisal of staff and pupils or patients.

It is interesting to note that Owens (1991), speaking from the American public school experience, reports that schools are far more organizationally complex than has been traditionally understood. He describes them as being currently bureaucratic in the management of routine aspects but using a human resources approach in the actual teaching in the classroom.

The school as an organization

Before examining in greater detail some of the approaches used by the specialist change-agent or 'consultant', it is necessary to consider the school as an organization, in the expectation that a clearer idea of its nature will lead to more appropriate and effective interventions. As open systems, schools have all the by now well-known attributes defined by general systems theory. One can, for example, identify recurring cycles of input, throughput (or transformation) and output, kept in dynamic equilibrium by means of feedback of information exchanges with a changing environment across a permeable boundary, so that these processes act as corrective devices or regulators. They are, in fact, a kind of energy imported from the environment, the right balance of which is essential for survival and enables institutions to evade entropy over long periods of time, as some of our long-established schools have succeeded in doing.

Schools as socio-technical systems

However, there are three factors in particular which must be understood and borne in mind when working with schools. First, schools are inherently socio-technical systems, i.e. they are open systems in which the technical or educational subsystem is in close and constant interaction with the psycho-social subsystem. The presence of this socio-technical interaction and its importance was originally demonstrated by Eric Trist and his associates in the Tavistock Institute of Human Relations Coal Mining Studies (Trist and Bamforth, 1951); they for the first time applied general systems theory to an enterprise as a whole. It became clear that the 'technic', i.e. the method of working and the way this is organized, has an effect on social relationships among workers and between them and those in charge; and furthermore, that these social relationships in their turn have a profound influence, for good or ill, on the efficiency with which the work is accomplished, as well as the health and satisfaction of those involved. For concise and clear summaries of socio-technical systems theory and related research see Pasmore *et al.* (1982) and Trist (1978).

In relation to schools, these studies underline the importance of the curriculum and methods of teaching, not only in themselves, but also for the effect they have on the social relationships within the staff group as well as among pupils and between them and their teachers. Neither learning nor teaching are possible outside of a network of personal relationships. There is therefore a constant reciprocal interaction between the technical and the social subsystems and between them and the environment, progressing, not so much in a circular motion, as in loops, propelled along a time dimension. Together they form, as it were, an organizational matrix, which acts like a net to hold the whole system together within its boundary. Such a matrix allows for choices, i.e. different ways of achieving the same goal in line with the principle of equifinality: each school will evolve its own characteristic ways of functioning, its own rules, organizational climate and ethos, and reach its own compromises between the technical and the social subsystems in different situations. This is typically achieved by a process of optimizing and maximizing (Vickers, 1965) in the service of the overall objectives and philosophy or 'mission' of the enterprise (Selznick, 1957).

Socio-technical systems analysis has so far been applied in the main to enterprises employing physical technologies. Studies of service organizations have been rare in spite of its obvious relevance to them, the one by Macy and Jones (1976) of a hospital being one of the few examples.

Another exception is Owens (1991); in discussing systems theory and organizational behaviour he says that 'socio-technical concepts help us to understand the dynamic inter-relationship among the structure, tasks, technology and human aspects of educational organizations as a force in evoking and moulding the behaviour of people' (Owens, 1991, pp. 84–5). The fact that educational organizations are *open* systems has additional consequences: two major clusters of forces define their nature – professional standards and expectations plus broader social cultural influences. We might note that sometimes these two clusters may conflict. Viewing the school as an open socio-technical system enables one to see the internal arrangements as at once unique and part of an interaction with its larger supra-system.

Subsystems as groups

Second, as with all systems, schools consist of subsystems arranged in a hierarchical order and in interrelation with each other for the purpose of achieving specific objectives. These different parts of the system are made up of groups headed by individuals so that the basis of the structure is the relationship within and between groups, their leaders and the head of the organization. The leaders of each group ideally act as links (Likert and Likert, 1976) connecting one group to another; for example, in a secondary school each 'faculty' such as humanities, mathematics, sciences, etc. will have its own head and these subject heads will meet together with the deputy head in charge of the curriculum, the latter in turn will meet the other deputies and the head. Primary schools have a simpler structure, with the head in much closer contact with the individual class teachers. Between the primary school head and the class teachers there will be only a deputy, who will also have a class to teach, or there may be a separate head of an infant department. A well-designed structure will allow all subgroups to interlink in a flexible way to give maximum information flow and to facilitate decision-making and planning by ensuring that every party affected is represented.

It follows that since subsystems are made up of groups, the organization will be subject to group processes and the dynamics of group life as well as the power struggles and politics involved in any hierarchical structure.

Schools and individual growth

Third, schools, unlike most organizations, have to make allowance for the immaturity of pupils and their gradual growth towards maturity, which calls for constant readjustment on the part of adults of the socio-technical balance. This is inevitably a source of strain as part of the job that teachers do, just as, for example, having to deal with illness, suffering and death is a strain for doctors, nurses and others working with patients in hospitals. Children inevitably challenge the adulthood of adults and will quickly expose any area in the adult's personality which is vulnerable to a confrontation with immaturity. This fact has been seminal in the development of Caplan's (1970) mental health consultation model and remains a vital factor affecting staff in schools and other organizations dealing with children and young people. There is a further distinctive consequence for schools as organizations arising from the immaturity of its charges: this is the overlap between the task of the school and that of the family, i.e. the nurture, socialization and acculturalization of the young, together with the transmission of knowledge and skills. This overlap and shared responsibility for the development of the new generation creates a particular ambivalent relationship and tension between parents and teachers, which calls for constant attention and boundary management between home and school (Taylor, 1982).

Models of intervention: historical overview

Historically it was the difficulties encountered by schools with individual pupils at the social interaction level (i.e. behaviour) or of the technical level of learning and teaching (i.e. academic progress) or both, which prompted them to seek help from likely specialists. Psychologists devised ways of identifying slow-learning and otherwise handicapped pupils and staffing a gradually expanding school psychological service, which was provided by local education authorities. From the early 1920s child guidance clinics were established (following the American model) where psychiatrists, social workers and educational psychologists worked together to identify children's problems (emotional disorder, conduct disorder, mental retardation, etc.) and to recommend treatment as appropriate.

133

The treatment most often recommended was removal of the child to a different environment and this took the form of a growing number of special schools. Treatment of any kind was scarce, but the diagnosis at least absolved teachers and others from responsibility and located the difficulty firmly in the child. The implication that the school or the individual teacher might adapt more effectively to the needs of the child was seldom acknowledged and followed through. It seemed easier for those who were dissatisfied with the status quo to carry out educational reforms by founding private 'progressive' schools rather than attempt to change established school systems.

With the expansion of child guidance clinics and school psychological services during and after the Second World War more professionals were available to see children and parents and visit schools, but this was outmatched by an enormous increase in referrals and the problem of long waiting lists seemed insuperable. A shift from a direct service to clients or patients to an indirect, consultative service to schools and other primary care givers was an obvious solution.

One of the earliest and certainly the most influential conceptualizations of consultation as a model for change was that of Gerald Caplan. As a member of a small psychiatric team in Israel in the early days after the Second World War (1948–52) he was faced with the problems thrown up by thousands of displaced, traumatized children who were arriving in Israel and who had to be cared for by the state. The impossibility of seeing so many children individually forced the team to develop ways of helping the adults who cared for them instead.

Caplan postulated that workers were more likely to lose their professional objectivity when presented with problems which touched vulnerable areas in their own personality and called this 'theme interference'. For example, a teacher with unresolved problems to do with control was more likely to encounter difficulties when challenged by an unruly youngster, and would probably react in a stereotyped way, according to some personal formula. A successful resolution of a problem created by such a situation would result in a modification in her work in relation to this vulnerable area, which would enable her to deal with similar problematic circumstances successfully in future. Caplan never lost sight of the economic argument for consultation, forced on him by circumstances, that help given to a primary worker to resolve problems in relation to one child would enable that worker to deal with similar problems in other children. He continued to develop and refine his model for the next twenty years, publishing a comprehensive account in 1970 under the title *The Theory and Practice of Mental Health Consultation*.

Mental health consultation represents a shift from the previous clinical model in a number of significant ways:

1 The focus of attention was no longer exclusively the individual client, in this case the child, but was enlarged to include the *setting* in which the difficulty occurred, i.e. the pupil–teacher relationship, the relationships in the class group and the organizational context of the school.
2 The consultant worked with the consultee, i.e. the teacher, not with the child, and the relationship between consultant and consultee was a co-ordinate one.
3 The aim of the consultation was limited to enable the consultee to contain and resolve the difficulties encountered with the client, not to reform, cure or treat the child, nor for that matter the consultee.

Taken together, these shifts firmly differentiate consultation from clinical treatment on the one hand and the giving of technical advice on the other, and establish it as an interventive approach aiming to promote the mental health of individuals in the operation of large systems like schools. It particularly relates to the psychosocial aspects of the system and the special circumstances arising from the immaturity of pupils as outlined above.

Noting that problems were often presented as crisis situations Caplan used crisis theory further to support his consultation model. According to crisis theory, change is more easily brought about when there is an upset in the steady, homeostatic state, such as when people's emotions are aroused. This is an important factor in systems interventions of all kinds, from individuals to families and organizations, the question of course remaining as to what represents an optimal degree of homoeostatic upset.

Mental health consultation has made its greatest impact in the United States. It is a complex and sophisticated model to follow, as it presupposes a sound clinical core in training. Educational psychologists in Great Britain have on the whole found it more congenial to concentrate on consultation based on behaviour modification techniques that remain centred on the individual child. These are no less complex but being based on learning theory are more in keeping with the academic background common to the majority of training courses.

At the same time there were parallel developments in organizational psychology, with social scientists grappling with problems such as absenteeism, motivation to work, personnel selection, work stress and what came to be known as 'the quality of working life'. In the USA, from the early 1920s, the Hawthorn Studies exerted a great influence (Roethlisberger and Dickson, 1947). They were seen as demonstrating the presence and power of informal social relationships in groups of workers in industrial settings, and how these group processes could result in behaviour which undermined the goals of management; this was a finding not replicated in schools in Britain until the late 1960s (Hargreaves, 1967).

From the late 1930s there was an increasing shift in researches from the individual to the group. A great deal of interest was aroused by Lewin and his research team by a series of seminal studies involving group dynamics, for example on the effects on groups of youngsters of different leadership styles (Lewin *et al.*, 1939). This interest was boosted in the Second World War and by such influential work as that of Bion (1961), who drew attention to the powerful influences of a group's unwritten agenda or 'basic assumptions' on the performance of its actual task. The post-war years saw a veritable explosion of experimentation with groups of all kinds, stimulated by public as well as professional enthusiasm: experiential groups, therapy groups, self-help groups, training groups and work with natural groups such as families.

Two developments with groups in particular added to the store of consultative approaches: one was Balint's (1957) work with general practitioners, meeting in small groups at regular times over an extended period, with the doctor–patient relationship as exemplified by the general practitioners' own case material being a focus for discussion. As Balint put it, the aim was to bring about a 'limited, though considerable' change in the doctor's personality, which would enable the doctor to contain and resolve the difficulties encountered in his relationship with his patient; it was not to make the GP into a psychotherapist, nor, for that matter, into a patient at the receiving end of psychotherapy from the group. A broad similarity with Caplan's mental health consultation model will be apparent in spite of differences in technique. Work discussion groups based on the Balint and related models for teachers, social workers, nurses and others in positions of caring for people became one of the most successful variations of mental health consultation (Caplan, 1974).

The second influence came from group relations training, developed at Bethel and the Tavistock (Higgin and Bridger, 1965; Low and Bridger, 1979), the first training conference being held in Britain in 1957. In a T-group (i.e. training group), the consultant sits in a group which is pursuing its task and from time to time comments on the processes, particularly those dysfunctional to the task, which he observes. The consultant avoids intervening in the *content* of the discussions. The technique, used in its 'pure' form by the T-group consultant is, of course, also useful in other work with groups; the Balint group leader, for example, will make process comments when deemed appropriate.

Consultation with a focus on 'process' has increasingly come to be used with staff groups of special schools, children's homes, therapeutic communities and all kinds of helping agencies, as psychiatrists, social workers and psychologists have profited from the greater availability of group training opportunities to provide them with the necessary skills. Process consultation has since been applied to organizational consultancy and described by Schein (1969). The focus in process consultation has moved a long way from the individual client, being firmly centred on the process of decision-making, planning and on the working relationships of the staff consultee group.

Consultation defined

This brief historical perspective on the development of consultation approaches – defined here as attempts on the part of specialists to help organizations attain greater efficiency in achieving their objectives – has shown a progression, from change in the micro- to change in the macro-field. A focus on the individual has moved to one on interpersonal relationships, and one on the psychodynamics of small groups has changed to the interrelationship between technical task and social systems, and their joint optimization. It will be evident that this constitutes a parallel to the change in the way we think about our world over this span of time. A reliance on linear chains of cause and effect characteristic of traditional sciences has given way to a growing recognition of the importance of context and the implications of Einstein's Theory of Relativity. This is a disturbing theory because it provides no easy certainty, recognizes a multiplicity of inter-related determinants, and is altogether less neat and tidy and more complex. Truth is no longer absolute and general, but hedged about with contingencies, even though these are more likely to correspond with reality.

As Owens (1991) points out, there is no one universal 'best' way of dealing with organizational issues. A systematic understanding of the dynamics of organizational behaviour is required to be able to analyse a specific situation.

Consultation from a socio-technical systems point of view, based as it is on relatedness and relativity, must deal with these complexities. It involves the use of knowledge and skills already developed at the personal, inter-personal and group level, together with elements which have evolved from the theory itself, such as the use of autonomous work groups, technical skill development, formation of an action group to develop systems changes, feedback on data and performance and so on. However, what we have discussed so far are theories and tactics and what is as yet lacking is a methodology.

A MODEL FOR CONSULTATION

An action research approach to consultation in schools

For systems consultancy in schools a type of action research has been found a useful operational model. It provides a framework to contain and a structure to guide the complex developments that are likely to emerge on a variety of fronts once a consultation has got under way. Derived from

Lewin (1952), who foreshadowed systems thinking with his field force theory, action research consists of repeated cycles of a progression of steps:

Formulation of a problem or question;
Fact-finding analysis of data;
Feedback of findings and discussion of implications;
Planning;
Implementation of action;
Evaluation.

Evaluation leads to further questions and a possible repetition of the cycle. On the other hand, the cycle may stop before it has run the whole course if satisfactory closure has been achieved, motivation has run out, or it is impractical to proceed. This cyclical process is above all a *collaborative* endeavour. The action researcher does not start with *a priori* assumptions that change is desirable or the primary aim of the exercise. The task of the action researcher is to help the client organization to ask answerable questions, to generate valid information and assist in the making of informed and responsible choices. It may well be wiser to leave things as they are once the alternatives have been considered. This is not quite the same as saying that everything will be exactly as it has been before, and it highlights the distinction between organizational and structural change and change in people. Each stage of the cycle separately and together affects people even if no material change takes place.

Problem formulation and fact finding

The initiative for expressing a 'felt need' or a problem inevitably rests with the client and this is more likely to happen if the consultant is already a familiar figure in the school and has earned the confidence of the staff. The following are examples of initial questions put by the heads of two comprehensive secondary schools situated in different areas:

School A: How can we improve the low attainment of many of our pupils?
School B: Why do we have problems with some of our first year pupils?

After a good deal of discussion among relevant staff the questions were rephrased in a more answerable form as follows:

School A: What is the standard of our lowest achieving pupils and who are they?
School B: What can classroom observation tell us about the interaction of first year pupils?

It will be apparent that behind each of these rephrased questions lay wider issues.

In school A it was the fact that there was no special needs department as such. Each teacher was to tailor the lesson material to the varying needs of pupils. One part-time teacher saw pupils at the request of class teachers in an *ad hoc* manner. An English teacher with an interest in special needs, who had been appointed at the beginning of the school year, found the system unsatisfactory and had already discussed some individual pupils with the consultant in the course of the year. The head was concerned to improve the standard of the school, which had a middle-of-the-road reputation and was not popular with parents concerned with academic performance. The issues discussed ranged from whether the special help given to pupils needed to be increased, to whether there should be a special needs department. The consultant suggested that some data would be useful on which to base the decision and offered to organize a survey of the attainments of the next intake of pupils in the autumn term with the help of a colleague. The offer was accepted and dates both for the survey and a feedback meeting were agreed.

In school B the discussion focused on the transition from primary to secondary school, an area to which the school already gave a good deal of attention, for example by maintaining close links with its feeder schools and by an integrated humanities course which reduced the number of teachers pupils were exposed to in their first year. There were many examples of pupils for whom transition proved a stimulus, but there were others for whom it was a source of stress. Problems which seemed to have lain dormant or were only simmering in primary school became hot issues, which caused a good deal of trouble and concern. One hypothesis put forward was that the problem lay with individual pupils, many of whom lived in troubled home circumstances, which made for difficult relationships and behaviour in school; another was that the group dynamics of the class pushed individual pupils into dysfunctional roles.

It was agreed to mount a project with the overall brief of studying the transition of pupils to secondary school and to reflect on the school's role in facilitating that transition, on the assumption that early attention to areas of difficulty would prevent problems arising in the future. A steering committee was set up consisting of the head of the school and other relevant senior staff members, with the consultant and two colleagues from the clinic. This committee was to take overall responsibility for the project. In addition five educational psychologist trainees were to be involved in the work, with the first year tutors and humanities teachers being seen as the relevant reference group from amongst the teaching staff. The project was scheduled to run from October to June and various meetings of the steering committee as well as a feedback meeting to the whole staff and a final review meeting were timetabled into the staff programme for the year.

To test the classroom dynamics hypothesis the project was to begin with classroom observations carried out by the clinic team. The school was already planning a pupil check-list to provide a basis for the identification of individual pupils in need of help in line with the first hypothesis. This was to be completed by tutors and humanities teachers jointly at the end of the autumn term and included observations by teachers of individual pupils' behaviour, personality characteristics and health. The results were to be analysed by the clinic team and presented together with the classroom observations at the feedback meeting.

Meanwhile the clinic team had to reach a decision about the methodology to be used for the classroom observations. Since classroom research has become acceptable, a large literature has accumulated, with consistent arguments as to the merits of systematic as against ethnographic (e.g. Woods, 1979) observation. The team finally decided to draw up a series of questions to orientate observations, also to leave observers free to develop their own time-sampling systems and to focus their observations as they wished. Some chose an individual pupil, others a small cohesive group of two or three pupils who always sat together. All observations were written up and discussed at fortnightly meetings of the clinic team. The observations included lessons in all subjects in every class except for games, for which pupils were transported to games fields away from the school. They also included a whole day observation for each class and an interesting observation of first year classes in the dinner queue.

It gradually became apparent that the original objective of observing pupils' classroom interaction was unrealistic, since for the most part the interactions that did take place were between pupil and teacher. There was no legitimate space for pupils to interact and pupil-to-pupil contact was confined to occasional whispered comments or requests and clandestine activities carried on when the teacher's attention was focused elsewhere (e.g. one girl showing snapshots to another under the desk).

Feedback of findings, discussion of implications and implementation of action

In school A the feedback meeting included the headmaster, the head of first year and the two teachers who had been involved in the preliminary discussion, as well as the consultant and her colleague, an experienced special needs teacher, who together had carried out the survey and analysed the results.

Low achieving pupils seemed to fall into three categories:

1 a small group which scored very low in reading, writing and arithmetic;
2 a large group with scores higher than the first group but which still fell within a defined remedial range;
3 a small group which scored above average in arithmetic but fell in the special needs range in reading and writing.

It was accepted that a programme should be devised which would enable small groups of pupils from each category to be taught separately. What the groups needed was not only carefully prepared material to suit each individual, i.e. the appropriate technique, but an equally important 'social remediation', i.e. the group would be used to build morale and generate a work culture which recognized the capacities of pupils and their ability to take responsibility for their own learning (Singer *et al.*, 1975).

Further joint meetings took place in various groupings to carry out this plan and incorporate it in the timetable. The consultants continued to make frequent visits to the school for the rest of that year to help work through the implications of the scheme with the rest of the staff and assist with technical information about teaching materials and discussions of methods of teaching, the management of groups and the evaluation of progress. No formal special needs department was set up, although the English teacher was given a scaled post and took responsibility for the administration of the scheme. A simplified screening procedure was worked out and used by the staff the following year when the visits of the consultants tapered off.

In school B the feedback was scheduled for the first full staff meeting in the spring term, after a preliminary feedback to the steering committee. This was a matter of expediency since it would have been impractical to call a meeting solely of teachers involved with the first year. Although some teachers felt that they need not have come to the meeting as they did not teach a first year class, there was sufficient general relevance in the issues discussed to provide interest for all. The meeting, however, was a large one, consisting of some eighty people, and needed to be carefully structured.

Since the feedback on the classroom observations concerned all first year teachers this was given to the whole group. The project team reported that the observations had not yielded useful data on the interaction of individual pupils or on the dynamics of the class group. The main interaction observed in classrooms was between the teacher and the class as a whole. This interaction took the form of a variety of patterns which we called the 'learning styles' promoted by the teachers. The predominant style consisted of an introduction given by the teacher followed by pupils working on their own on a task set by the teacher, usually from prepared worksheets.

Throughout the lesson, therefore, there was no legitimate reason for pupil interaction and the only acknowledged source of help was again the teacher. There were exceptions; for example, in French, music and physical education the teachers interacted with the whole class for a much greater proportion of time and would alternate this with short periods where the class was split into subgroups and set the task of practising together or learning from each other. The predominant style expected pupils to concentrate on their private study and gave the unintended message that pupils were not expected to learn co-operatively or to control themselves.

We subsequently found several relevant studies in the literature on this topic, including a study on the transition of pupils from primary to secondary school by Galton and Willcocks (1983).

The meeting was then divided into separate groups for each class with a double agenda:

1 Presentation of pupil check-list analysis.
   A separate chart was produced for each class recording a summary of the information, the method of analysis was explained and the results discussed. It soon became apparent that the information was considered to be far too confidential and it was decided that the charts should be kept under lock and key by the head of first year. The pupil check-list played no further part in the project.
2 Discussion of feedback and decision on the next step.
   The final part of the meeting was given over to a discussion of teachers' reactions to the feedback as a whole and issues which they felt should be explored further. The minimum 'next step' proposed was for each group to agree on a date for another meeting. There was obviously some overlap where teachers taught in more than one class and not all teachers were interested in taking matters further. However, in most classes there was a spontaneous grouping round the form tutor and the project worker and some of the more enthusiastic teachers.

The second phase of the project dates from this important feedback meeting with the staff. It was evident that if the project was to proceed there would have to be a face-to-face group working together on commonly agreed objectives. The former observers therefore took on the role of facilitators, each with their own class group of teachers. The course of the project now diversified, each class group arranging their own meetings and making their own decisions about how they wanted to continue. One group, for example, wanted to investigate the issue of learning styles further and organized mutual observations of each other's lessons, giving up their free periods in order to do this. The project worker helped the group to organize this and met with them to discuss their experience. Another group decided to share with each other 'what worked' with their particular class, which had been identified as difficult. In this way positive ideas were transferred across lessons. The teaching became less stressful and more enjoyable and the negative reputation of some individual pupils and the class as a whole changed for the better.

In parallel to this diversification of activities, some members of the project team, working individually or in pairs, carried out complementary projects, such as an investigation into first year pupils' perception of secondary school, which involved all the pupils in the first year in writing an imaginary letter to a friend about their experience of the transition; a study of the social interaction of the six partially hearing pupils in the first year, which involved some exploration of the liaison between the attached partially hearing unit and the main school; and a review of the first year tutor system, raising such issues as the timetabling and use made of tutor periods and the selection of tutors.

Evaluation

In school A evaluation took the form of monitoring the progress of pupils in the special needs groups, which was encouraging. Progress was, on average, greatest in category 3 and least in category 1. Feedback from the two teachers taking the groups, from the pupils themselves, as well as the head and the rest of the staff was positive and morale seemed to have lifted. The attention given to the progress of low achieving pupils had sparked teachers' interest in the progress of the rest of the pupils, which was being pursued independently of the first project. The scheme was extended to the second year for those children who had still not reached the minimum standard used for their original selection.

However, this account has a sequel. In the early summer of the second year the consultant received a telephone call from the head teacher and was taken aback to hear him say that the scheme was causing trouble for the school as 'we had not reckoned with parents!'. News of the scheme must have spread in the local community, for the school had had an unprecedented number of 'first choice' applications from pupils who 'needed help'. He was taking up the matter of a more equitable distribution with the local education officer and wanted a supportive report from the consultant. The moral of this story is that no system, any more than no person, is an island.

In school B evaluation took place at the final review meeting, to which all staff were invited as well as at the subsequent final meeting of the steering committee and of the project team. Since there were no hard data by which to evaluate degrees of success or failure of the various aspects of the project, evaluation depended on formal consensus reports from various groups and informal contributions from individuals.

From both the school's as well as the project team's point of view the positive aspects of the project lay in the work of some of the class groups and the teachers' mutual observation of lessons. Teachers appreciated the opportunities for reflection, discussion and planning, which had an immediate relevance to their handling of class groups and relationships with individual pupils. The mutual observations led to discussions about learning and teaching, resulting in experimentation and change which was felt to be beneficial to pupils as well as for the teachers' own professional development. There was a proposal that a lesson period should be time-tabled for those teachers who wanted to continue with the observations, but it seemed unlikely that this would be practicable.

The major difficulty encountered by the project team was the lack of availability of teachers for meetings, which presented quite a formidable obstacle to the work. Since teachers are busy teaching or dealing with pupil issues all day and the hour from 4 to 5 o'clock was regularly booked for different staff meetings this is not surprising. Teachers often gave up their lunch hour or precious free period in order to meet and project workers made every effort to be as flexible as they could, bearing in mind their own commitments. Without such personal effort and commitment the work could not have proceeded.

Discussion

With these two brief descriptions still fresh in our minds this might be the right moment to consider the advantages and constraints of the action research approach to school consultation.

Constraints of the action research approach

1 Action research is usually slow to get off the ground, at any rate from the client's point of view. But this is necessarily so, as establishing a colla-borative relationship is invariably time-consuming and difficult. Schools have a culture of action and lengthy discussions at the beginning of anything happening are not congenial. The use of a questionnaire early on can sometimes speed up this stage.
2 Competing bids for staff from different outside agencies can interfere with a proper engagement with any one of them. The school which has many consultants going in and out looks a lively, busy and vital place. Froth can indeed be fun, but when it dies down leaves hardly a trace.
3 The presenting problem may not be the most important problem or remain the only problem. The consultant must stay alive to the impli-cations of reframing and the need for constant revision of the contract and in particular the renegotiation of sanction to keep pace with developments.
4 The timing and method of feedback is crucial, but the consultant may have little choice about its timing because of the constraints of the timetable and having to choose a date far ahead.
5 The dual goals of action research can be conflicting. There can be a varying emphasis either on the action or the research component and the latter can be at different levels. In the examples cited the research yield was mainly, though not altogether, specific to the particular situations. Even so, the demands for help and for action can conflict with the

demands of fact finding and research, especially if one person is to fulfil both. The solution then is to split the roles between two people.

6 The final point concerns consultation and altruism. There is a profound conviction in our culture that valid, unadulterated assistance or counsel, be it from a neighbour, friend, therapist or consultant, must be disinterested, all-giving and non-receiving. The prototype is presumably the idealized mother who takes care of the needs of her child with no thought to her own. We know, of course, that things are more complicated than that, but the ideal lives on. Until recently it was more difficult for community service organizations like schools to keep a realistic view of the 'consulting contract'. Now, public service organizations have to operate, like industry, in the 'market place' and the consultancy fee has to be explicit and form part of the preliminary negotiations.

In most cases the consulting team will approach the task with enthusiasm and commitment, generated by the desire to prove itself and perhaps to produce a good piece of research, while the client organization may be ambivalent; it will wish to have its problems solved, but will want this to be at the least expense in terms of change. However, the concrete barrier to unrealistic expectations – the fee – will be missing in the case of the public institution.

Related to this issue were the attitudes expressed about our use of educational psychology trainees as a resource for consultation projects in schools. The Tavistock Clinic provides a direct and indirect mental health service and is also a research and a major postgraduate training institution in this field. A large part of its services are provided by the members of training programmes, just as is the case with trainee nurses and doctors in hospitals. However, in schools the consulting team's motivation has been called into question by a remark indicating that the primary objective of its involvement is to provide a learning experience for trainees rather than for the organization. It would be interesting to see whether such feelings are more pronounced in the case of educational psychology trainees, who have, until entering the course, been operating as teachers in schools.

Advantages of action research

1 An obvious advantage is that action research combines research and application. It can be likened to the discovery method of learning or learning from experience. The fact finding, being tailored to the particular needs of the organization at the time, is immediately relevant and available for processing by the system.
2 Action research looks at whole phenomena and promotes change at the system level. Whichever slice of the organizational cake is taken as the starting-point, it will inevitably contain elements pertaining to the whole

and once set in motion, the fact finding feedback process gathers its own momentum and spreads through the system, eventually leading to a process of self-generating change.

3 Being based on collaboration, action research is not something that one party does to another. Rather, it is a natural evolution to which both parties contribute, leading to development and growth. In this sense it has no end, only punctuation marks.

Tactics and techniques

If action research provides a methodology for consultation to socio-technical systems, what are the tactics and techniques which would help the researcher? Some tactics have already been mentioned in passing, such as the reframing of problems and questions and the need to keep the contract up to date to ensure continuous sanction (Clark, 1972). Others are role analysis (e.g. of special needs teachers and tutors), boundary management (e.g. forming small special needs groups) and analysis of the socio-technical system (e.g. class observations, survey).

Techniques, by which here is meant how best to conduct oneself in a consulting relationship, are seldom explicitly described by social scientists. Concerns with technique seem to belong to clinicians, who are perhaps somewhat inclined to anthropomorphize the institution and treat it like a patient. However, techniques cannot be transferred wholesale from one system to another, as Palazzoli, best known for her innovatory work with families, discovered in her researches on consulting to large systems (Palazzoli et al., 1976, 1983).

System change and action research

The mechanism whereby action research sets in motion an evolutionary growth process is in fact the same as occurs naturally in open systems existing within an environment, i.e. it is triggered by feedback and followed by adaptive change within the system.

Feedback, in the form of information, produces, as it were, a state of cognitive dissonance (Festinger, 1958) within the members of the system who then have to strive to achieve a resolution of the dissonance by adapting to the changed situation. Action research succeeds best when there is already some dissonance felt within the system owing to feedback from the environment that all is not well, i.e. when there is a natural underpinning. If this 'felt need' in the client is low for whatever reason, the probability is that action research will not make a significant impact, since the spur for adaptation, i.e. change, will be lacking. If the dissonance is acutely felt it constitutes a 'crisis', and motivation to change is likely to be greater.

We know that change in human beings is a complex process involving, amongst more pleasant reactions, resistance, anxiety and stress (see for example, Marris, 1974). People have to let go of old attitudes, assumptions and behaviour before they can take on new. There are, of course, alternatives available as to what the new should be, the choice being ultimately related to which model of humanity and which values are preferred. Every institution develops its own philosophy and one of the functions of leadership is to define and redefine this philosophy and make it explicit. It is part of the consultant's job to facilitate this task. An institution's philosophy exerts a powerful influence on its members and shapes the organizational culture. Any change in organizational practice must be in line with its philosophy, otherwise the 'culture' of the organization will not constitute a good host for the embryo of change to grow and any changes that are introduced will 'wither away', as Bain (1982) puts it so graphically in the beautiful action research described in *The Baric Experiment*.

Meanwhile, developments in technology, such as the advent of the microchip, are having fundamental repercussions on society, introducing a new socio-technical paradigm of work, in Kuhn's (1970) sense of the word, not just a variant of what has gone before, i.e. not first order change, but a work culture which is different in kind, demanding second order change (Emery, 1982; Watzlawick *et al.*, 1974).

These developments have profound implications for education. It is time to think seriously about how schools can adapt to the changing demands on them so that they will continue to fulfil their function of preparing future generations of young people for changing environmental conditions.

10

CONSULTATION TO SCHOOL SUBSYSTEMS BY A TEACHER

Muriel Barrett

A number of inner-city education authorities are no longer able to make special provision for children with special educational needs (SEN). Even when statementing procedures are completed, many children have to be contained in classes that may become too large to meet their needs. Many are excluded from the school system and since the Education Reform Act 1988 increasing numbers of excluded children are becoming members of subculture subsystems outside school.

Teachers express increasing concern about the education of children and young people who, from their behaviour in school, are thought, or known, to be suffering distress. This may involve integrating into more than one family, or into a different culture; experiencing physical, sexual or emotional abuse; facing unemployment; living in bed-and-breakfast accommodation or in inadequate housing; contemplating suicide or having to manage the sudden loss of primary care givers (attachment figures).

Many of these children feel angry, betrayed and unsupported by the adults most important to them in their family systems. For some, belonging to a school system provides a substitute base that is secure because they experience consistent and caring behaviour from adults and, generally speaking, are accepted by their peers. They may be unable to give their attention to cognitive tasks and as Maher (1987) found, many abused children find their scholastic skills are adversely affected. However, consciously or unconsciously, many of these children value what the school has to offer (Hetherington, 1991).

THE EXTENDING ROLE OF TEACHERS

The majority of teachers are skilled practitioners who provide a classroom atmosphere that is conducive to learning, and play, for children of all school ages. Most teachers enjoy teaching and show a capacity for caring: caring about their professional standards; noting how cognitive skills relate to individual ability; planning creatively and, of equal importance, monitoring the social interaction of children with their peers and adult members of the school.

Currently teachers are under increasing pressure from society to extend their roles. Not only is there an expectation that they can prove their didactic skills, by meeting the requirements of the national curriculum, but also that they reach a high level of skill in understanding and managing children's behaviour, in particular those described as having special educational needs (Education Act 1981).

In 1990 the National Children's Bureau published an introduction to the Children Act 1989. Under the heading 'Policy and practice in education' it stated that over 42,000 children are in care and there are 'many more at risk of abuse'. The emphasis on 'interagency co-operation' and 'working in partnership with parents' which is regarded as a major theme of the Act is particularly relevant to teachers who have day-to-day responsibility for 15,000 hours at least of secondary-age children's lives (Rutter *et al.*, 1979). The majority stand at the interface of many children's two systems, family and school, and will need to understand this legislation if they are to safeguard the interests of children with whom they work.

With the implementation of the national curriculum, teachers themselves may feel they are becoming learning-disabled. There is an expectation that they will be able to inculcate an excitement about learning at the same time as having to help disenchanted children of all abilities to attain certain prescribed national levels of achievement.

A TEACHER IN THE ROLE OF CONSULTANT

Attachment theory (Bowlby, 1969, 1973, 1980) has informed my work both as an educational therapist (Barrett and Trevitt, 1991) and in my role as a teacher consultant. This role symbolizes a secure base from which members of my own profession can explore their work with children and young people, whose behaviour is often chaotic and destructive. The consultation provides a working space in which to examine the here and now of an interactive process. Exploratory behaviour fosters their questioning of self as a member of different systems and leads to an awareness of their own internal working models, an image of self with other. The concept of separation includes anger, sadness and loss. Consultees can examine these feelings through the experience of the breaks and endings in their work with a consultant and think about what similar experiences mean to the children they are teaching. If members of a subsystem can update or re-assess their internal working models of self with other, a potential for change becomes available to them.

A teacher in a consultative role attempts to facilitate the capacity of other teachers' learning by exploring the process of their interactive practice with children and adults. Consultant and consultee can discover how they make use of their teaching skills and themselves as a tool. They can develop an awareness of the feelings elicited in them by the behaviour of others, and understand their own response to it. The questions can then be asked: Can behaviour reflect the feelings that exacerbate or ameliorate a child's anxiety and attitude to teachers and learning? Do their own reactions have an impact on a child?

I have found, in my work with individual teachers, that they feel under additional pressure because they are working with children whose behaviour and cognitive skills are unacceptable to the whole system. They can feel de-skilled, and lack confidence in their ability to understand the children they are teaching.

How then can a member of their own profession enable classroom, advisory or learning-support teachers, or classroom assistants, to gain 'psychological' insights? Schools, in some areas, make use of the clinical training and experience of members from other professions (Hanko, 1990).

A teacher in a consultative role arrives as an unknown quantity at a first meeting with the consultees, and may constitute a threat: 'Here is a member of our own profession who knows something we do not.' Being known to be a practising teacher, but representing a health service institution which could be perceived as non-educational, has frequently resulted in an ambivalent reaction from consultees.

PREPARING A SECURE BASE FOR LEARNING: INTRODUCTIONS

I usually begin by recounting my experience of mainstream primary teaching, and my work with learning-disabled secondary school groups in on- and off-site units, relating these to experiences we have in common. I then outline my clinical work with individuals, peer groups, families and community workers.

During the introductory period I have found that one is less likely to 'succeed' when working with a subsystem if some attention is not paid to the whole. It is important to spend time learning about the culture of the whole organization, the belief system and hierarchical structure as well as the lines of communication and boundaries as described in Chapter 1. It is of paramount importance to discover a subsystem's understanding of what the consultation process can achieve, and also how it sees its role in the context of the larger system of which it is part.

ATTEMPTS TO ENGAGE A GROUP IN A SUBURBAN PRIMARY SCHOOL

The three county advisers responsible for the management skills and policy of a school's special educational needs provision invited me to consult to a group consisting of junior school SEN staff; they were the deputy head teacher, who was acting head for one term, the infant head teacher and one adviser.

I met the three advisers on three occasions to discuss the feasibility of undertaking this task. One adviser took direct responsibility for liaising with the education office, the school psychologist and an SEN inspector. I was informed that the SEN teachers had expressed concern about the differing rates of 'intellectual and emotional' development of children in the school. My intended approach and management details were discussed in these meetings. This led to an informal visit to the school to meet the teaching staff, ancillary workers and children and to 'observe the school at work and at play'. The children were racially mixed, the majority coming from high-rise flats which almost encircled the two single-storey buildings.

At my final meeting with the advisers I was presented with a title for my 'course'. Arrangements were confirmed in writing, stating that my work would begin in the following term. Prior to the first meeting I telephoned the school, and arrived at the confirmed time and date in the room designated for our work together.

On my arrival at the school meeting we were informed by the head teacher that, (1) the adviser had not arrived; (2) she knew nothing about the arrangements which had been made during her absence in the previous term; (3) there was a crisis involving parents, police, the deputy head, two class teachers and the school keeper; and, finally, there was to be an important local education authority (LEA) meeting which she and two teachers wanted to attend.

The mayhem that followed these statements took some time to subside. I sat down, took out my papers and waited. The group continued to discuss amongst themselves; some were seated, others moved in and out of the room and the activity continued in the corridor. A child entered and left. I felt anxious but had plenty of time to observe the interactive behaviour of the group and wondered how I would engage them. Defining and agreeing a primary task can take an inordinate amount of time unless one can discover a channel of openness within the membership of the group. How then could I begin to harness what Richardson (1975) refers to as the 'emotional forces' of this apparently disparate group? Their energy seemed to be flowing at a highly defensive level. Were they operating in an emotionally negative mode and therefore unable to take in my words at a cognitive level (see Bowlby, 1985)?

The channel of openness came in one teacher's apology for the mayhem. My response was to announce (I use this word advisedly), that, as our time was now already limited, perhaps we could begin. Time seemed to be the only boundary available to contain some of the feelings emanating from the group in front of me. The junior head teacher left.

I re-introduced myself, mentioned my institution and my professional background, gave a brief account of my current work and then said that I understood they were interested in considering how the rate of the physiological development of junior school children may affect their emotional and intellectual development. The announcement of the topic resulted in everyone speaking at once but not to me. I reflected on my role. Were they testing out my ability to 'teach' them how to manage difficult children and reluctant learners by behaving in this way themselves? This thought seemed very relevant to the situation that I found myself facing and being a part of, and led me to question two other aspects of my position. Could the situation in some way be reflecting the attitude from the teaching profession in more general terms about the role of specialist teachers? And, what had been the hidden agenda of the advisers whose role would not usually encompass advising on emotional development?

How then to establish a secure base? My self-as-system as defined by Duhl (1983) enabled me to contain my own anxiety about how to proceed. I felt excluded, but remained in touch with a capacity to function and stay with the task. When I expressed my regret that we seemed unable to begin, a response came from the teacher who had earlier made an apology on behalf of the group. She asked if I would share the source of my information relating to the title of the 'course'. To give myself a thinking space I repeated the title. I said I understood the request had arisen out of a conference that some of them had attended. Everyone at once exchanged views, while I was totally ignored.

I waited and listened to the exchanges and made eye contact with a few teachers. When I asked if they were prepared to share their views with the whole group no one took up this option. I empathized with their confusion as there seemed to be some misunderstanding as to the purpose of our meetings but asked if we could use the time left to us to decide whether or not we should contemplate working together (see Conoley and Conoley, 1982).

I tried to contain some of the hostile feelings, apparently aroused by my words, although possibly attributable to the sudden arrival of the adviser. The reactions to my question were mixed. Two people left immediately, without expressing an opinion, to attend the local education authority meeting mentioned earlier. One member addressed me but directed her criticism to the adviser who had arranged two such important meetings at the same time. Another said, 'What you said was very interesting but it can't help us. We talk to one another all the time, we don't need these meetings.' This teacher seemed able to voice openly some of the group's hostility. This critical outburst silenced the group, although some nodded agreement. The 'open channel' member attempted to lead the group into a continuation of the task. She stated firmly her personal reservations about my approach to working with children, but conceded that they knew very little about their emotional development. This was contradicted by the most overtly hostile member who reiterated her statement that they did nothing but talk about the children they taught. The tone of the general discussion gave me the impression that all members were at least now engaged in a common task so I posed the question, 'Should we try to work together?' This was answered by the 'open' member who re-stated her scepticism and proceeded deftly to criticize her colleague: 'Yes, we do indeed talk about children in our breaks, but I feel that these discussions contain little that is constructive about how to manage or understand emotional outbursts.' Was she questioning my lack of constructive management of the group who appeared to be demonstrating such behaviour?

Our allocated time had elapsed and I suggested that we met once more to explore the possibilities of working together but that we may discover that it was not feasible. I thanked them for staying with me to clarify what had clearly been a misunderstanding of the brief by most of the participants.

The realization that I too had been misled in some way as to the real nature of the consultative work enabled me to recognize the similar feelings emanating from the group. In subsequent meetings I stayed with the anger of the group, which sometimes developed inappropriate subsystems or became interlocked in critical conflict or retreated into non-communication. Each individual was in danger of interacting in a dysfunctional manner, and placing the blame on to the whole system or those outside it. The group worked hard, wrote up and discussed its work, and this led to a recognition of its members' interdependence.

We found a secure base in the presentation of a child with a medical condition about which I knew nothing. By sharing the anxious feelings aroused by the concept of 'not knowing' the group began to explore and play with ideas which led to an open communication between the school's two systems.

My work in this primary school led me to recognize what factors affect a group's ability to become a creative source of a working interaction. Is the consultation imposed on a subsystem by what Apter (1982) called 'outside resource people and change agents', or does it arise from within a group? The imposed approach may imply a lack of confidence in the professional competence of a system or subsystem; the self-selected approach seems to ease the point of entry.

THE IMPOSED APPROACH IN AN INNER-CITY COMPREHENSIVE SCHOOL

A newly-appointed head of a special educational needs department, Mr B, and I had been invited, for the first time, to a regular meeting between the head teacher, the school's year heads and a child psychologist from the local family health clinic. It was known that I came from the same institution but was a teacher. The meeting was to review the past year's work and to plan for next year's intervention. During this meeting a proposal was made that I should offer consultation to Mr B's department, where his appointment was welcomed. It was reported that the SEN subsystem had previously been a failure.

Immediately after the meeting I approached Mr B and shared my misgivings about the manner of our introduction and that we had been presented with the *fait accompli* that we would be working together.

We met a week later and Mr B, initially, seemed very reluctant to have 'my' consultation imposed upon him. I suspected this was partially due to my being another teacher who was working outside a school system. Sensing his unease, I suggested that he might not yet feel ready to take on a regular commitment until he had established himself in a school and a role that was new to him, but he welcomed the opportunity to discuss the children for whom he was now responsible in his first appointment to an inner-city school. We arranged a meeting with his staff, some of whom were part time and agreed that I would meet the head teacher to outline our proposals and to confirm the arrangements in writing.

The point of entry: Resistance to the establishment of a secure base

I was welcomed and introduced to Mr B's department staff and talked about my teaching and clinical work. The group's response was one of interest. They readily agreed to give a weekly individual 'presentation' of their work and immediately began to formulate their current practice and timetabling problems. Their open manner led me to assume that my preparatory meeting with Mr B meant that the group would be readily engaged. This assumption proved to be correct for every member except Mr B. Certainly I had either overlooked or had not sufficiently acknowledged this man's 'needs'. I noted his apparent resistance to learning. He was unable to accept any comments made by me about anyone else's contributions. Everything was questioned and ideas doubted; his manner became rather hostile.

Individual exploratory behaviour

Mr B was the last member to discuss his work, in a presentation that illustrated not only a blocking out of feelings, but included an unwillingness to explore cognitively. I was reminded of children who are resistant to learning as described by Barrett and Trevitt (1991). This highly skilled, organized and dedicated head of an SEN department hesitantly began his presentation. He justified his reluctance to discuss the child by saying that he had been prevented from doing so, either because he was always being called to meetings or because the child was absent. He eventually described the child in question as 'disruptive in class and one who is very difficult in my group'. His notes were written on pieces of scrap paper and he gave such minimal information that there was very little material on which the group could work. One teacher said the child resisted producing any work for her. The presentation ended with a rather aggressive slapping down of his brief notes on the table as he stated that there was nothing to say about the boy.

By his nonverbal communication and withholding of material I felt my teaching skills were being challenged by Mr B. His staff seemed unusually inhibited but said the boy was intelligent. When I expressed my thoughts about the angry frustration that this boy's behaviour would elicit in me, other group members began to think about their own interaction with him. They acknowledged that it was difficult to teach him because he did not easily relate to his peers. By focusing on the triggers of interactive behaviour that were thought to exacerbate the boy's resistance to completing a task, we discussed the use of games, drawing, modelling, or stories, that might encourage the boy to express his feelings and to relate to his peers more appropriately. (Educational materials provide a boundary within which children feel it is safe to express feelings about cognitive tasks, self and others.)

The following week Mr B immediately talked about the boy he had presented. He reported that by hearing that we had been able to empathize with the boy's behaviour, and at the same time acknowledge our own feelings, he had recognized how angry and incompetent the boy had made him feel and that he, subsequently, had a much better week with him. Mr B discovered, during a discussion about the children's projects, that the boy could not tolerate hearing that another child's work was better than his and, rather than 'fail', he did not try. (By my indirect comments about children's interactive behaviour the consultees reflect on their own interactions with me and each other.)

Updating internal working models

From this time Mr B and his group of full- and part-time teachers developed as a dynamic subsystem who directly challenged my views about the links between behaviour, feelings and learning.

The group suddenly decided it needed more information about the family systems of children being discussed. This request led to an interesting turning point. The teachers recognized that having more details of the children's history could lead only to speculation about how this could be affecting their behaviour in a school and could detract from focusing on the here and now of teaching and learning. The work remained within the boundary of the subsystem for several months, with occasional verbal flurries into the status of the specialist teachers *vis-à-vis* the whole staff group. (It may be recalled that the special needs subsystem prior to Mr B's appointment had been deemed a 'failure'.) Occasionally the group expressed their dismay that subject teachers made no allowances for 'their' children's difficulties.

Mr B seemed surprised when I asked if he had thought of inviting a subject teacher to join us for part of a meeting when a particular child was to be discussed. I had the impression that he was even more surprised when these invitations were accepted and serious thought was given to his staff's opinions. There was one exception, a head of the history department, who verbally dismissed a boy, Sean, as 'a waste of space'.

Separation: subsystem *vis-à-vis* the whole system

After an Easter break a serious difference of opinion between the special needs staff group and the above-mentioned history department head was aired. The subsystem with which I was working realized it had some 'power' *vis-à-vis* the whole system.

The issue related to a form of punishment for the boy Sean who 'disappeared' before a history lesson; he had visited a local paper shop. The head of history had told Sean that he could not leave the school premises during school hours, even to play football, a game at which he excelled. On the same day the boy had been told that the SEN department was to visit the local football club as part of a project. Parental permission had been sought, and granted, for this outing. Sean was left feeling confused and upset.

Mr B requested a meeting with the head teacher and the history department head; here he offered to speak to Sean's mother to discuss the matter. He had brought to this meeting the project work done by Sean about football and commented favourably on his progress. The head teacher accepted the comment and the offer; an alternative punishment was found for the boy.

In the group Mr B asked for a discussion on how to talk to parents. From this arose some work on the limits of what can be achieved by a subsystem, which emphasized what could be achieved at the interface between a school and a family system at a time of crisis (Steele and Raider, 1991).

THE SELF-SELECTED APPROACH

A member of staff, Mrs J, from a special unit in the same school, had twice joined the consultations, described above, when children with major emotional and social skills problems were being considered for referral to her unit. A majority of them were in trouble with the law.

Mrs J telephoned me at the clinic to say she liked the way I worked and wanted an appointment to discuss consultation to her unit. Our meeting began with a straightforward statement: 'We need your help.' The staff members' prime concern was the children's peer group dynamic and their own interactive role within the unit. She wished to discuss her department's role in the whole school system, its relationships with the school's other subsystems and with the community. She expressed some confidence about its contact with parents.

The SEN head, Mr B, welcomed the initiative of the unit head. (An ongoing overlap of teaching between the two groups operated because of the house and tutor system of this school.) The head teacher now seemed to be the person experiencing the consultant as being imposed upon him by the 'self-selected' approach of Mrs J. This was despite the fact that I had carried out exactly the same procedure for both groups: interviews with the head to discuss the proposal, meeting the school counsellor and educational psychologist and confirming the times and dates in writing. The resistance from the head teacher came in the form of two areas of anxiety about my input: would I be 'doing' psychotherapy and what about confidentiality, as I was not a member of the school system?

A secure base?

In the preliminary discussions with Mrs J and the introductory visit to the special unit, I had been impressed by her openness and that of her colleague. My reaction, therefore, to the first consultation with them was one of surprise. Almost before I had time to sit down, and without reference to any context, they rushed into an overwhelming description of one child's destructive behaviour. The staff base seemed secure; mine did not. To give myself a thinking space I empathized with their feelings of fearfulness and impotence and made a note of the child's age and first name. I then suggested, as the child's behaviour was being contained by them at the moment, that they might give me some factual information about the composition of the unit? For example, how many groups were there and did the attendance overlap? Was the child in question a member of more than one unit group? Giving them this rather concrete task lessened the shared anxiety level about the child and the high anticipation of achieving too many, perhaps unrealistic, goals. Before leaving I referred back to the child who was at present causing the unit so much concern and asked the staff to record a three-minute observation of behaviour, within the unit, at any time during the next week.

Exploratory behaviour, internal working models, updating and separation

On my arrival for the second meeting Mrs J gave me a printed rationale of the unit, plus the detailed timetable, prepared for the school staff, which answered my previous week's questions. She said, 'Thank you for holding on to our anxiety about Laurie last week. You made us feel that we were actually providing him with a safe place while his life was so chaotic.' The boy was a member of three different groups and the two teachers had independently observed his interactive or solitary behaviour. Notes had been recorded and compared and were read to me. A working relationship was immediately revealed as they exchanged opinions and thought about the actions they had taken. They decided to approach other members of the school staff in an attempt to change Laurie's timetable so that he would attend just one group. This plan of action highlighted the issue of boundaries in the 'here and now' for the group. I said that we could not accomplish all the tasks they hoped to achieve in the time we had available each week. If we focused on the behaviour and learning skills of the children the question of boundaries would arise naturally from time to time.

The two members of the unit staff wrote (with a copy for me) detailed accounts of their interactions with all the children they were teaching. They frequently noticed where their own input could have changed a situation; they could hold children in mind and enable them to communicate their feelings, especially about cognitive learning and feeling 'thick'. There was a willingness to question, to doubt and to show a capacity for learning from acknowledged mistakes. Mrs J and her colleague chose to examine the dynamic of the children's peer group in their circle time discussions. In the middle of reading one of her accounts Mrs J discovered that she and her colleague had missed the main thrust of the children's exchanges, their sexual concerns. They were expressed in the form of exaggerated behaviour, verbal exchanges, drawings or plasticene models. Once these concerns were acknowledged and addressed in the group circle the next day the children could explore them further.

Later that year the question of the survival of the unit was raised, after there had been a full inspection of the school. The growing confidence of the staff in their work with the unit children, a willingness to consult with any other staff member, regular meetings with the head teacher, year heads, school counsellor, plus their work with parents, police, magistrates and social workers was justified. This small subsystem maintained a balance between its own carefully considered policy and practice, and the whole school system of which it became an integral part. The unit was not closed.

COMMENT

Children are placed in a 'special needs' subsystem when the whole school system appears to have 'failed' them. Consultation to a part is unlikely, *per se*, to change an underfunctioning whole. A teacher consultant has the opportunity to create a working space for teachers, on a regular time-limited basis, which may have the potential for shifting an entrenched stance that has become counter-productive for adults and children alike. The outcome may be similar whether the consultation is imposed or self-selected, but a wish for change from a consultee is likely to influence the point of entry.

Lawrence and Miller (1976) described much of their consultative work as helping individuals to discover their capacity for self-management, so that in their work in a variety of roles and contexts they are not merely reacting and adapting to environmental pressures but constantly acting upon their environment, and changing it into what they want it to be.

A school subsystem working with a teacher consultant can provide an opportunity for the group to reflect on its relationship to the whole institution and how its behaviour will have an effect on the whole school policy and belief system. My work with school subsystems encourages me to think that individuals can become empowered in the context of the consultative work in a group. When teachers appreciate the 'psychological' and therapeutic skills they have, their professional confidence in self-management and in their capacity to influence their environment to bring about change is increased.

11

THE CHILDREN ACT 1989
Implications for the family and the school
Caroline Lindsey

The legal framework of our society influences and reflects the beliefs and the behaviours of its members. There are two main ways in which the Children Act can be considered as influencing the interaction of the educational system (that is, the organization of the school and the teachers within it) with the family system (that is, the children, who are the school's pupils, their parents, siblings and extended family). First, the Act determines the ways in which concerns about children are to be dealt with and how their well-being is to be promoted. Its key principles need to be understood by professionals in the school setting, both to enable them to relate to other health and social services professionals and to serve the interests of the pupils and their families. Second, the thinking on which the Children Act is based has far-reaching implications for the educational system, both in terms of practice – how children are educated – and in terms of resources.

The Children Act 1989, implemented in October 1991, represents a major restructuring of child care legislation in England and Wales, providing a comprehensive and integrated statutory framework to ensure the welfare of children. The Act covers nearly all the law, both private and public, relating to the care and upbringing of children and the social services to be provided for them. There have been a number of important influences on the development of the Act, including Government Reports (Social Services Committee, 1984), the findings of Child Abuse Inquiries (Butler Sloss, 1988; Department of Health, 1991; Lyon and Cruz, 1990); the Law Commission's Report on Child Care Law (1988), as well as the views of child care practitioners, research and pressure groups such as the Family Rights Group.

THE WELFARE PRINCIPLE

The fundamental principle underlying the Act is that the child's welfare is paramount. Whilst the term 'welfare' is not defined, the Law Commission (White *et al.*, 1990) considers that material welfare is essential but secondary to the need for stability, security, love and understanding, care and guidance. Warm and compassionate relationships are regarded as fundamentally important for the full development of the child's own character, personality and talents. The Act contains a check-list of relevant factors to be taken into account when considering the welfare of the child in court proceedings. The first of these is 'the ascertainable wishes and feelings of the child concerned (considered in the light of his age and understanding)'.

This is the first time that the courts are directed to take the child's wishes into account. The child cannot decide what should happen but must be heard and listened to. Adults are obliged to consider the child's perspective. The need to listen to the child raises the dilemma of how to understand what the child says and the need to balance the child's wishes with protection. We know that 'without context, words and actions have no meaning at all' (Bateson, 1979), and that the context in which the child's statement is to be understood is likely to be the family relationship. Sometimes, in the cases coming to court, what the children may say they wish is what they believe a loved and/or feared parent would want to hear them say. This may be particularly true of the anxiously attached child, who fears further rejection, or for those who have experienced long-standing abuse, where the relationship with the abusive parent is all important and when the fear of breaking up the family is as great as that of the continuation of the abuse.

It is therefore particularly important that those skilled in listening to children and facilitating their communication are involved both in helping those whose task it is to ascertain the children's wishes and in direct work with the children concerned, where appropriate e.g. very young children and the emotionally disturbed.

Teachers are often the trusted adults to whom children tell their secrets, their hopes, fears and wishes, in a variety of ways, in conversation, through play, writing and drawing. Teachers need clear guidelines which enable them to deal sensitively and appropriately with the information, in the interests of the child. The interests of the child may not always be the same as those of the parents, which may also create a dilemma.

The general principle of the need to listen to children's views in considering their future is, by contrast with the Children Act, not referred to in the Education Reform Act 1988 nor in the 1993 Education Bill. There is, however, a Circular 22/89 from the Department for Education and Science which does refer to the need to involve 'older children and young persons in discussions on their special educational needs and any proposed provision'. Children subject to an Education Supervision Order under the Children Act are the only children with a statutory right to be consulted about school choice. Research studies have shown the efficacy of listening to pupils' views (Davie *et al.*, 1989). Davie (1993) draws attention to the findings of the Elton Committee of 1989, which investigated discipline in schools. It received evidence from the National Children's Bureau which advised the importance for schools of finding ways to heed the views of pupils (Davie, 1989).

CONSENT TO ASSESSMENT AND TREATMENT

By further contrast with the Children Act, where assessment and treatment must have the agreement of the child, if of sufficient understanding to make an informed decision, the Education Act 1988 lays down that children must receive a mandatory curriculum up to the age of 16 and that their progress must be assessed. It could be argued that the right to refuse assessment and treatment is of a different order from the obligation to receive education and have progress monitored. Nevertheless, the rights of children recognized in the Children Act reflect the understanding of systemic thinkers that effective dialogue on which learning is based is dependent on responsiveness to feedback. Even within the constraints of the National Curriculum, useful opportunities may be created for pupils and teachers to reflect on how and what they are being taught.

The principle of ascertaining children's wishes and their consent to assessment and treatment, if of sufficient understanding, may be applied by extension to the practice of psychological testing by educational psychologists, usually but not always as part of the process of preparing a statement of special educational needs. The parents' permission is sought for this procedure but there is no obligation to consult the child. However, greater co-operation is likely to be gained from the child if the purpose of the assessment is fully explained and the child's agreement is obtained. Time taken to give feedback to the child as well as to the parents respects his or her involvement in the process and may offer the opportunity for understanding and change.

The welfare check-list also includes the need to pay particular regard to:

the child's physical, emotional and educational needs;
the likely effect of any change in circumstances on the child;
the age, sex, background and any relevant characteristics;
any harm which he has suffered or is at risk of suffering;
how capable each of his parents and any other person in relation to whom the court considers the question to be relevant, is of meeting his needs;
the range of powers available to the court under this Act in the proceedings in question.

The underlying philosophy of the Act is that children are best looked after in their own families and where possible the integrity and independence of the family should be respected. Courts are instructed not to intervene or make an order unless to do so would be of positive benefit to the child. It is sometimes difficult for teachers, because of their identification with their pupils, to accept that the best some families can do for their children is not sufficient for them to reach their potential and that although their parenting falls short of desirable standards, this does not necessarily justify statutory intervention.

DELAY

The court is enjoined by the Act to have regard to the general principle that delay is likely to be prejudicial to a child's welfare and to conduct proceedings as quickly as possible, using timetables. The time-scale of proceedings should be in accordance with time in the life of a child, not that of an adult. This important recognition of the damage done to children and their relationships with their parents, by delay in decision-making about their future, has implications for the field of education. Statementing for special educational needs is an obvious example, where there has been widespread professional experience of serious delay in the process of assessment and decision-making to the detriment of children, their families and their schools.

PARENTAL RESPONSIBILITY

The Law Commission was concerned that the law did not adequately recognize that parenthood is a matter of responsibility rather than of rights. The Act makes a change from parental rights to parental responsibility, to denote the duties, rights and authority that a parent has. Only through adoption do parents lose their parental responsibility. On separation and divorce, both parents retain their parental responsibility and neither parent is excluded from the parental role. This means, for example, that both parents continue to be entitled to receive reports from the school and to participate fully in decisions about the child's education.

Instead of arrangements for custody and access, the courts now have the power to make a range of orders, known as 'Section 8' orders, namely: residence orders – determining where the child is to live; contact orders – determining who the child is to see and hear from; prohibited steps orders – a specific embargo upon the exercise of parental responsibility; and specific issues orders – intended to enable either parent to bring a specific question relating to the child before the court.

On the reception of a child into care, parents will be allowed to exercise their parental responsibilities to the extent that this is in the interests of the child, according to the judgement of the social worker.

PARTNERSHIP WITH PARENTS

Another key concept arising from the guidance to the Act is the need for partnership with parents. Collaboration is to be the aim whether services are being offered under voluntary or statutory arrangements. Partnership together with parental responsibility, as well as the obligation to discover children's wishes, implies that professionals must endeavour to inform fully and involve parents where possible, and children where appropriate, in decision-making. But where partnership threatens the protection of the child, the child's welfare is paramount.

The concept of partnership has obvious implications, too, for practice in schools. Its impact has been felt by most professionals in the case conference, where despite initial anxieties, parental participation has generally been shown to enhance their understanding of the concerns and actions taken by professionals. Parents reported that they felt heard and that their views contributed to the outcome (Holmes *et al.*, 1991).

Collaboration with parents in the school setting has been demonstrably effective, for example, in the involvement of parents in reading schemes. When children with behavioural problems see that their parents and their teachers are working together to manage the difficulties, they experience more consistency and feel more contained. Early warning about concerns which may be arising needs to be seen as an appropriate involvement of parents, who might have some useful explanation to offer, rather than as an admission of failure on the part of the school, and therefore left until the end-of-term open day or report. Neither of these latter two methods of communication do much for partnership with parents.

CHILDREN IN NEED

Under Section 17, local authorities have a 'duty to safeguard and promote the welfare of children who are in need within their area and to promote the upbringing of such children by their families, by providing a range and level of services appropriate to those children's needs'. A child is defined as being in need if:

he is unlikely to achieve or maintain or have the opportunity of achieving or maintaining a reasonable standard of health or development without the provision of services by a local authority;
his health or development is likely to be significantly impaired or further impaired without the provision for him of such services; or
he is disabled.

Health includes physical and mental health and disability includes 'mental disorder'. The help that should be offered to meet the identified need must be appropriate in terms of the child's race, culture, religion and linguistic background.

Health and education, as other services such as housing and voluntary agencies, are expected to assist social services in their provision for children in need. The local authority is intended to develop a policy on family support services for children and their families, and also day care and education provision for children under statutory school age. Obviously these developments are limited by the lack of resources for implementation but the hope would be that these services would prevent the need for reception into care and other statutory interventions.

As part of the provision for children in need, children are no longer received into voluntary care but may on request be accommodated by the local authority. Parents are able to remove the child without notice unless there are grounds for taking emergency procedures to protect the child.

CHILD PROTECTION: SIGNIFICANT HARM

Another new concept introduced in the Act is that of significant harm. The court may make a care or supervision order only if it is satisfied that:

the child concerned is suffering significant harm or is likely to suffer significant harm; and
the harm or likelihood of harm is attributable to the care given to the child or likely to be given to him if the order were not made, not being what it would be reasonable to expect a parent to give to him; or
the child's being beyond parental control.

The definition of harm includes ill treatment, which covers psychological, emotional, physical and sexual abuse, and neglect. It also includes the impairment of health and development, where health means physical or mental health and development means physical, intellectual, social and behavioural development. Harm has to be shown to be attributable to the absence of a reasonable standard of parental care and the court has to be satisfied that the parents are not willing or able to modify the way they care for their child, or that the child rejects them.

It is important to note that the likelihood of future harm may now be taken into account, in contrast with the previous legislation, apart from wardship proceedings.

Many of the signs that children are suffering from significant harm will first be noticed in the school setting. Concerns, for example about physical injury or malnourishment, unexplained developmental delay, failure to learn and serious emotional disturbance need to be raised with the parents and with the social services, where appropriate. As has already been noted, children may reveal their experience of abuse, either directly or indirectly, to teachers. But they may also tell other children who, in turn may report their story. Parents, too, may share serious worries about their parenting with teachers, who then have to decide whether and from whom to seek further help.

There are, of course, also the situations where the harm which the child experiences is perpetrated in the school setting, by teachers, other adults or pupils, for example, by means of inappropriate punishment, physical or psychological maltreatment or sexual abuse.

ORDERS

It is not within the scope of this chapter to describe the changes to the legislation in detail. The interested reader is referred to the Children Act 1989, the Department of Health's *An Introduction to the Children Act, 1989* (1989) and White *et al.*, *A Guide to the Children Act, 1989* (1990). There are, however, two orders of particular relevance to the school setting, which will be considered.

Emergency protection order

Amongst the range of orders available to the court under the Act, it is important to note the important change from the place of safety order to the emergency protection order. The Cleveland Enquiry (Butler Sloss, 1989) highlighted the defects of the place of safety order, which lasted up to twenty-eight days, without the possibility of appeal, and allowed local authorities to make far-reaching decisions about children without consultation with parents or recourse to the court. The emergency protection order lasts for a maximum of eight days with one period of extension for up to seven days. It may be made when there is reasonable cause to believe that the child is likely to suffer significant harm.

Education supervision order

The local education authority can no longer make an application in care proceedings, in cases where the child is not being properly educated, for example where there is non-attendance at school. But, in consultation with the social services, an application can be made for an education supervision order, lasting from one to three years. The supervisor has the duty to advise, assist and befriend the child and his parents, and give directions which will secure that the child is properly educated. Before giving any directions, the supervisor has to ascertain the wishes of the child and his parents, in particular their wishes as to what school he should attend. If there is a failure to comply with the directions, the supervisor has to notify the social services, who then have a duty to consider what further action to take. Whilst the Review of Child Care Law thought that failure to attend school is not sufficient grounds for reception into care, on occasion persistent failure to attend school may still satisfy the criteria for significant harm and hence for care proceedings. At the time of writing the education supervision order has not yet been very widely used.

WELFARE OF CHILDREN IN INDEPENDENT SCHOOLS

The proprietor of any independent school providing accommodation now has a duty to safeguard and promote the children's welfare. The local authority in which the school is, must take reasonable steps to enable it to determine that this is happening and has powers to inspect the premises and records and see the children. Failure to comply with the promotion of the child's welfare may lead to being struck off the register of independent schools or disqualify the person from his role as proprietor or teacher.

CONCLUSION

This chapter has attempted to address the effect of the Children Act on the interface between the family and the school by examining its key principles. Some contradictions between the Children Act and educational legislation have been highlighted. Attention has been drawn to the importance of recognizing the child's perspective.

From a systemic point of view, the Act is a remarkable attempt to facilitate the maintenance of significant family and other relationships and their influence in the lives of children. This is to be achieved by support of the families of children in need and by the principle of partnership with parents and collaboration between agencies, as well as by minimizing state intervention in the lives of families and by recognizing the enduring nature of parental responsibility.

12

ISSUES FOR TRAINING

Emilia Dowling and Elsie Osborne

In this final chapter we draw together some of the key lessons of the book and the issues they raise for professional training. The perspective we attempt to describe is capable, we believe, of useful application in many contexts.

It is, of course, possible for a systemic approach to be generalized after specialized training in family therapy or consultation. But our aim in this chapter is to pay attention to how we can address more generic training courses in order to enrich and widen the theory and practice of many of the professionals involved directly in work with families and schools, including psychologists, social workers, learning support staff and the teachers themselves.

Since supervision is the core of much professional training we consider these issues of particular importance for supervisors, since they have an opportunity to provide a model of an interactional perspective and of the use of feedback. A section of the chapter therefore looks at some of the opportunities and issues supervision raises.

Throughout we draw on our own experience of many years in training educational and clinical psychologists at qualifying and post-qualifying level, and in multi-professional courses. We begin, therefore, by considering the contexts in which the learning of the two groups of psychologists, educational and clinical, take place.

THE CONTEXT OF THE LEARNING

Many professionals working with children are required as part of their brief to work with families and schools. However their professional training falls short of equipping them to deal adequately with both of these two systems. This is true of educational and clinical psychologists since, traditionally, the locus of work of the educational psychologist is the school psychological service and that of the clinical psychologist working with children is the hospital-based child and family psychiatric clinic, paediatric department or primary care base. Educational psychologists act as specialist consultants to the education service on children's learning and adjustment to school. An important part of the preparation for this role takes place in their teacher training and experience, and the educational context is the particular focus of the one-year postgraduate course in educational psychology which follows. Neither of these training periods allows for any major experience in the understanding of the dynamics of family systems or the development of skills in working with families (Taylor, 1982).

Within a generic training for clinical psychologists, the share devoted to children and families is inevitably limited, with much of the emphasis on mental illness and learning difficulties in adults. Those who have specialized in child mental health often experience uncertainty in venturing to follow the child into an unfamiliar school setting, which in any case is the educational psychologist's territory, although attempts have been made by individual clinical psychologists to apply their behavioural treatment expertise in the classroom (Douglas, 1982).

In the face of this state of affairs each profession is liable to get stuck in its own handed-down role in assessing individuals and families from their particular perspective using their own familiar network, i.e. health, education or social services. Thus the split between the individual child and his or her home or school context is perpetuated and mirrored in the relationship of the professionals concerned. It is our view that it is limiting to look on the family and school systems as separate entities since the child has to function in both. There is no impermeable boundary between these two systems and a flow of reciprocal influences takes place over extended periods of time during a child's development (see Chapter 1).

LEARNING AND CHANGE

The process of learning involves change: changes in what we know (cognitive level), in what we perceive and feel (perceptual and affective level) and in what we do (interactional level).

During the course of training, individuals may experience first and second order change. Watzlawick defines *first order change* as 'change from one behaviour to another within a given way of behaving'. *Second order change* involves 'the change from one way of behaving to another' (Watzlawick *et al.*, 1974, p. 28).

We regard this difference as fundamental, since we view trainees' development as encompassing both. Learning new ideas and specific techniques will come to form part of the range of responses available to them in their practice (first order change), as well as the development of different views and beliefs about human behaviour (second order change).

Learning then becomes a co-evolutionary process, whereby the trainees contribute with their ideas and grow and develop in an interactional context, which may be dyadic (as in individual supervision or tutorials) or in work groups.

One of the main areas for second order change is the development of the belief that there are different views about a situation and in fact the notion of an absolute 'truth' becomes redundant. Giving up the notion of 'a truth' involves a radical change in attitude which enables trainees to explore with an open mind the different perspectives in a situation. This is particularly relevant when working with families and schools, as a child's difficulty may well be perceived in very different ways by parents and teachers.

Both family and school are seen as open systems needing to maintain a state of equilibrium within a changing environment. Each system is exposed to homoeostatic reactions to demands for change which may be functional or dysfunctional; and each maintains a more or less permeable boundary across which an information exchange with the environment and each other can take place. If this process is inadequate or faulty, the child, as the linchpin between the two systems, could become a casualty. The notion of circular causality helps trainees understand reality as an inter-locking series of events, which can be read from any one of several starting-points, i.e. punctuated in different ways to affect meaning. For example, a boy was referred for poor academic performance and poor relationships. The boy's mother was considered to be uncaring by the class teacher and headmistress, who reported that she seldom responded to invitations to come to the school and seemed unfriendly and uncommunicative. In a family interview with the psychologist the mother revealed that she felt criticized by the teachers. She said she hated going to the school as she had had her fill of criticism at home from her own mother without looking for more. If only her son would behave himself at school and learn all would be well.

In such a situation the problem is traditionally assigned to the child. But by enlarging the context to include the family one could equally punctuate the cycle to see the problem as being the mother or grandmother. Looking further in the direction of the school other circumstances might emerge which would have relevance, such as the social climate in the classroom, the relationship of the boy to the teacher or the relationships in the staff group.

The shift from a linear to a circular perspective is an important process in the course of the trainees' development as it frees them from identifying with a particular individual in the system and helps them towards being able to hold a more neutral position.

INTERSYSTEMIC PROCESSES

Next to boundaries, context and circular causality, is the importance for each particular system of its own idiosyncratic rules and ethos which keep it in a 'steady' state and which may be incongruent with other systems and lead to misunderstandings and difficulties. Each system consists of subsystems, in relation to one another – parents–siblings, staff–pupils – arranged in a hierarchical order. Confusions between subsystems or hierarchical roles are not only dysfunctional but also contagious and in our experience often have an uncanny way of being recreated across systems and contexts.

When training professionals working with families and schools it is helpful to encourage them to recognize the intersystemic processes which practitioners need to be particularly aware of, namely *mirroring* and *triangulation*. One example will serve to illustrate both phenomena: the family consisted of a 40-year-old single mother and her 8-year-old son, living with her parents. She had never disengaged from her parents to lead an independent life. The boy was *triangulated* between mother and grandmother, who fought out their long-standing battle of who should be in control by arguing about who should have authority over the boy. This situation was *mirrored* at school where it was not clear whether a newly appointed headmistress or a powerful and influential deputy headmistress was in charge. In each case the secondary gains for the people involved reinforced the status quo and kept it going. Such duplication of a problematic situation in both contexts reinforces the dysfunctional pattern and indicates to the practitioner that her interventions should give priority to a change in this alignment.

It will be evident that the assimilation of new concepts will bring in their wake new perceptions and new lines of intervention. As Goethe said, 'We see what we know.' An important aspect of training is to open people's eyes to what they know but have not yet seen.

TRAINING AIMS AND PHILOSOPHY

Trainees need to be encouraged to get a 'feel' of what it might be like to experience a particular problem from different angles: that of the child, a parent or a teacher. Helping them to examine different views of reality frees them from seeking the 'right' one. This challenge to trainees' belief systems promotes changes in attitude which will enable them to view events from many different points of view.

It is important for them to learn to recognize and verbalize the difficulties of the situation and to express in a humble and sympathetic way caution regarding the scope and consequences of change. This is particularly relevant to schools, since teachers are committed professionals who often only seek the help of other professionals as a last resort after everything has been tried (Chapter 9). Their professional training inculcates a judgemental attitude. Increasingly teachers are expected to make constant evaluations of their pupils and are themselves judged by their pupils' success or lack of it in the examination system.

171

As part of our training philosophy, we share our own struggles with families and schools with an emphasis on looking for new solutions rather than dwelling on causes or apportioning blame. The same approach is used with material that trainees bring from their own current experience. For example, instead of dwelling on the obstacles presented by a 'difficult head', trainees are encouraged to explore the context in which the head teachers have to function; it may then transpire that they are undermined by other staff preventing commitment to any one line of action. The focus of the work then moves from individual 'pathology' to the relationship between the head teacher and staff.

We encourage trainees to recognize the 'grammar' of the relationships, i.e. the rules, without getting trapped in the 'story'. Once recurrent patterns of interaction are identified it is possible to formulate a structured way in which they might be altered. The emerging patterns themselves point to the areas that need to be restructured, maybe through the use of tasks. Trainees can then use their creativity to devise a task which will be congruent with the context in which the problem occurs.

We look for development in the following areas:

Changes in attitude: Being open to hear and accept different beliefs and views about a situation; being aware of the context in which difficulties occur; being aware of how their own belief system influences their response to a situation.

Changes in practice: Paying attention to recurrent patterns of interaction; being mindful of who in the system should be invited to attend an interview; thinking about the effects of change in the wider context; taking the risk of putting new ideas into practice.

Relationship to schools: Dealing with the school as an organization; seeing both the referred child and the teacher's role within the context of the school system.

Linking the family and school systems: Considering the possibility of having family–school interviews and when appropriate being able to raise issues that would previously have been tackled separately with the parents or the teachers.

In general we aim for a framework which enables trainees to move towards an interactional view in their thinking and practice.

AN INTERACTIONAL PERSPECTIVE IN SUPERVISION

Supervision, as an essential part of training, offers its own opportunities for the introduction of systemic techniques, but our main interest is in other functions than its straightforward didactic one. The attitudes demonstrated by a supervisor are probably more influential than any which are advocated by book or lecture, and much of what we have been suggesting previously is related to approaches or attitudes. Examples are: a non-judgemental, non-blaming perspective towards clients, an understanding of the importance of feedback, an emphasis on alternative perspectives and on shifting the viewpoints that are based on one person's perception only.

The closeness of the relationship which develops within individual supervision sessions means that supervisors have to be especially alert to the nature of the interactions, as they take place, between themselves and their supervisees. This constant monitoring is over and above the need to create a good, trusting relationship in the first instance.

For example, a supervisee brought many complaints about the head teacher with whom she was currently involved, and made a clear bid to engage the supervisor as an ally against the head. She was reminded by the supervisor of the context in which the head teacher was working, and requested to make a deliberate attempt to stand, as it were, in the head's shoes. In the reflective atmosphere of a supervision session it is possible to search for the rational factors which might lie behind apparently irrational behaviour. This example also indicates the supervisor's need to retain a task oriented approach in the face of attempts to create a collusive relationship which would not be in the interests of the supervisee's work.

The interaction between supervisor and supervisee has many other aspects and may, in itself, mirror the transactions between supervisee and client. Part of the basis for the support which is an essential function of supervision lies in the possibility it offers for the acceptance of the feelings which are raised in the course of working with other people's problems. So to acknowledge the pressures which arise from the context in which families and schools function is also, indirectly, to show an awareness of the importance of the supervisee's own context and pressures. Sometimes the similarities may be very close, as for example, when a trainee started to test out the supervisor's tolerance and patience by forgetting to carry out administrative tasks and by arriving late for sessions. Focusing on the interactional process within the session led to an understanding of how the trainee was pressing the supervisor in a manner which reflected the dismissive way he felt he was being treated by his clients. This offered alternative possibilities for coping with the feelings raised. The manner in which the supervisor tackled the trainee's temporary failure in responsibility could provide a model for the trainee in approaching his clients. From another perspective, discussion of the client's problems in working with the trainee could provide comment, indirectly, on the trainee's own feelings.

The supervisor has a unique possibility for passing on a truly interactive perspective, based on an empathic understanding as well as a theoretical one. This implies a need, however, for the supervisor to monitor interactions within a supervision session constantly and to struggle with feelings about the supervisee, rather than to attempt to discount them or to set them aside.

An understanding of the pressures which impinge on the supervision session itself, as well as on the supervisee's working context, will readily occur within a systemic approach, for example, where there is a shift towards more emphasis on appraisal within supervision or where there is anxiety about confidentiality. The influences and pressures on the supervision relationship are discussed more fully elsewhere (Osborne, 1993).

Supervision may offer a particularly useful way of introducing a more interactional perspective to qualified practitioners. A survey carried out in 1991–2 by a standing committee on supervision set up by the British Psychological Society Division of Educational and Child Psychology Training Committee found a considerable unmet wish amongst practising educational psychologists for supervision, to provide a chance to discuss and consider their work in depth. (The results are summarized by Pomerantz, 1993.) The support which supervision can offer to a hard–pressed profession is greatly strengthened and enriched by an interactional and systemic perspective being brought to bear.

The teaching profession might itself consider the advantages of later, ongoing supervision as a means of supporting the practising teacher. Unfortunately the word is especially liable amongst teachers to imply an overseeing and evaluating function, associated only with the incompletely qualified. Elsewhere, for instance amongst psychotherapists and some social workers, supervision may be linked to the close and intense preoccupation with intrapsychic dynamics which is characteristic of individual psychotherapy. Family therapy has developed its own tradition of live supervision as a shared activity, including viewing from behind a one-way screen (Whiffen and Byng-Hall, 1982). Each of these groups may find some aspects of the approach described as having some relevance for their own practice.

CONCLUSION

To summarize, in this chapter we have outlined some of the features which we consider to be relevant in training professionals working with families and schools.

In the area of supervision there are particular opportunities for working with an interactional perspective, as well as providing an especially influential model of the attitudes which are fundamental to a systemic approach.

A particular aspect worth emphasizing is the process of change in belief systems which will enable trainees to seek and understand different views of a situation or a problem and, therefore, accept that there might be different solutions. This co-evolutionary process towards a position which accepts different perspectives rather than seeking the 'right' one, will, we hope, enable the trainees to work collaboratively with their clients, whether they are parents, teachers or children.

NOTE

This chapter draws on the material from Chapter 11 in the first edition. We are grateful to Denise Taylor for her agreement to use it.

BIBLIOGRAPHY

Ackoff, R. L. (1960) 'Systems organizations and interdisciplinary research', in F. E. Emery (ed.) *Systems Thinking*, Harmondsworth: Penguin Books.

Ainsworth, M. D. S., Blehar, M. C., Waters, E. and Wall, S. (1978) *Patterns of Attachment: a Psychological Study of the Strange Situation*. Hillsdale, NJ: Erlbaum.

Andersen, T. (1987) 'The reflecting team', *Family Process*. 26, pp. 415–28.

Anderson, N., Goolishian, H. and Winderman, L. (1986) 'Problem determined systems: towards transformation and family therapy', *Journal of Strategic and Systemic Therapies*, 5 (4), pp. 1–19.

Aponte, H. J. (1976) 'The family–school interview: an ecostructural approach', *Family Process*, 15, pp. 303–13.

Apter, S. J. (1982) *Troubled Children Troubled Systems*, New York: Pergamon Press.

Argyris, C. (1964) *Integrating the Individual and the Organization*, New York: John Wiley.

Auerswald, E. H. (1985) 'Thinking about thinking in family therapy', *Family Process*, 24 (1), pp. 1–12.

Bain, A. (1982) *The Baric Experiment*, Occasional Paper No. 4, London: Tavistock Institute of Human Relations.

Balint, M. (1957) *The Doctor, his Patient and the Illness*, London: Pitman Medical.

Bandura, A. (1969) *Principles of Behavior Modification*, New York: Holt, Rinehart & Winston.

Barrett, M. and Trevitt, J. (1991) *Attachment Behaviour and the Schoolchild: an Introduction to Educational Therapy*, London and New York: Tavistock/ Routledge.

Bateson, G. (ed.) (1973) *Steps to an Ecology of Mind*, St Albans: Paladin.

Bateson, G. (1979) *Mind and Nature: a Necessary Unity*, London: Wildwood House.

Berg, I., Hullin, R., McGuire, R. and Tyrer, S. (1977) 'Truancy and the courts: research note', *Journal of Child Psychology and Psychiatry*, 18, pp. 359–65.

Bernstein, B. (1970) 'Education cannot compensate for society', *New Society*, 15 (387) 26 February, pp. 344–7.

Bertalanffy, L. von (1950) 'The theory of open systems in physics and biology', *Science*, 3, pp. 25–9.

Bion, W. R. (1961) *Experiences in Groups*, London: Tavistock Publications.

Bowlby, J. (1949) 'The study and reduction of group tensions in the family', *Human Relations*, 2 (2), pp. 123–8.

176

Bowlby, J. (1969) in *Attachment and Loss*, vol. 1, *Attachment*, London: Hogarth Press and Institute of Psychoanalysis; New York: Basic Books.

Bowlby, J. (1973) *Attachment and Loss*, vol. 2, *Separation: Anxiety and Anger*, London: Hogarth Press and Institute of Psychoanalysis; New York: Basic Books.

Bowlby, J. (1980) *Attachment and Loss* vol. 3, *Loss: Sadness and Depression*, London: Hogarth Press and Institute of Psychoanalysis; New York: Basic Books.

Bowlby, J. (1985) 'The role of childhood experience in cognitive disturbance', in M. J. Mahoney and A. Freeman (eds) *Cognition and Psychotherapy*, London: Plenum.

Boxall, M. (1976) *The Nurture Group in the Primary School*. London: Inner London Education Authority.

Bramley, W. (1990) 'Staff sensitivity groups: a conductor's field experience', *Journal of Group Analysis*, 23 (30), pp. 301–16.

Burden, R. (1978) 'Schools systems analysis: a project-centred approach', in B. Gillham (ed.) *Reconstructing Educational Psychology*, London: Croom Helm.

Burden, B. (1981a) 'The educational psychologist as instigator and agent of change in schools: some guidelines for successful practice', in A. McPherson and A. Sutton (eds) *Reconstructing Psychological Practice*, London: Croom Helm.

Burden, B. (1981b) 'Systems theory and the relevance to schools', in B. Gillham (ed.) *Problem Behaviour in the Secondary School*, London: Croom Helm.

Burden, R. (1989) 'Assessing classroom ethos: some recent promising developments for the systems oriented educational psychologist', *Educational Psychology in Practice*, April, pp. 17–22.

Butler Sloss, Lord Justice (1988) *Report of the Inquiry into Child Abuse in Cleveland in 1987*, London: HMSO.

Button, L. (1981) *Group Tutoring for the Form Teacher*, London: Hodder & Stoughton.

Byng-Hall, J. (1991) 'The application of Attachment Theory to understanding and treatment in family therapy', in C. Murray Parkes and J. Stevenson-Hinde (eds) *The Place of Attachment in Human Behaviour*, London: Tavistock Publications.

Cade, B. (1979) 'The use of paradox in therapy', in S. Walrond-Skinner (ed.) *Family and Marital Psychotherapy: a Critical Approach*, London: Routledge & Kegan Paul.

Campbell, D., Draper, R. and Huffington, C. (1988) *Teaching Systemic Thinking*, London: DC Associates.

Campbell, D., Draper, R. and Huffington, C. (1991) *A Systemic Approach to Consultation*, London: Karnac Bocks.

Campion, J. (1984) 'Psychological services for children using family therapy in the setting of a school psychological service', *Journal of Family Therapy*, 6 (1), pp. 47–62.

Campion, J. (1985) *The Child in Context*, London: Methuen.

Cannon, W. (1939) *The Wisdom of the Body*, New York: W. W. Norton.

Caplan, G. (1970) *The Theory and Practice of Mental Health Consultation*, London: Tavistock Publications.

Caplan, G. (1974) 'Mental health consultation: retrospect and prospect', paper by US Department of Commerce Workshop on Mental Health Consultation.

Caspari, I. and Osborne, E. (1967) 'The neighbourhood schools service of the Tavistock Clinic', in *Counselling in Schools*, Schools Council Working Paper No. 15, London: HMSO.

Children Act (1989) The, London: HMSO.

Clark, A. W. (1972) 'Sanction: a critical element in action research', *Journal of Applied Behavioural Science*, 8, pp. 713–31.

Coleman, J. S. (1966) *Equality of Educational Opportunity*, Washington: US Government Printing Office.

Conoley, J. C. and Conoley, C. W. (1982) *School Consultation: a Guide to Practice and Training*, New York and Oxford: Pergamon Press.

Conoley J. C. and Conoley C. W. (1990) 'Staff consultative work in schools', in N. Jones and N. Frederickson (eds) *Refocusing Educational Psychology*, London: Falmer Press.

Cooklin, A. I. (1982) 'Change in here and now systems vs systems over time', in A. Bentovim, G. Gorell Barnes and A. Cooklin (eds) *Family Therapy: Contemporary Frameworks of Theory and Practice*, London: Academic Press.

Cooklin, A. I., McHugh, B. M. and Dawson, N. K. (1993) 'Family therapy basics', a computer and video distance learning pack, London: Marlborough Family Service.

Cooper, P. and Upton, G. (1990) 'An ecosystemic approach to emotional and behavioural difficulties in schools', *Educational Psychology*, 10 (4), pp. 301–21.

Craft, M., Raynor, J. and Cohen, L. (eds) (1980) *Linking Home and School*. London: Harper & Row.

Dare, C. (1982) 'Families with school going children', in A. Bentovim, G. Gorell Barnes and A. Cooklin (eds) *Family Therapy: Complementary Frameworks of Theory and Practice*. London: Academic Press.

Davie, R., Phillips, D. and Callely, E. (1984) *Evaluation of Inset Course on Behaviour Problems*, Report to Welsh Office, Cardiff: Department of Education, University College

Davie, R. (1989) 'The National Children's Bureau: evidence to the Elton Committee', in N. Jones (ed.) *School Management and Pupil Behaviour*, Lewes: Falmer Press.

Davie, R. (1993) 'Listen to the child: a time for change', *The Psychologist*, 6 (6), pp. 252–7.

Davis, L. (1977) 'Evolving alternative organizational designs: their socio-technical basis', *Human Relations*, 30, pp. 261–73.

Dawson, N. K. and McHugh, B. M. (1986a) 'Families as partners', *Pastoral Care in Education*, 4 (2), pp. 102–9.

Dawson, N. K. and McHugh, B. M. (1986b) 'Application of a family systems approach in an education unit', *Maladjustment and Therapeutic Education*, 4 (2), pp. 48–54.

Dawson, N. K. and McHugh, B. M. (1987) 'Talking to parents of children with emotional and behavioural dificulties', *British Journal of Special Education*, 14 (3), pp. 119–21.

Dawson, N. K. and McHugh, B. M. (1988) 'Claire doesn't talk: behavioural or learning difficulty', *Gnosis*, 12, pp. 8–11.

Dell, P. F. (1982) 'Beyond homeostasis: towards a concept of coherence', *Family Process*, 21 (1), pp. 21–41.

Department of Health (1989) *An Introduction to the Children Act, 1989*, London: HMSO.

Department of Health (1991) *Child Abuse: a Study of Inquiry Reports, 1980–1989*, London: HMSO.

Dewey, J. and Bentley, A. F. (1949) *Knowing and the Known*, Boston, Mass.: Beacon Press.

Donaldson, M. (1979) *Children's Minds*, Glasgow: Fontana/Collins.

Douglas, J. (1982) 'Behaviour therapy in a systems framework', *Bulletin of the British Psychological Society*, 34, February, pp. 64–7.

Douglas, J. W. B. (1964) *The Home and the School*, London: MacGibbon & Kee.

Douglas, J. W. B., Ross, M. M. and Simpson, H. R. (1968) *All our Future: a*

Longitudinal Study of Secondary Education, London: Peter Davies; reprinted 1980 in *Educational Analysis*, 2 (2).

Dowling, E. (1990) 'Children's disturbing behaviour: whose problem is it? An account of a school based service for parents and teachers', *Association of Child Psychology and Psychiatry Newsletter*, 12 (4), pp. 8–11.

Dowling, E. and Osborne, E. (1985) *The Family and the School: a Joint Systems Approach to Problems with Children*, London: Routledge & Kegan Paul.

Dowling, E. and Taylor, D. (1989) 'The clinic goes to school: lessons learnt', *Maladjustment and Therapeutic Education* 7 (1), pp. 24–31.

Dowling, J. R. (1980) 'The adjustment from primary to secondary school', *British Journal of Educational Psychology*, 50, pp. 26–30.

Duhl,B. (1983) *From the Inside Out and Other Metaphors*. New York: Brunner Mazel.

Dupont, S. and Dowdney, L. (1990) 'Dilemmas in working with schools', *Newsletter, Association for Child Psychology and Psychiatry* 12 (1), pp. 13–16.

Education Act (1981) An Act to make provision with respect to children with special needs, Department of Education and Science, London: HMSO.

Emery, F. (1982) 'New perspectives on the world of work: socio-technical foundations for a new social order?', *Human Relations*, 35 (12), pp. 1095–122.

Emery, F. and Trist, E. (1965) 'The causal texture of organizational environments', *Human Relations*, 18, pp. 21–32.

Entwistle, N. (1990) 'Student learning and classroom environment', in N. Jones and N. Frederickson (eds) *Refocusing Educational Psychology*, London: Falmer Press.

Festinger, L. (1958) 'The motivating effect of cognitive dissonance', in G. Lindzey (ed.) *Assessment of Human Motives*, New York: Rinehart & Winston.

Fine, N. J. and Holt, P. (1983) 'Intervening with school problems: a family systems perspective', *Psychology in the Schools*, 20 (1), p. 59–66.

Fischer, C. T. (1979) 'Personality and assessment', in R. S. Valle and M. King (eds) *Existential–Phenomenological Alternatives for Psychology*, New York: Oxford University Press.

Frederickson, N. (1990) 'Systems approaches in educational psychology practice: a re-evaluation', in N. Jones and N. Frederickson, *Refocusing Educational Psychology*, London: Falmer Press.

Freund, J. C. and Cardwell, G. F. (1977) 'A multi-faceted response to an adolescent's school failure', *Journal of Marriage and Family Counselling*, 3 (2), pp. 49–57.

Galloway, D., Ball, T., Blomfield, D. and Seyd, R. (1982) *Schools and Disruptive Pupils*, Harlow, Essex: Longman.

Galton, M. and Willcocks, J. (eds) (1983) *Moving from the Primary Classroom*, London: Routledge & Kegan Paul.

Gath, D., Cooper, B., Cattoni, F. and Rockett, D. (1977) *Child Guidance and Delinquency in a London Borough*, Oxford: Oxford University Press.

Gillham, B. (ed.) (1978) *Reconstructing Educational Psychology*, London: Croom Helm.

Gillham, B. (ed.) (1981) *Problem Behaviour in the Secondary School*, London: Croom Helm.

Goffman, E. (1961) *Asylum*, Harmondsworth: Penguin Books.

Gorell Barnes, G. (1975) 'Seen but not heard: gateway to the future', *Social Work Today*, 5 (22), pp. 689–93.

Gorell Barnes, G. (1982) 'Pattern and intervention', in A. Bentovim, G. Gorell Barnes and A. Cooklin (eds) *Family Therapy: Complementary Frameworks of Theory and Practice*, London: Academic Press.

179

Gorell Barnes, G. (1985) 'Systems theory and family theory', in M. Rutter and L. Hersov (eds) *Child Psychiatry: Modern Approaches*, 2nd edn, Oxford: Blackwell Scientific Publications.

Haley, J. (1976) *Problem Solving Therapy*, San Francisco, Jossey Bass.

Handy, C. and Aitken, R. (1990) *Understanding Schools as Organizations*, Harmondsworth: Penguin Books.

Hanko, G. (1990) *Special Needs in Ordinary Classrooms: Supporting Teachers*, Oxford: Basil Blackwell.

Hargreaves, D. H. (1967) *Social Relationships in a Secondary School*, London: Routledge & Kegal Paul.

Hargreaves, D. H. (1978) 'Deviance: the interactionist approach', in B. Gillham (ed.) *Reconstructing Educational Psychology*, London: Croom Helm.

Hetherington, E. M. (1991) 'Coping with family traditions: winners, losers and survivors', in M. Woodhead, P. Light and R. Carr (eds) *Growing up in a Changing Society*, London and New York: Routledge.

Higgin, G. W. and Bridger, H. (1965) *The Psychodynamics of an Inter-Group Experience*, London: Tavistock Publications.

Hobbs, N. (ed.) (1975) *The Futures of Children*, San Francisco, Jossey-Bass.

Hoffman, L. (1981) *Foundations of Family Therapy*, New York: Basic Books.

Hoffman, L. (1988) 'A constructivist position for family therapy', *Irish Journal of Psychology*, 9 (1), pp. 110–29.

Holmes, E. (1982) 'The effectiveness of educational intervention for pre-school children in day and residential care', *New Growth*, 2 (1), pp. 17–30.

Holmes, S. (1982) 'Failure to learn: a systems view', *Australian Journal of Family Therapy*, 4 (1), pp. 27–36.

Holmes, S., Sharland, E. and Jones, D. P. H. (1991) 'Parental participation at initial case conferences in Oxfordshire', unpublished paper.

Hoyle, E. (1969) *The Role of the Teacher*, London: Routledge & Kegan Paul.

Imber-Black, E. (1989) 'Women's relationships with larger systems', in M. McGoldrick, C. M. Anderson and F. Walsh (eds) *Women in Families: a Framework for Family Therapy*, London and New York: W. W. Norton.

Jencks, C., Smith, M., Acland, H., Bane, M. J., Cohen, D., Gintis, H., Hayns, B. and Michelson, S. (1972) *Inequality: a Reassessment of the Effect of Family and Schooling in America*, New York: Basic Books.

Johnson, D. (1982) 'Families and educational institutions', in R. N. Rapoport, M. P. Fogarty and R. Rapoport (eds) *Families in Britain*, London: Routledge & Kegan Paul.

Jones, N. and Frederickson, N. (eds) (1990) *Refocusing Educational Psychology*, London: Falmer Press.

Kaplan, L. (1971) *Education and Mental Health*, New York: Harper & Row.

Katz, D. and Kahn, R. L. (1969) 'Common characteristics of open systems', in F. E. Emery (ed.) *Systems Thinking*, Harmondsworth: Penguin Books/Allen Lane.

Keeney, B. (1983) *Aesthetics of Change*, New York: Guilford Press.

Kelly, J. G. (1968) 'Toward an ecological conception of preventive intervention', in J. Carter jnr. (ed.) *Research Contributions from Psychology to Community Mental Health*, New York: Behavioral Publications.

Kuhn, T. S. (1970) *The Structure of Scientific Revolutions*, 2nd ed, Chicago: University of Chicago Press.

Kofka, K. (1935) *Principles of Gestalt Psychology*, London: Routledge & Kegan Paul.

Lacan, J. (1977) *Ecrits: a Selection Translated from the French* by Alan Sheridan, London: Tavistock Publications.

Lacey, C. (1970) *Hightown Grammar: the School as a Social System*, Manchester: Manchester University Press.

Lawrence, W. G. and Miller, E. J. (1976) 'Epilogue', in E. J. Miller (ed.) *Task and Organization*, London: John Wiley.

Law Commission (1988) *Report on Review of Child Care Law, Guardianship and Custody*, Law Commission Report No. 172, London: HMSO.

Lewin, K. (1952) *Field Theory in Social Science: Selected Theoretical Papers*, ed. D. Cartwright, London: Tavistock Publications.

Lewin, K., Lippitt, R. and White, R. K. (1939) 'Patterns of aggressive behaviour in experimentally created "Social Climates" ', *Journal of Social Psychology*, 10, pp. 271–99.

Likert, R. and Likert, J. G. (1976) *New Ways of Managing Conflict*, New York and London: McGraw-Hill.

Love, L. R. and Kaswan, J. W. (1974) *Troubled Children: Their Families, Their Schools and Treatments*, New York: John Wiley.

Low, K. B. and Bridger, H. (1979) 'Small group work in relation to management development', in B. B. Smith and B. A. Farrell (eds) *Training in Small Groups*, Oxford: Pergamon Press.

Lyon, C. and de Cruz, P. (1990) *The Child Abuse Inquiry Reports in Child Abuse*, ch. 10, Bristol: Jordan.

McGeeney, P. (1974) 'Reaching home', in M. Marland (ed.) *Pastoral Care*, London: Heinemann Educational Books.

McNab, S. (1993) 'Connecting with constructivist thinking: some preliminary thoughts', unpublished paper.

Macy, E. and Jones, A. (1976) *The Socio-technical System at Bethesda Hospital*, Ann Arbor, Ill.: Institute of Social Research.

Madanes, C. (1981) *Strategic Family Therapy*, San Francisco, Jossey Bass.

Maher, P. (ed.) (1987) *Child Abuse: the Educational Perspective*, Oxford: Basil Blackwell.

Marland, M. (ed.) (1974) *Pastoral Care*, London: Heinemann Educational Books.

Marris, P. (1974) *Loss and Change*, London: Routledge & Kegan Paul.

Miller, E. J. (ed.) (1976) *Task and Organization*, Chichester: John Wiley.

Minuchin, S. (1974) *Families and Family Therapy*, London: Tavistock Publications.

Minuchin, S. and Fishman, H. (1981) *Family Therapy Techniques*, Cambridge Mass.: Harvard University Press.

Morgan, G. (1986) *Images of Organization*, London: Sage Publications.

Murray, L., Kempton, C., Woolgar, M. and Hooper, R. (1992) 'The impact of postnatal depression on infant development', *Journal of Child Psychology and Psychiatry*, 33 (3), pp. 543–61.

National Children's Bureau (1990) *An Introduction to the Children Act*.

Osborne, E. (1983) 'Teachers' relationships with the pupils' families', in I. Salzberger-Wittenberg, G. Henry and E. Osborne (eds) *The Emotional Experience of Learning and Teaching*, London: Routledge & Kegan Paul.

Osborne, E. (1989) 'Educational therapy', *Journal of Educational Therapy*, 2 (3), pp. 1–17.

Osborne, E. (1993) 'Some external pressures and influences on face to face supervision', *Educational and Child Psychology*, 10 (2), pp. 25–30.

Owens, R. G. (1991) *Organizational Behavior in Education*, 4th edn, Englewood Cliffs, NJ: Prentice Hall.

Palazzoli, M. S. (1980) 'The problem of the referring person', *Journal of Marital and Family Therapy*, 6, pp. 3–9.

Palazzoli, M. S. (1982) 'Behind the scenes of the organisation: some guidelines for the expert in human relations', *Journal of Family Therapy*, 6, pp. 299–307.

181

Palazzoli, M. S. (1983) 'The emergence of a comprehensive systems approach', *Journal of Family Therapy*, 5 (2), pp. 165–77.

Palazzoli, M. S., Cirillo, S., D'Ettore, L., Garbellini, M., Chezzi, D., Lerma, M., Luccini, M., Martino, C., Mazzoni, C., Mazzaucchelli, F. and Nichele, M. (1976) *Il Mago Smagato*, Milan: Feltrinelli Economica.

Palazzoli, M. S., Boscolo, L., Cecchin, G. and Prata, G. (1978) *Paradox and Counterparadox: a New Model in the Therapy of the Family in Schizophrenic Transaction*, London and New York: Jason Aronson.

Palazzoli, M. S., Boscolo, L., Cecchin, G. and Prata, G. (1980) 'Hypothesizing circularity-neutrality: three guidelines for the conductor of the session', *Family Process*, 19 (1), pp. 3–12.

Parkes, C. and Stevenson-Hinde, J. (1982) *The Place of Attachment in Human Behaviour*, London: Tavistock Publicatons; New York: Basic Books.

Pasmore, E., Francis, C., Haldman, J. and Shain, A. (1982) 'Socio-technical systems: a North American reflection on empirical studies of the seventies', *Human Relations*, 35, pp. 1179–204.

Penn, P. (1985) 'Feet forward: future questions, future maps', *Family Process*, 24 (3) Sept., pp. 299–310.

Plas, J. (1986) *Systems Psychology in the Schools*, New York: Pergamon Press.

Plowden Report (1967) *Children and their Primary Schools*, Central Advisory Council for Education, London: HMSO.

Pomerantz, M. (1993) 'The practice of supervision for local authority educational psychologists', *Educational and Child Psychology*, 10 (2), pp. 16–24.

Power, M. J., Alderson, M. R., Phillipson, C. M., Shoenberg, E. and Morris, J. N. (1967) 'Delinquent schools?', *New Society*, 19 October, p. 542.

Reynolds, D. (1976a) 'A delinquent school', in M. Hammersley and P. Woods (eds) *The Process of Schooling*, London: Routledge & Kegan Paul.

Reynolds, D. (1976b) 'When pupils and teachers refuse a truce: the secondary school and the creation of delinquency', in G. Mungham and G. Pearson (eds) *Working Class Youth Culture*, London: Routledge & Kegan Paul.

Reynolds, D. and Murgatroyd, S. (1977) 'The sociology of schooling and the absent pupil: the school as a factor in the generation of truancy', in H. C. M. Carroll (ed.) *Absenteeism in South Wales, Studies of Pupils in Their Homes and Their Secondary Schools*, Swansea: University College of Swansea, Faculty of Education.

Richardson, E. (1967) *Group Study for Teachers*, London: Routledge & Kegan Paul.

Richardson, E. (1975) Selections from 'The environment of learning', in A. D. Colman and W. H. Bexton (eds) *Group Relations Reader*, Sausalito, Calif.: Grex.

Roethlisberger, F. J. and Dickson, W. J. (1947) *Management and the Worker*, Cambridge, Mass.: Harvard University Press.

Rutter, M., Maughan, B., Mortimore, P. and Ouston, J. (1979) *Fifteen Thousand Hours: Secondary Schools and Their Effects on Children*, London: Open Books.

Salzberger-Wittenberg, I., Henry, G. and Osborne, E. (eds) (1983) *The Emotional Experience of Learning and Teaching*, London: Routledge & Kegan Paul.

Sampson, O. (1980) *Child Guidance: its History, Provenance and Future*, Leicester: British Psychological Society, Division of Educational and Child Psychology.

Schools Council (1968) *Enquiry 1: Young School Leavers*, London: HMSO.

Schein, E. H. (1969) *Process Consultation: Its Role in Organizational Development*, Cambridge, Mass.: Addison-Wesley.

Schein, E. H. (1985) *Organizational Culture and Leadership*, London: Jossey Bass.

Schein, E. H. (1987) *Process Consultation*, vol. 2, *Lessons for Managers and Consultants*, Reading, Mass.: Addison-Wesley.

Selznick, P. (1957) *Leadership in Administration*, Evanston, Ill.: Row Peterson.

Singer, L. S., Whitson, M. B., Fried, M. L. (1975) 'An alternative to traditional mental health services and consultation in schools: a social systems and group process approach', in A. D. Coleman and W. H. Bexton (eds) *A Group Relations Reader*, Sausalito, Calif.: Grex.

Social Services Committee, Second Report (1984) 'Children in care' (the Short Report), London: HMSO.

Steele, W. and Raider, M. (1991) *Working with Families in Crisis, School-based intervention*, New York and London: Guilford Press.

Stevenson-Hinde, J. (1990) 'Attachment within family systems: an overview', in *Infant Mental Health Journal*, 11, pp. 218–27.

Stoker, R. (1992) 'Working at the level of the institution and the organisation', *Educational Psychology in Practice*, 8 (1), pp. 15–24.

Stringer, P., Stow, L., Hibbert, K., Powell, J. and Louw, E. (1992) 'Establishing staff consultation groups in schools', *Educational Psychology in Practice*, 8 (2), pp. 87–96.

Taylor, D. (1982) 'Family consultation in a school setting', *Journal of Adolescence*, 5, pp. 367–77.

Taylor, D. (1986) 'The child as go-between: consulting with parents and teachers', *Journal of Family Therapy*, 8 (1), pp. 79–89.

Taylor, D. and Dowling, E. (1986) 'The clinic goes to school: setting up an outreach service', *Maladjustment and Therapeutic Education*, 4 (2), pp. 12–18.

Thompson, S. and Kahn, J. H. (1970) *The Group Process as a Helping Technique*, Oxford: Pergamon Press.

Toffler, A. (1970) *Future Shock*, New York: Random House; London: Bodley Head.

Tomm, K. (1988) 'Interventive intervening, Part 3: intending to ask linear, circular, strategic and reflexive questions', *Family Process*, 27, pp. 1–15.

Trist, E. (1978) 'On socio-technical systems', in W. Pasmore and J. Sherwood (eds) *Social Technical Systems: a Course Book*, San Diego, Calif.: University Association.

Trist, E. and Bamforth, K. (1951) 'Some social land psychological consequences of the long wall method of coal-getting', *Human Relations*, 4, pp. 3–38.

Tucker, B. Z. and Dyson, E. (1976) 'The family and the school: utilizing human resources to promote learning', *Family Process*, 15, pp. 125–41.

Turner, G. (1983) *The Social World of the Comprehensive School*, London: Croom Helm.

Vickers, G. (1965) *The Art of Judgement*, London: Chapman & Hall (also in Methuen University Paperbacks, 1968).

Von Foerster, H. (1984) 'On constructing a reality', in P. Watzlawick (ed.) *The Invented Reality*, New York: W. W. Norton.

Walrond-Skinner, S. (1976) *Family Therapy: the Treatment of Natural Systems*, London: Routledge & Kegan Paul.

Walrond-Skinner, S. (1978) 'Indications and contra-indications for the use of family therapy', in *Journal of Child Psychology and Psychiatry*, 19 (1), pp. 57–62.

Walrond-Skinner, S. (ed.) (1979) *Family and Marital Psychotherapy*, London: Routledge & Kegan Paul.

Watzlawick, P., Weakland, J. H. and Fish, R. (1974) *Change: Principles of Problem Formation and Problem Resolution*, New York: W. W. Norton.

Wedell, K. and Lambourne, R. (1980) 'Psychological services for children in

England and Wales', Occasional papers, vol. 4 (1 and 2), Leicester: British Psychological Society, Division of Educational and Child Psychology.

Whiffen, R. and Byng-Hall, J. (eds) (1982) *Family Therapy Supervision: Recent Developments in Practice*, London: Academic Press.

White, R., Carr, P. and Lowe, N. (1990) *A Guide to the Children Act 1989*, London: Butterworths.

Woods, P. (1979) *The Divided School*, London: Routledge & Kegal Paul.

NAME INDEX

Ackoff, R.L. 3
Ainsworth, M.D.S. 37
Aitken, R. 42
Andersen, T. 91
Anderson, N. 12–13, 90, 122
Aponte, H.J. 2, 15, 71, 78, 100
Apter, S.J. 153
Argyris, C. 128
Auerswald, E.H. 101

Bain, A. 147
Balint, M. 136
Bamforth, K. 131
Bandura, A. 5
Barrett, M. 58, 149, 154
Bateson, G. 5, 161
Bentley, A.F. 3
Berg, I. 83
Bernstein, B. 128
Bertalanffy, L. von 3, 130
Bion, W.R. 110, 136
Bowlby, J. xiii, xv–xvi, 37, 149, 151
Boxall, M. 114
Bridger, H. 136
British Psychological Society Division
   of Educational and Child Psychology
   Training Committee 174
Burden, R. 2, 41, 47, 60; assessment
   48; joining process 21; organizational
   structure 9, 19
Butler Sloss, Lord Justice 160, 166
Button, L. 80
Byng-Hall, J. xiii, xvi, 37, 174

Cade, B. 26
Campbell, D. 11, 22–3, 38–9, 40, 41–2
Campion, J. 13, 33
Cannon, W. 6
Caplan, G. 38, 133, 134–5, 136

Cardwell, G.F. 71
Caspari, I. xvi
Clark, A.W. 146
Cleveland Enquiry 160, 166
Coleman, J.S. 127
Conoley, C.W. 39, 152
Conoley, J.C. 39, 152
Cooklin, A.I. 89, 85
Cooper, P. 2, 20
Craft, M. 2
Cruz, P. de 160

Dare, C. 9
Davie, R. 161–2
Davis, L. 130
Dawson, N.K. 88
Dell, P.F. 6
Department of Education and Science
   161
Department of Health 160, 166
Dewey, J. 3
Dickson, W.J. 135
Donaldson, M. 44
Douglas, J. 127, 169
Dowdney, L. 60
Dowling, E. 60, 61, 62, 88
Dowling, J.R. 117
Duhl, B. 152
Dupont, S. 60
Dyson, E. 2, 70, 71, 79, 85

Elton Committee 161–2
Emery, F. 130, 147
Entwistle, N. 44

Festinger, L. 146
Fine, N.J. 2
Fischer, C.T. 48
Fishman, H. 95

185

Frederickson, N. 2, 31, 40, 47
Freund, J.C. 71

Galloway, D. 7, 9, 15
Galton, M. 142
Gath, D. 128
Gillham, B. 2, 7, 47
Goffman, E. 128
Gorell Barnes, G. 6, 9, 18, 102

Haley, J. 17, 26, 29, 59, 88
Handy, C. 42
Hanko, G. 109, 150
Hargreaves, D.H. 12, 47, 127, 135
Hetherington, E.M. 148
Higgin, G.W. 136
Hobbs, N. 71
Hoffman, L. 6, 28
Holmes, E. 114
Holmes, S. 2, 164
Holt, P. 2
Hoyle, E. 103

Imber-Black, E. 11

Jencks, C. 127
Johnson, D. 2
Jones, A. 132
Jones, N. 47

Kahn, J.H. 110
Kahn, R.L. 4, 130
Kaplan, L. 70
Kaswan, J.W. 2
Katz, D. 4, 130
Keeney, B. 3
Kelly, J.G. 32
Kofka, K. 3
Kuhn, R.S. 147

Lacan, J. 75
Lacey, C. 127
Lambourne, R. 47
Law Commission 160, 163
Lawrence, W.G. 159
Lewin, K. 3, 136, 138
Likert, J.G. 132
Likert, R. 132
Love, L.R. 2
Low, K.B. 136
Lyon, C. 160

McGeeney, P. 70
McHugh, B.M. 88

McNab, S. 28
Macy, E. 132
Madanes, C. 26
Maher, P. 148
Marland, M. 78–9
Marris, P. 147
Miller, E.J. 109, 159
Minuchin, S. 9, 21, 24, 29, 89, 95
Morgan, G. 10
Murgatryd, S. 9
Murray, L. 37

National Children's Bureau 149, 162

Osborne, E. xvi, 58, 88, 174;
    hierarchical structure 19; home visits
    19; polarization 14
Owens, R.G. 128, 130–1, 132, 137

Palazzoli, M.S. 24, 26, 56, 95, 120, 146
Parkes, C. 37
Pasmore, E. 131
Penn, P. 23
Plas, J. 3, 5, 40–1, 100
Plowden Committee 70, 127
Pomerantz, M. 174
Power, M.J. 127, 129

Raider, M. 156
Reynolds, D. 9, 128
Richardson, E. 110, 151
Roethlisberger, F.J. 135
Rutter, M. 2, 10, 128, 149

Saltzberger-Wittenberg, I. 108, 110
Sampson, O. 46
Schein, E.H. 10, 136
Schools Council 70
Selznick, P. 132
Singer, L.S. 141
Social Services Committee 160
Steele, W. 156
Stevenson-Hinde, J. 37
Stoker, R. 2–3
Stringer, P. 86

Taylor, D. 2, 15, 18, 31, 71; boundary
    management 133; consultative
    service 60, 61; training 169
Thompson, S. 110
Toffler, A. 130
Tomm, K. 22
Trevitt, J. 58, 149, 154

Trist, E. 130, 131
Tucker, B.Z. 2, 70, 71, 79, 85
Turner, G. 7

Upton, G. 2, 20

Vickers, G. 132
Von Foerster, H. 28

Walrond-Skinner, S. xvi, 6, 29, 46
Watzlawick, P. 26, 29, 95, 147; change
    169; reframing 23–4
Wedell, K. 47
Whiffen, R. xvi, 174
White, R. 160, 166
Willcocks, J. 142
Woods, 140

SUBJECT INDEX

ability/intelligence: testing 47–8, 50, 51–3; *see also* assessment, special needs

abuse 121, 161; *see also* child protection

action research 129, 137–47; advantages 145–6; constraints of approach 144–5; evaluation 143–4; feedback and implementation 140–3; problem formulation and fact finding 138–40; system change and 146–7; tactics and techniques 146

advice-giving 38, 39

assessment: changing approaches to 47–8; consent to 162–3; interactional perspective 49, 50, 51–3

attachment theory xiii–xiv, 37–8, 149

attitudinal changes 172

attitudes towards learning 116

belief systems 11–12, 68; challenging in classroom interventions 95–100

blame 31–3, 88–9

boundaries, 20, 67–8

care-giving task 112, 113–14

causality, circular, 4–5, 31–3, 170

change: action research *see* action research; experiencing 95–100; learning and 169–70; resistance to 34–5; schools and 42, 43, 127–31

change-agents 130

child guidance movement xi, 33, 45, 46; model of intervention 133–4

child protection 165–6

Children Act (1989) 149, 160–7; child protection 165–6; children in need 164–5; consent to assessment and treatment 162–3; delay 163; orders 166–7; parental responsibility 163; partnership with parents 164; welfare in independent schools 167; welfare principle 160–2

children in need 164–5

children's wishes 161

circular causality 4–5, 31–3, 170

circular questioning 22–3

classroom interventions 95–100

clinic setting: meetings with family and teacher 103–6; sharing information with teachers 106–8

closed systems 33

cognitive psychology 44

coherence 6

communication 60; children's wishes 161–2; failures 73; between families attending Marlborough Family Service Education Unit 93–4; joint systems approach 15; problem-oriented systems 12–13

consent to assessment and treatment 162–3

consultation: and altruism 145; action research model *see* action research; models of intervention 134–7; to primary schools 112–26 (dual roles 125–6; initial considerations 112–20; setting up the consultation 120–1; tasks 121–4; techniques 124–5); by teachers *see* teacher consultancy; theories and systems approach 38–9

consultative service 43, 59–68; clinical examples 63–4; drop-in for parents 62–3; drop-in for teachers 65–6; and headteacher 66–7, 68; task of consultation 67–8; territory 61, 68; workshops for parents 66

contact orders 163
context: learning 168–9; school 112; systems theory 4
crisis theory 46, 135
culture 10–11, 128

decentralization 130
delay, Children Act and 163
delinquency 127
development 112, 113; schools and individual 133; stages 117–20; *see also* transitions
differentiation 42
discipline 116
discussion groups, teachers' 108–10
dual roles 125–6

Education Act (1981) 12, 47, 149
Education Reform Act (1988) 12, 47, 148, 162
education supervision order 161, 166–7
educational psychologists (EPs) *see* psychologists/psychological services
educational social worker (ESW) 54, 56, 57
educational task 112, 113
educational therapy 58
emergency protection order 166
equilibrium 34–5
ethos 10–11, 128

failure, success and 50
families: clinic-based meeting with teachers 103–6; common elements of family and school systems 8–12; failure to respond to referral 59–60, 77–8; feedback to 49; primary school pupils and their families 115–20; *see also* parents
family tasks 51–3
family therapy 1–2, 30–1; structural 9; suitability 46; supervision 174; systemic 40–1, 58
feedback: action research 140–3; to families 49; loops 7–8
feelings 37–8
form tutors 78–9, 80–1, 86–7
future, questions about 23

gender-related beliefs 11
general practitioners (GPs) 136
general systems theory *see* systems approach

group relations training 136
groups: intervention models 135–7; nurture groups 114; subsystems as 132–3; work discussion groups with teachers 108–10

harm, significant 165–6
headteachers: and change 129; consultative service and 66–7, 68; role 103
hierarchical structures 8–9, 19
home-school liaison 70; *see also* partnership
home visits 18–19, 90–1
homeostasis 6–7, 34

independent schools 167
individual growth, pupils' 133
infant-school pupils 115–17, 119; *see also* primary schools
information exchange: feedback model 7–8; with teachers in clinical setting 106–8
in-service training 124
interactional perspective xi–xii, 45–58, 59; choice at referral stage 48–9; cycles of interaction 4–5, 31–3, 170; family tasks 51–3; feedback to families 49; long-term school refuser 54–7; problem formulation 22; success and failure 50; supervision 172–4
intersystemic processes 170–1
intervention: expectations of 17; models of 133–7
intervention strategies 12–14
intervention techniques 21–8
isolation 93

joining process/manoeuvres 21
joint interventions 69–87; clinical practice examples 71–7; school case examples 81–5; school-family intervention project 77–81
joint systems approach 15–29; aims 15; avoiding triangulation 20; forms of intervention 15–16; initial stages 17–19; intervention techniques 21–8; keeping boundaries 20; relevant questions 16–17; respecting existing hierarchies 19
junior-school children 117–20; *see also* primary schools

Langtry Young Family Centre 114
learning: attitudes towards 116; and change 169–70; context 168–9; *see also* secure base
legislation 1, 12, 66–7, 149; *see also* Children Act, Education Acts
life cycle stages 117–20
local management of schools (LMS) 66–7, 130
long-term school refuser 65–7

management 42
Marlborough Family Service Education Unit 88–101; classroom, families and engagement process 93–5; classroom interventions 95–100; referral and initial contact 89–93; relationship with child's school and teachers 100–1
mental health consultation model 134–5
meta rules 9–10
mirroring 171

National Curriculum 149, 162
need, children in 164–5
nursery-school children 115–17, 119; *see also* primary schools
nurture groups 114

open systems 33–4, 132, 170
orders 163, 166–7
organizational psychology 135
organizations: effects on people 128; hierarchical 8–9, 19; schools as 41–3, 131–3; *see also* systems approach

paradoxical intervention 25–6
parental responsibility 164
parents: consultation to primary schools 122–3; consultative service drop-in 62–3; consultative service workshops 66; overlapping concerns with teachers 114–15; partnership with 164; split 73–5; *see also* families
partnership with parents 164
positive connotation 24–6
primary schools 112–26; consultation process 120–6 (setting up 120–1; tasks 121–4; techniques 124–5); context 112; developmental stages 117–20; dual roles 125–6; home-school liaison 70; organizational structure 132–3; overlapping

concerns for parents and teachers 114–15; pupils and their families 115–17; tasks 112–14; teacher consultancy 150–3
problem definition 21–2
problem-determined systems 12–14
problem formulation 22, 138–40
process consultation 136–7
prohibited steps orders 163
protection, child 165–6
psychodynamic approaches 36–8; *see also* attachment theory, groups
psychologists/psychological services 2–3; assessment role 47; difficulty of reaching needy families 60; historical review 46–8; independence 35; joint interventions *see* joint interventions; models of intervention 133–7; NHS reforms 87; rejection of clinical approach 30–1, 47; response to referrals 77–8; setting up outreach services 60–1; supervision 174; trainees 145; training and learning context 168–9; *see also* child guidance, clinic setting, family therapy, referrals
punctuation 5–6
pupils' individual growth 133

questions: circular 22–3; future 23; relevant for intervention 16–17

recursive phenomena 5
referrals 124–5; child guidance model 45; choice 48–9; families' failure to respond 59–60, 77–8; interactional perspective 48–9, 53, 56, 58; Marlborough Family Service Education Unit 89–93
reframing 23–6
relocating problems 57
residence orders 163
rules 9–10

school refuser, long-term 54–7
schools: and change 42, 43, 127–31; common elements of family and school systems 8–12; context 112; and individual growth 133; Marlborough Family Service Education Unit and relationship with 100–1; nature of school setting 103; as organizations 41–3, 131–3;

resistance to change 34–5; as socio-technical systems 131–2; subsystems *see* subsystems; target for change 127–47; tasks 112–14; training aims and relationship with 172; *see also* primary schools, secondary schools

secondary schools: action research and transition to 139–40; 141–3, 143–4; delinquency rates 127; home-school liaison 70; subsystems 132; teacher consultancy 153–8

'Section 8' orders 163

secure base for learning 150, 152–3, 157; resistance to establishment of 154

security xiii–xiv

separation 117–20, 149; subsystem and whole system 156

significant harm 165–6

socio–technical systems 131–2

soft systems methodology (SSM) 40

special needs action research 139, 140–1, 143

special needs unit 153–8

specialists, proliferation of 130

specific issues orders 163

standard assessment tests (SATs) 47

starting school 117, 118–19

structures, hierarchical 8–9, 19

subsystems: as groups 132–3; teacher consultancy 148–59; and whole system 156

success, failure and 50

supervision 172–4

suspensions 15

systems approach xi–xii, 1–44, 101, 172; action research and system change 146–7; cause, effect and blame 31–3; common elements to family and school systems 8–12; consultation process 122; equilibrium and resistance to change 34–5; independent psychologist 35; intersystemic processes 170–1; interventions strategies 12–14; joint systems approach *see* joint systems approach; key concepts of general systems theory 4–8; open and closed systems 33–4; schools and change 42, 43, 130; schools as socio-technical systems 131–2; subsystems *see* subsystems; supplementary

frameworks 36–43; systems perspective 3

task setting 26–8; *see also* family tasks

Tavistock Clinic xv, 37, 54, 145

Tavistock Neighbourhood Schools Project xvi

teacher consultancy 148–59; attempts to engage a group 150–3; imposed approach 153–6; secure base for learning 150; self-selected approach 156–8

teachers: clinic-based meeting with family 103–6; consultation to primary schools 123; consultative service drop-in 65–6; difficulty of asking for help 129, 171; extending role 148–9; in-service training 124; Marlborough Family Service Education Unit and relationship with 100–1; mutual observations 142, 143–4; overlapping concerns with parents 114–15; sharing information with 106–8; supervision 174; work discussion groups 108–10; working with out of school setting 102–11

territory: consultative service 61, 68; social workers' problems 18

theme interference 134

training 168–75; aims and philosophy 171–2; context of learning 168–9; group relations training 136; in-service for teachers 124; interactional perspective in supervision 172–4; intersystemic processes 170–1; learning and change 169–70

transitions: life cycle stages 117–20; primary-secondary school 139–40, 141–3, 143–4

treatment, consent to 162–3

triangulation 171; avoiding 20

tutors: form 78–9, 80–1, 86–7; year 79, 80–1, 86

violence 91–2, 100–1

welfare, Children Act and 160–2, 167

work discussion groups 108–10

year tutors 79, 80–1, 86